WASTED TIME

WASTED TIME

EDWARD HERTRICH

DUNDURN
PRESS

Editor: Laurie Miller | Designer: Laura Boyle | Cover image: istockphoto.com/BrilliantEye

Library and Archives Canada Cataloguing in Publication

Hertrich, Edward, author
      Wasted time / Edward Hertrich.

Issued in print and electronic formats.
ISBN 978-1-4597-4351-9 (softcover).--ISBN 978-1-4597-4352-6(PDF).--
ISBN 978-1-4597-4353-3 (EPUB)

      1. Hertrich, Edward. 2. Hertrich, Edward--Imprisonment.
3. Prisoners--Ontario--Biography. 4. Millhaven Institution. I. Title.

HV9505.H47A3 2019   365'.6092   C2018-905749-1
                                              C2018-905750-5

Conseil des Arts du Canada | Canada Council for the Arts | Canada | ONTARIO ARTS COUNCIL CONSEIL DES ARTS DE L'ONTARIO an Ontario government agency un organisme du gouvernement de l'Ontario

We acknowledge the support of the Canada Council for the Arts, which last year invested $153 million to bring the arts to Canadians throughout the country, and the Ontario Arts Council for our publishing program. We also acknowledge the financial support of the Government of Ontario, through the Ontario Book Publishing Tax Credit and Ontario Creates, and the Government of Canada.

Nous remercions le Conseil des arts du Canada de son soutien. L'an dernier, le Conseil a investi 153 millions de dollars pour mettre de l'art dans la vie des Canadiennes et des Canadiens de tout le pays.

Care has been taken to trace the ownership of copyright material used in this book. The author and the publisher welcome any information enabling them to rectify any references or credits in subsequent editions.   — *J. Kirk Howard, President*

The publisher is not responsible for websites or their content unless they are owned by the publisher.

Printed and bound in Canada.

Dundurn Press
Toronto, Ontario, Canada
dundurn.com, @dundurnpress

CONTENTS

INTRODUCTION

WHILE I WILL APPRECIATE any interest our youth may have in the contents of this book, I place greater emphasis on my hope to inspire adults to contemplate my life; to contemplate their own past mistakes. And to look toward their charges; for our young deserve to have an interest shown in each of their lives. They deserve to receive assistance when they become confused in their life choices. They deserve for us to genuinely care, to show them proper direction, and guidance. To intervene when negative influences present themselves. Everyone knows the young will err. We know that, for we all were young once. Who among us has never made a mistake? Some were just fortunate not to have been noticed. It is incumbent upon older people to restore a youth upon a proper path, with dignity and self-esteem intact. To do otherwise would be to fail them. To do otherwise would be to help create the monsters and demons we find within our society.

It is far easier to open a closed heart than to open a closed mind.

One simply requires compassion and understanding.

The other requires strength and determination.

The following pages chronicle my life. They are memories, my memories, and as such are fact to me. Many of these facts can be supported by government records. The contents of this book are in no way meant to glamourize the violence and the drug subculture that I experienced. There was no glamour. Every violent act involved some degree of concern, including various levels of fear. Every "high" was simply that, an aberration from reality. Every contact with law enforcement was met with deep consternation and regret.

Movies and novels. Fact or fiction. Criminal lifestyles portray illusions of power, wealth, and excitement. These tales are etched upon the imaginations of youth. In some areas of society, these illusions are bolstered by today's criminal elements. The superficiality of their lifestyle is hidden. Like moths to a flame, our young are drawn. To experience. To experiment. Negative occurrences do repel almost all, mainly without their peers noticing. Those that continue the experience do learn the reality of life outside the law. An unkind legal system. A harsh correctional system. Most every criminal offender, regardless of age, comprehends the risk to their liberty prior to their acts. Still, some stubbornly pursue the lifestyle, leading them to the world of concrete and steel. A world that tests one's strengths and vulnerabilities.

Events will occur within this world that will impact individuals to varying degrees. Fortunately, many will traverse their sentence without physical harm. None escape with indifference. Most choose rightly, never to return. To remain upon a proper path. Those few who do return recognize their luck will last for only so long. There is always a bigger, meaner dog in the yard. Sometimes there is a pack of dogs. Either way, at the end of a lengthy criminal career, whether one is whole or crippled, retirement without reward is inevitable. And sometimes sudden.

PROLOGUE

THE YEAR WAS 1962. In just over a year, the president of the United States of America, John Fitzgerald Kennedy, would fall to an assassin's bullet. I was in my first grade of elementary school at Regent Park Public. I was six years old.

I had begun to walk up the eight concrete steps that led off school property and onto the path home for lunch. A sudden rush of older children began to race up the steps, passing me. I was accidentally bumped hard from behind. Losing my balance, I fell headfirst into the edge of one of the steps. The concrete sliced deep into my forehead.

As I got back onto my feet, I held one hand against the gash, pressing hard. I attempted to retrieve my fallen textbook with the other hand. "Leave that," an older child said, taking my free hand. She led me back into the school and down the hallway to the principal's office. The girl kept yelling for help. The principal appeared. "What's wrong?" she asked. "Him," the child said simply.

The principal fastened her gaze on me. "And what is wrong with you?" She smiled. I removed my hand and looked down at my palm. It was red and sticky. As I lifted my head back up to look at her, the blood gushed forth from the deep wound. It flowed down my face. The principal fainted. She hit the floor, flat on her back. Teachers milling about in the hallway raced to her assistance. As they drew closer, they noticed me. They left the principal lying there. One teacher picked me up, while another applied pressure to the wound. A third teacher had immediately raced out the back door of the school, over to the adjacent 51 Division police precinct. In no time at all, I was carried into the back of a police paddy wagon. With sirens blaring all the way, I was whisked to the emergency doors of the nearby Hospital for Sick Children in downtown Toronto. At six years old, I had just been given my first ride in the back of a paddy wagon — the first of over a thousand.

PART ONE

I

The Younger Years

REGENT PARK, CANADA'S FIRST social welfare housing project, is located in the city of Toronto, in the province of Ontario. The neighbourhood sits one mile east of the city's downtown core, just north of the shore of Lake Ontario. It covers an area four city blocks by four city blocks. Since its inception in the 1950s, low-income families have been provided "affordable" housing there. Based on the number of family members, they were either placed in row houses or an apartment in one of the many three- and six-storey rust-coloured buildings. Five high-rise buildings also provided domiciles within the project. The infrastructure of brick and concrete left no illusion that this "neighbourhood" was anything but a project. From the onset, Regent Park was regarded as a "high-crime" area — the highest, most every year, in the city. Notorious for violence, renowned for drugs, Regent Park made knowledgeable people regard its borders with great trepidation.

In the summer of 1956, my family took up residence in one of the many row houses. I spent the first sixteen years of my life as a resident of South Regent Park.

Considering the hardship each family in Regent Park endured, people were generally friendly to each other, but aloof. Those more familiar, whether by proximity or social ties, would converse. People respected each other's privacy, unless action dictated otherwise. Child endangerment definitely prompted intervention. Interloping, otherwise, was regarded with disdain.

Men, fathers, were rarely seen. They worked long hours, were dead, or divorced of their families residing in Regent. The project housed two elementary schools, with another on its border. The children attended class together, and played together. The women busied themselves maintaining households, while nurturing their young. Like that of my mother, who bore eleven children, their lives were strenuous. For us children, ignorant of the outside world or its responsibilities, life was good.

I recall the sky being unusually grey. Not blue at all, for a midsummer morning. I had toddled out of the family backyard to sit with a neighbour, a girl my age, on the curb of the parking lot that lay out back of our row houses. She was sad. We began to look at all the debris that the wind had blown into the trench our feet now rested upon. Beer bottle caps, empty cigarette packages, bubble gum wrappers. At four years old, we imagined these as treasure.

A loud bang pierced the air, accompanied by a woman's screams. We looked over our shoulders to see the girl's mother racing frantically along the side of the row houses. Another bang followed. We looked over our other shoulders to see the girl's father standing outside his backyard. Before the third bang had a chance to reverberate, I was airborne. Flying high up in the air, I landed on my mother's hip. *Where had she come from?*

"You, too," she snapped, as she yanked the little girl off the curb. She took off running, a child on each hip, back to the safety of our house. She locked the back door and peered out through a window.

I never heard the last bang, but I heard the story of an unfaithful wife who had escaped death, and a distraught husband who, after failing to hit his target, sat in his chair and ended his own life. The remaining family moved soon after. I felt sad for the little girl, and I would miss her company.

My own family was no stranger to domestic violence. My alcoholic father had struggled against the burden of raising eleven children on a paltry wage and his need to be "the man" amongst his friends at the local taverns. After administering several physical beatings upon my mother and eldest siblings, he was, I am told, convinced to leave the family abode at the insistence of a loaded shotgun. I was five years old. Growing up in Regent Park, I found domestic violence to be a prevalent factor in the lives of many families. Of course, it was sheltered "in-house" as much as possible. The Children's Aid Society was regarded in the neighbourhood as "home wreckers" and "child stealers," and the police were always the enemy of the people.

My best friend as a child was my next door neighbour, Wayne. He was the middle brother of three, who all suffered the affliction of muscular dystrophy, wheelchair-bound, with no muscle control. I would talk and watch TV with them daily. We played board games, such as checkers or chess, but I would have to move the men for them. Once I was big enough to push Wayne in his wheelchair, we'd go around the neighbourhood, to the corner stores, the restaurant. As I got older, around nine, he had me push him to salvage yards and the dockyard beside the lake. Wayne seemed to know everyone, and all the men would give him coinage. We would be rich when we returned, upwards of three dollars apiece.

One morning, he talked me into pushing him down to the CNE grounds. The Exhibition had just opened, and we wanted to see the midway and go on some of the rides. So we set out. We got lost. With night having fallen, and rain coming down, I pushed Wayne into a corner store in the city's northwest end. The woman took one look at us, Wayne in his wheelchair, and called the police. We both knew our addresses, so the police drove us home. Both our mothers thanked the police profusely. Wayne's mother was kissing his head. My mother was tanning my ass. They still let us hang around together. Wayne would pass away at an early age because of his disease. His two brothers suffered the same fate.

I was very fortunate as a young boy to meet a wealthy family from Scarborough. The Lowes approached my school's principal searching for an underprivileged girl to spend the holidays with their lone daughter. They had two sons, as well, but no one to provide their daughter company. Since my family had eight girls, they were directed to my house. My mother was receptive to the idea, but none of my sisters would go alone. I was sent with them in the hope of quelling any homesickness they might feel. I loved the vacations with this family. Four of my sisters would try, but all returned home early. They did not like the daughter. Being with the two sons, I had no such problem. I was taken to Fantasy Island in New York, to productions of *Camelot* and *The Nutcracker Suite* at the prestigious (then) O'Keefe Centre. We'd go to the drive-in, movies, the Exhibition, tours of old Fort Henry, and country farms.

The best part of this relationship for me was the attention I received from the couple. They'd dote on me, even tucking me in bed at night after we said our prayers. This was all new to me. They'd take me for haircuts at a real barbershop, buy all the clothing I needed, and the food they would serve was a huge upgrade from the diet I received with all my other siblings on a welfare budget.

After a couple of years of holidays, the couple approached my mother with their hope of adopting me permanently into their family. I had no idea they would do that or I could have told them that was a huge mistake. My mother was aghast. She forbade them from seeing me. She could not believe they would expect her to give up any of her children, regardless of the large numbers in our family. As a youngster, I just assumed the Lowes had given up on offering opportunities to the "underprivileged" and had let me go. I would see them many years later, as an adult. And sometimes, as an adult, I would wonder where my life would have gone if my mother had agreed to the adoption; but I would dwell on that only briefly.

Regent Park Public School ended at grade six. Further upgrading had to be continued at other schools. At grade six graduation, my friend Perry would be awarded the school valedictorian award. I was very happy for him. We'd become friends as soon as his family had moved into Regent. But my mother was incensed. I had attended the school, completing each year with straight As or A pluses. Perry had only transferred in for the last two years. We'd hung around together, and he was my study partner. Our grades reflected our closeness. My mother felt I was overlooked in favour of the school's "minority equality" agenda (Perry was Japanese).

I always felt the grade six music teacher was the deciding factor. He had lobbied hard on Perry's behalf. He had wanted me to attend his private "tutoring" lessons after school, and I had refused. He had even asked my mother to talk to me about it, but I would not budge. He was the only teacher that ever gave me "the creeps." After graduation, my mother would make Perry feel uncomfortable when he called on me, and she definitely forbade me from assisting him in any further home studies. She wanted me to disassociate myself from Perry, but I drew the line there. I felt she was being unfair. I remained friends with Perry until his family moved out of the project a year later. I would read in the Toronto tabloids many years later that he had achieved the distinction of being "the most-robbed pharmacist in the city." He worked just a city block southwest of our old school. The music teacher would also find himself referenced in a Toronto tabloid, but as an offender in a child sexual molestation case. I was happy Perry gained a profession; sad for the violence he was a victim to. As for the music teacher, I felt total vindication about my juvenile decision to avoid him.

I had only one real confrontation in Regent Park Public School, and it came during my last year. A new girl, Karen, had transferred in. One day, as school let out, and Perry and I were walking out of the schoolyard, we saw a huge crowd gathering. Curious, we went to see what was going on. Two boys were holding Karen's arms down while another boy was trying to kiss her. She was moving her head to avoid that and sobbing. I grabbed the main antagonist and threw him on his butt into the crowd. Then I threatened the other two to let her go. They did. I told the whole crowd to leave her alone, or they would have to deal with me. Then Perry and I walked her home. It really was no big deal, but Karen and her parents thought so. We became good friends after that, and remained so throughout the years.

I attended grades seven and eight at Park Public School, also within the "project." I met two boys my age who would be my closest friends during that period. Arnold was a year older, but far more mature. He loved his alcohol, and the girls. Bobby was different. He loved his chemicals, particularly solvents. Girls were also a major focus in his life. The pair would fall in love with new girls almost weekly. Sometimes the same girl, and then that would be a problem. They would argue and fight. I was constantly asked to choose a side, but I wouldn't.

I would "go steady" with many girls, and either "pack them in" or get "packed in." I really cared less. It was juvenile stuff. I was just doing what all the other kids did. My grades were far more important to me than feeling a boob. It may have been the fact that I had seven older sisters that made the exercise less appealing to me at that time. I'm not sure. I am sure that after grade eight I was totally interested in the girls around me. They, however, were interested in the older boys, or those who were involved in crime or the drug subculture. This did not escape my notice. I began to wonder if I'd missed a step in my personal development.

As far as my upbringing went, I felt fortunate. Not knowing the benefits of a middle- or upper-class life, I wanted for little. With such a large family, I didn't lack company or protection — except when one of my older siblings would minorly assault me. I was the second-youngest of eleven, and as kids will be kids, I'd do something to anger one of them now and again. And again.

After elementary school, my focus shifted from books of knowledge to gaining social acceptance from the older teens. I hadn't matured to the point of fully appreciating those closest to me. As a young teen, I was both diminutive and passive. I had school friends, but I wanted to be a part of the "in" crowd. The cool kids. I associated myself with the local drop-in community centre, a hangout for the older teens I began to mimic. Smoking cigarettes. Drinking alcohol. My abuse of further substances was quick to follow. It was the time of Woodstock. Jimi Hendrix, Janis Joplin, and the Rolling Stones filled the airwaves. Cheech and Chong provided comedy for the "new drug" era. Marijuana, hashish, and LSD (acid) flooded the project. Mescaline, MDA, peyote, and a number of other chemical drugs seeped in. Methamphetamine sat just on the cusp. It seemed the more times I used drugs, the more I was accepted by the group. And I wanted to be accepted.

My mother was anguished by my change in lifestyle. She held hope that I would be successful in life. That hope was fading fast.

High school began for me in Toronto's West End, at the Central High School of Commerce, outside of the project, halfway across the city, and away from my friends. One of my sisters (three years my senior) had preceded me into this school. Other than her, who I rarely saw, I knew no one. The first thing I learned in high school was that I was poor. Other students did not bring their lunch in a brown paper bag. They ate at restaurants, pizza shops, or the local stores around the school. Or they lived nearby. Their clothing was relatively new, and far more expensive than my own. The vast majority had graduated from the same area schools, and so they all knew each other. Nobody else from Regent Park who graduated that year had chosen this commercial school so far away. From Regent Park they went to area commercial, technical, or vocational schools, if they didn't have the misfortune to go to reform school.

I was not ostracized at Central Commerce. Being smaller than most every male student, definitely poorer, and a total stranger, my self-esteem was severely tested. I liked two girls, totally different from each other but both more mature than I. Dorie was Jewish, and cute as a button, experienced in older boys and drugs. Lina was an Italian goddess whose father knew it, and he never let her out of his sight after school. Each day I would see him on his porch waiting for her to exit the school. The first year, I made a strong effort, effecting good grades, as well as excellent attendance. That did little to alleviate my daily depression. When the school year ended and summer was upon us, I revelled in illicit drugs and alcohol once again with my peers in the project.

Over the summer, I hung out with an older teen named Ray. We would meet in the mornings or early afternoons and go to various places, stealing bicycles. We had a fence (a buyer of stolen merchandise) in the project, and we would be paid on delivery. We also stole from cars, storage lockers, from almost anywhere. It paid for food, beer, and drugs.

Jessie, a girl from my new high school, had moved into the project, and we became friends. One night, I introduced her to the drop-in centre. We sat and talked for a few hours and then I walked her home. Well, almost. As soon as we got to the road across from her building, we saw a lot of police cars. One cop in front of the building yelled, "That's him. You. Don't move!" He was directing his comments at me. I had a small bag of pot on me, as usual. I knew I was in danger of being arrested. I looked at the closest cop. He had the reputation for being the fastest cop in Regent, and he was waiting for traffic to clear so he could run across the road.

I wasn't waiting. I turned and ran. Halfway down the street, I turned to look back. He was pursuing me and gaining ground fast. I headed for a wall that adjoined two sets of row houses. It had a couple of small indents that I used daily. I never broke stride as I hurdled the wall just as the cop's hand brushed the sole of my sneaker. I heard him hit the wall with a grunt. Landing on the other side, I sped to the closest high-rise building and into one of the many ground-floor apartments of people I knew. We turned out the lights and peered out the window. I could see the cop now gingerly making his way back up to the building, his counterparts, and his vehicle. A few minutes later, I snuck through the project in the shadow of night, back to my house.

Bobby was outside the door. He was sniffing a rag soaked with nail polish remover. Again. He had serious issues. His hand was bloody. "Can I come in?" he asked.

"No, my mom's home, and you stink," I answered. "I'll see you tomorrow." His other hand was bleeding pretty good. "What did you do to yourself?" I asked.

"Oh, punched out some windows at 600," he said. That was my new friend's building. "I was angry. You got five bucks?" he asked. I gave it to him and went inside.

Not long after, the phone rang. It was the lead counsellor from the drop-in, who happened to be Bobby's oldest brother. "The cops are here, they want to talk to you. Either you come down now, or I'll give them your address." I looked at my mom, and then told him, "I'm on my way."

The Regent Park Community Centre was a two-and-a-half-storey brick building in the middle of South Regent, on Sackville Street. Its basement floor contained a washroom, a couple of small side rooms primarily used for arts and crafts for the younger kids, and at the rear a large room with Ping-Pong, shuffleboard, and bocce-ball tables. The main floor housed a "hangout" room, painted black with black lighting and all kinds of splashes of different-coloured paints to give a psychedelic effect. The main rear room was much bigger, with large steps to sit on at the back, a stage at the front. Movies were shown there every so often, but usually it was just a place to sit around and listen to music. The upstairs floor had the offices of the counsellors who worked in the centre.

As soon as I entered the upstairs office, the one cop jumped off the couch and pulled up his pant leg. He had skinned himself pretty good on the wall. "You little bastard —" he started.

"Hold on," interrupted the counsellor, glaring at me. "You upset a lot of people tonight in their homes, not to mention the damage you did to the building. I'm ready to ban you from the centre, and I just might kick your ass every time I see you," he threatened.

"I didn't do shit," I answered, "and we both know either of my brothers would kick your ass if you laid one hand on me."

The cop jumped in. "If you didn't do anything, why did you run?"

"You were chasing me," I reasoned. Then I looked at the counsellor. "Me and you have to talk away from them," I said.

He looked at the cops. "Please. He's not going anywhere. Just give us a minute in the hall." They acquiesced.

"I was here with a girl when those windows got smashed. Ask anyone downstairs," I told him.

"How did you know about the windows if it wasn't you?" he growled. I told him about running into Bobby. He knew us two were often mistaken for each other, and he knew his brother had problems. "Shit," he muttered.

"Yeah, shit," I agreed. "I ran because I had a bag of pot on me. I didn't know anything about the vandalism."

"I know I have no right to ask, but would you do me a favour? Don't mention my brother. I'll arrange for them to bill you, no criminal charges, and when you get the bill, bring it to me and I'll pay it." I agreed. I wouldn't have mentioned Bobby, but I would have fought it in court before I paid a nickel.

The cops agreed to the counsellor's terms and left. But not before telling me that they would get me one day.

And these two would.

卌

The four thirteen-storey high-rise buildings in South Regent had fire-escape staircases on either end. These sheltered areas provided a space where the youths could get high or drunk without being seen by the law, especially during inclement weather. These stairwells would always smell like stale beer, urine, and, on good days, marijuana.

The middle floors were ideal in the event of police chases. There were a great many of those, but no one ever seemed to get caught. We could see out the narrow windows on each landing, or hear people entering the fire escapes, and could see partway down the stairwells who was coming. The cops just could not manoeuvre around the stairwells as quickly as the neighbourhood kids. We'd slide along the round metal railings, sling-shotting our rear ends around and down each flight with the help of the vertical pole at each floor. We could descend seven floors to the ground before they could make it down three flights. Going up the concrete steps, the cops had too much equipment to hang onto as they chased us. If the exits were blocked, then we'd extend the cat-and-mouse game up and down the staircases until the foot patrol grew tired, or we would simply deke into one of our friends' apartments. On good-weather days, we'd sit outside in the parking lots to socialize and get high. We always had to watch for local foot patrols, though.

A couple of weeks later, I walked Jessie home again. As we reached the building, some teens were having a party in one of the ground-floor apart-ments. "Look at this asshole," one yelled out the living room window, and soon there were a few guys there.

"Hey, baby, lose the loser and come in here."

"We'll show you a good time."

"Hey, buddy, what are you looking at? You want your face kicked in?"

We just kept walking. We took the stairwell up to her third-floor apart-ment, where we said good night. Back down on the first floor, I unhooked the cover of the lighting fixture and took out one of the long fluorescent tubes. Then, I went and knocked on the door of the partygoers. "What do you want?" the teen opening the door said. I punched him square in the face, knocking him back into the apartment. I followed. A second teen jumped up off the couch. I smashed the glass tube across his face, sending him to the floor. I then went after the other two who had been instigating through the window earlier.

The cops charged me for assault.

A week after that, Bobby talked me into accompanying him down to the Old City Hall. He had a court date to appear for some minor theft. After court, we crossed over to Nathan Phillips Square and smoked a cou-ple of joints. Then we went to the Eaton Centre. Once inside, he headed straight to the jewellery display counters. As soon as the salesperson wasn't watching, he grabbed some items. "Here, put these in your pocket. I don't have a coat," he said.

"Fuck off," I answered.

"I do this all the time, don't worry. We'll go over to the pawnshops on Church Street and trade them for cash. I do it all the time."

Like an idiot, I relented. He walked out of the store ahead of me. I followed. A huge black hand grabbed my left shoulder. "Did you pay for that?"

"I don't have anything," I answered, and, looking at Bobby a good ten feet in front of us, I continued, "He does."

The man beckoned Bobby to come back. I was motioning him to run.

He walked back. As the store detective reached out to grab Bobby, I drove my elbow into his groin area. He let go of my shoulder. I spun off him and started to run back up the street. I got about three strides before I hit smack dab into the stomach of a uniformed policeman.

I was arrested and given a summons to appear in court. I quit hanging out with my sniffer friend. I was sixteen.

𝄇𝄇𝄇𝄇𝄇

The summer of 1972 was going downhill fast. I still had my stolen bicycle gig going with Ray. We'd go out almost daily. Every so often, the local cops would be sitting in their car when we'd ride into the project, and they would give chase. Their cars could not access the narrow concrete walkways, though, and they certainly couldn't run fast enough to catch a bike, but still, they'd try. We would watch from a distance after those chases, just to ensure they didn't see where our fence lived. Then we'd drop off our stolen merchandise and collect our monies.

One summer day, as we neared our target area, we passed a van with the keys still in the ignition. It was full of televisions. Ray ran to the driver's door and jumped in. "Let's go!" he yelled. "You're crazy," I said, and continued walking. He started the van up and pulled up beside me. "C'mon, this is a great score," he said. I looked at him hesitantly, then hopped in.

We drove to Scarborough, to his father's place, and stored the TVs. As we walked back to the van, I said, "Leave it. We'll take the subway home."

"Screw that, we're driving back to Regent." Ray laughed.

"Leave it," I said again as I continued walking past the van. He hopped in and started it up. I had gotten a half a city block before he pulled up beside me. "Come on, we'll be fine. Don't worry." Like an idiot, again I relented.

It had started out a beautiful, warm, clear day. But now the van was surrounded by police cruisers, and Ray had no other option than to stop. I was ripped out through the front passenger door and flung to the asphalt. With guns drawn. I was handcuffed and thrown into the back of one of the squad cars. I was taken to the nearest precinct, where I remained adamant that I was hitchhiking home when a friend from Regent picked me up. I hadn't seen any televisions. I was only in the van six blocks or so. Ray and I were taken downtown to the precinct in the area where the van was stolen. I was placed in a cell. Later on, Ray was placed beside me. He'd given the TVs back. We were both charged with theft, but released on our own recognizance. The police, however, had contacted my mother.

There is no worse feeling on this planet than when you have to look in the eyes of the person who loves you the most and see their pain. Pain that you caused. My mother punched me repeatedly in the face; but that compared little to the pain in my heart. I remember trying to justify my actions in my mind. It was not my fault that I was born into a poor family. It was not my fault that I had to steal to have money. But I still knew it was wrong.

My older brother (from jail) asked his lawyer, the Lion, to represent me. Ray, who was older than me, made a plea-bargain agreement for thirty days in custody. My charge was dismissed.

The four youths from the assault case were deeply admonished by the trial judge, even though they had decided to withdraw the charges against me. "Every one of you is bigger than this squirt," he told them, "and you called the police? Get out of my courtroom."

I was not so lucky with the store detective and his sore groin. He pressed hard, but, because it was my first offence, I received only a fifty-dollar fine.

My mother could not wait for school to start again.

||||

I had no illusions that my second year of high school would mirror my first. I was right. The few classmates I had made friends with the year prior were now in different classes. I was once again a stranger to the other kids. Although my grade ten scores remained passable, they faltered, along with my attendance. But I persevered.

My mother was summoned to the principal's office shortly after school began for my third year. She came, accompanied by my oldest brother, and with me in tow. "He never showed up for the first two weeks of school," the principal informed my mother.

"I wasn't sure when school started," I told him.

My mother looked at me sadly and half-whispered, "Don't lie."

Thwack, my brother slapped me in the back of my head. He was thirteen years my senior.

"And then he walked into a class of students who hadn't missed a day, and he scored the highest mark on an exam. How do you think those students felt?" the principal asked.

"Did he cheat?" my brother asked, eyeing me suspiciously.

"I don't know," the principal said. "Let's ask him."

All three adults fixed their gaze upon me. "It was an open-text exam," I whined. "Can I help it if the other kids can't read?"

Thwack, my brother slapped me again in the back of the head.

"I could suspend him for a month, but I think that would only be giving him what he wants." My family nodded. "I have to do something, though, so I will suspend him for one week to give him time to think about his future," he concluded.

"Okay," my brother said, "after that, he won't miss any more time.

"Right?" he asked me.

As I began to think about it, he gave me a third slap to the back of my head.

"Sure," I answered.

I went back to school, and my brother went back to prison. (He'd been in custody more often than not since I was born.) I carried my brown lunch bags once again, but instead of food, they now contained small bags of marijuana. I was eating at the pizza shops and restaurants now, compliments of the profits I made off the other students. I didn't attend school half the time, and when I did, I didn't attend half the classes. Instead, I spent my days in billiard halls or at the homes of friends in Regent Park.

I quit halfway through the school year. My mother was irate. I insisted I needed to earn a wage.

During the previous two summers, and on school days missed, I'd been out stealing. My mother had her suspicions, and agreed that work was an avenue to avoid this behaviour.

So, I went to work as an assembler for a large power systems company. I'd quit stealing, but still enjoyed smoking weed and having a couple of beers on the weekends. I enjoyed the job very much, and more so, I liked the people. Well, most of them. I lasted almost a full year.

I came into work one morning and found myself immediately involved in a dispute with one of the foremen. He had acquiesced to another worker's request to substitute me on the assembly line. I was to work in another department. Most probably to do the job the other worker didn't want. I never found out. My replacement was sitting in my chair, at my station, listening to my radio, while he drank his coffee. I knocked him on his ass. He ran to the foreman, who came screaming at me. I packed up my tools and left.

2

The Crazy Years

JUST AFTER I QUIT MY JOB, my oldest brother was once again released from prison. He'd bought the house two doors down from my mother's the last time he was home; he made good profit from the drug trade.

And it didn't take him long to pick up right where he'd left off. Before long, the RCMP were out front, swarming him, his car, the house. I was sitting two doors up, watching, and my brother yelled at me to call one of our sisters. *What can she do?* I wondered. This was the cops.

I called just the same. She sounded unusually alarmed and hung up. I walked out the front door, down the street, and around the corner. There, I put it in high gear and raced to my sister's. I saw her right away on her porch, looking furtively up and down the street. She held a large metal tool box. "Go inside and watch the kids," she told me. A taxi pulled up out front. She had tears in her eyes, and I suddenly understood her situation. "I have a better idea. You go inside. Where am I going?" I asked as I relieved her of the tool box.

My brother picked me up a couple of hours later. "You shouldn't have gotten involved," he scolded.

"She's my sister," I replied.

"What are you doing for money?" he asked.

"I sell a bit of pot here and there when I need it; other than that, I'll find a job somewhere."

"Well, if you're doing that, you may as well come with me and make some real money. What do you think?"

"Sure," I answered, without a thought. I was ecstatic. I was going to work with my big notorious brother. I didn't realize it at that very moment, but I had just made the worst mistake of my life. It was a decision that would haunt me for the next forty years.

HHH

My brother, through his partner, got me an apartment. I also got a car to drive, although I had no driver's licence. But, since I had no plans of stopping, and I knew how to drive, it didn't matter; the fine in those days for failing to produce a licence was twelve dollars.

I was versed over and over again on the importance of being vigilant of police surveillance, especially "tails" — cars following you while driving. I was taken to an apartment building nearby, where my brother introduced me to a very large lady and her young son. "This is our stash house," he told me. "No one comes here but us. The only way the cops can get here is if one of us screws up. Don't make that mistake. This lady could get in trouble, and if that happens, we have to get her out of it. Do you understand?" He was smiling at her as he told me this, and so I smiled at her, as well, and reassured her I understood. "No one comes here. Be careful," he repeated. I was then given a pager and placed "on call." I'd be told where and when to meet, who I was seeing, and how much product to bring. It was simple. It was trafficking in methamphetamine.

Now, I'd grown up in the projects, but I was totally in awe of the world of speed dealers and users. The first apartment I entered had no furniture save a large bed and two huge leather chairs in a back bedroom. Two girls, slightly older than I was, greeted my brother and me at the front door. They led us down the hallway to the bedroom. They were garbed only in panties and half-cut brassieres. I blushed. We entered the room as a man came out of the shower and proceeded to dress. He talked with my brother. He was very angry. He had to drive downtown. Some people owed him money, and now he was in a position of having to chase them down. He was fuming. He sat on a chair to put his boots on. "I'll kill them," he said, as he stamped his foot into a boot. Then he leaned back in the chair and went to sleep. Just like that. Out cold. I'd never seen anyone go from enraged to unconscious in one second. The two girls giggled. My brother laughed.

The two girls were then handed a bag to put away for their friend. They then turned their focus on me.

"Who is this little guy?"

"Oh, he's so cute," they teased.

"Would you like some cherry cheesecake?" they chided.

I was flushed.

"Cut it out," my brother told them. "You'll get to know him soon enough." Then he looked at me. "Ready to go?"

"Oh yeah," I answered, jumping out of the chair. I couldn't leave fast enough.

The girls giggled again. "See you soon," the taller one said. I looked back. She pulled one side of her panties halfway down and winked at me as she waved. I blushed again. I would live with each of these women for a time, separately, in the next few years.

Most of the people I met, I knew only by monikers — the German, the Crab, the Tall Guy, the Short Guy, the Fat Guy, the Little Fellow. The most animated, by far, though, was the King of Hearts. I met him one day as I was driving along the Danforth, a major Toronto thoroughfare, with my brother. He cut us off with his big black Cadillac and then braked. My brother stopped his vehicle and jumped out. The King of Hearts came swaggering up. "Brother!" he screamed as he hugged my brother. I stayed in the car watching all the pedestrians gaping at this spectacle. The King had a huge silver spoon, the size of a small saucer, hanging off an oversized silver rope chain he wore around his neck. On every finger, he had bejewelled gold rings. They talked for a few seconds, then parted ways.

After a few weeks of my new "employment," I was introduced to an attractive older woman from Jamaica. She was white, with blond hair and a great build. She was a marijuana cultivator, and also an importer of her product, Jamaican grass oil. I was given a bag to take to the stash house. Then I was told to go downtown to one of the head shops to procure a gross of five-gram glass vials. Those I dropped at my apartment. Then I picked up my brother's partner and we went shopping for alcohol to soften up the black tar oil and a turkey baster to transfer the oil into the vials. We also picked up dextrose, a baby-milk substance used to "cut" speed. I dropped the partner off at his car with the purchases.

I then went to visit a close friend from Regent. Neither of us lived there anymore, but we'd kept in touch. I brought a plastic bag containing a dozen or so joints. We smoked a couple in his apartment and had a beer. Then the phone rang. It was his sister. She wanted us to retrieve her from the project so she could join us. I was reluctant, but he convinced me. It wasn't that far away.

In Regent Park, everyone knew us, including the police. And as soon as we drove across the bridge, I saw them. Worse, they saw me — two beat cops who had chased me many times in the project. Now, I was trapped. "Shit," I said, as I reached into my shirt pocket and took out the plastic bag. There was a hole under the dash, so I stuck the bag up in there, flipping it toward the back. I proceeded through the light. They turned the corner and right onto the rear bumper of my car, horn blaring. I pulled over. One approached my window.

"Can I help you, officer?" I asked.

"Don't get fuckin' smart. Ownership, licence, you know the drill," he spat out.

"Is there a problem?" I asked innocently.

"That's it. Shut off the ignition and get outta the car!" he ordered.

His partner had come out on the other side and had my friend stand on the curb. "You, too," he said to me, pointing at the curb. I went and stood beside my friend. "Papers?" one asked. "Glovebox," I answered. Finding the ownership and mechanical fitness, he approached me. "Driver's licence?" I patted my pockets, reached in, and then feigned disappointment. "Oh, I must have left my wallet in my other pants," I told him.

"That'll be a fine," the cop informed me. "We're searching the car."

"Go ahead," I said.

"We weren't asking." The fat one scowled as they jumped into the front seat. My friend looked at me. He was nervous about the plastic bag. I just reassured him these two were idiots. "Aha! I got you," the one cop yelled, smiling. He held a half a cigarette of grass so old the paper was yellow. He'd pulled it out from under the floor mat.

"You have to be kidding me," I said.

"You have the right to remain …" and on he went with the standard drill.

"It's a big day for you guys, eh?" I sneered sarcastically.

"Take down your pants, we're searching you," one ordered.

"I'm not taking my pants down in the middle of a street. Go fuck yourselves!"

"We'll take you to the station then, and we're going to beat the crap out of you," the fat cop said.

"Go ahead," I dared. "I'm still not dropping my pants here."

The two looked at each other, and then one returned to their cruiser and got on the radio. My friend and I stood there for another twenty minutes. Then they handed me a summons to appear in court for the roach and a traffic ticket for failing to produce my licence.

"That was close," my friend said.

"You drive," I told him.

"I lost my licence," he told me.

"That's okay. I've never had one. Just drive," I said, handing him the keys.

"Where to?"

"Just go straight, I want to see something."

As soon as we moved, four other cars parked in the immediate vicinity began to move. I'd noticed them when I was standing on the curb. I knew Regent like the back of my hand, and there was no reason why cars would be stalled or waiting in the spaces these people occupied. There were two or three men in each vehicle.

I had my friend pull up in front of the nearby police station. I got out and went around to the driver's door. I stopped to give a fist pump to the idling cars stopped at the top of the street, then I got behind the wheel. I retrieved my bag of joints. The race was on. This was my first time being tailed in a vehicle. But I was in Regent. There was no way they were going to be able to maintain a tail on my car. This was my turf.

I owned it, I told myself as I wheeled this way and that through back alleys and side streets. Then I slid into the neighbouring Cabbagetown area.

About twenty minutes later, I merged into mainstream traffic, minus the tail. We never did pick up his sister that day.

I took my friend home, gave him a few joints. I smoked one and had a beer with him at his apartment. I wondered about the undercovers. Then my pager went off. It was the partner. "My place, seven o'clock," was all he said. I hung around for one more beer and then left. I watched for cops, but saw no one around or following me.

At seven, I took the empty vials up to the partner's apartment on the fourth floor. We were tenants of the same building. He already had the oil and alcohol from the stash house, so we went to work. I told him about the events of the day, but he shrugged it off as my imagination. Heating up grass oil, hard as tar, then diluting it with alcohol so that we could suck it up in the turkey baster to deposit it in vials was a messy job. Each vial would develop air pockets I had to pop in order to fill it. Finally, after cleaning off the last vial and cap, I set it down on the kitchen table. We were done.

Ke-rack! The front door of the apartment cracked in half, right across the middle. I assessed the situation: fourth floor, windows closed, blinds drawn, curtains pulled across them.

I had nowhere to run.

Ke-rack! The second swing of their sledgehammer knocked the door wide open. The narcs spilled into the apartment. "Don't fucking move!" a huge bearded cop screamed as he shoved a shotgun in my face. I looked at him, then slowly, very slowly, raised my left arm and moved the barrel to the side, away from my head. "I've gotta sit down," I told him. The cops were all over the apartment. They had 105 vials, each filled to capacity with Jamaican grass oil, staring them in the face, but they didn't look happy. They kept going into the back bedroom and talking.

After ten minutes, the lead narc took me into the bedroom with two other cops. "You think you're pretty smart blowing us off like that earlier tonight, eh, kid?" I feigned ignorance. "Down in Regent. You know what I'm talking about. You knew that was us," he said. I continued to play dumb. "Okay, where did the oil come from?" he asked.

"It was mine," I admitted. "I bought it off a guy in the bar last night. Thought I could make a few bucks."

"What guy? What bar?"

I gave him the name of a rundown East End watering hole and said earnestly, "The guy didn't give his name, but if I see him again, I'll call you guys." The cops looked at each other, then broke out laughing. "Sure you will, kid," the lead narc said, patting me on my shoulder. "Sure you will." He looked at his men. "Okay, pack everything up and let's get out of here." They all left. With us and the oil, too, of course.

At the station, they pulled the plastic bag of joints out of my shirt pocket and charged me with possession of those, as well. In the morning, we were both released on bail.

The partner could not wait to tell my brother about the tail in Regent. I found it ironic how the night before, just ahead of our arrest, in his opinion, the tail was just my imagination. My brother was pissed. "They fucking followed you? How many times did I tell you about that? Shit!" he ranted.

"I'm pretty sure they didn't," I said. (If they had, they would have hit my friend's apartment while I sat there, and they hadn't, I reasoned.)

"You're not positive, though, are you? Who did you tell about the oil?" he demanded.

"I didn't say anything to anyone," I answered angrily.

"You're full of shit. How else would they have got to you two idiots? Shit!" He continued his rant. I just stood there silently. "Okay," he said after a few seconds. "Well, they know what you look like now. So, if you want to keep working as the runner, the hair goes. Secondly, change the blue jean look. Go buy some dress pants and nice shirts. Shit, are you sure you never told anyone about the oil?"

I looked him in the eye and shook my head slowly. Then I went out and made an old Italian barber a very happy man.

‖‖‖

Bruno was a full-grown, attack-trained Doberman pinscher. The partner had bought him to protect a vacant house he was renovating for resale. Once inside, Bruno had other ideas. From the third floor, he spied a neighbour walking her dog. He backed up and ran headfirst right through the closed window. The smashed glass and Bruno fell onto the front lawn below. The lady got the door of her house closed behind her and her dog just as Bruno arrived. He tried to eat through her door. She called the Humane Society. Bruno was captured and placed in solitary confinement. His stubbed tail wagged a mile a minute as soon as he saw me come around the corner with his leash.

The humane society officer looked at me strangely as I admonished Bruno. "Idiot, next time, run down to the first floor, then jump out the window. You could have got hurt." After that, Bruno stayed with me, especially during business hours. He wouldn't let anyone near the car, and had occasion to bite both my oldest brother and an associate who snuck up on me in the car one day, trying to be funny. I liked that. One morning the landlord, thinking I wasn't home, used his key to access my apartment. I caught Bruno in mid-air as he lunged for the landlord's throat. "No dogs," he said, shaken, standing outside the apartment door. "Next time, knock," I told him. I kept Bruno.

A few nights after our release, the partner gave me a ride home, as my car had broken down. As we approached our building down a side street, I saw a few narcs from earlier that week. "Stop!" I said, pointing them out. "Let's get out of here. They haven't seen us."

Laughing, the partner replied, "Don't worry. They're just here for surveillance, to watch us." Then he pulled up right in front of the building, right in front of them.

Upon seeing us, they immediately pulled their guns out. One narc walked over to me with a sledgehammer. "You're just in time to see me knock on your door." He smiled.

"The landlord is already pissed with what you did to his door. Here, just use the key." I handed it to him. He took it and began to head into the building.

"Wait!" the partner yelled. "He has an attack dog in there!"

I couldn't believe he did that — warned the cop. The cop turned around, walked back up to me, and punched me hard in the face.

We were then placed in separate squad cars and were off to their police station again. When we entered, I saw the young boy from the stash house, and he saw us. "Mommy, your friends are here," he said. Right there, I knew we were in a world of trouble. As we were escorted down the hall, we passed a room that was occupied by the large lady. She uttered one word through her tears to me: "Please."

I was put in a small room with three of the narcs. The lead detective said, "Well, kid. We pretty much know everything. We've been onto your brother, his friends, and suppliers for a long time. We know you're the runner. You thought we were stupid over the oil bust, didn't you? We had you as soon as your brother called his partner on a wire-tapped line. All we did was trace the number to the location. We did think the glassware he was talking about was for a speed lab, and not some stupid vials for oil. [*So, that's how they found the apartment.*] And then your brother called the partner on the stash house line, and here we are. So, what I need to know is what involvement the large lady had in all this?"

The one thing I was thinking about is the only way the cops can find the stash house is if one of us screws up (well, he had), and we have to get the large lady out of trouble. I said, "She doesn't know anything. I couldn't trust my landlord, so we kept the tool boxes in her apartment. She doesn't know what was in them. She doesn't even know the combinations for the locks. I always had her leave the apartment when I went there." That was all I could do to help her. And that was exactly what she had said, other than she included everything she could about my brother and his partner. They'd been involved with her long before I'd come on the scene. After all, she was not a "player," she was a civilian, a mother with a young son.

My brother had arrived at the police station minutes behind us. We were placed in the cells for the night, then taken in the morning to the "bullpen" of the Old City Hall for a court appearance. I'd never been there before, and could not believe the amount of people crammed into that cage. All three of us were granted bail. The large lady had been released on her own recognizance. My brother and his partner had sureties present, so they were released. I was taken to the Don Jail in a police paddy wagon.

Stepping into the wagon, my wrists handcuffed to a strange older man on each side, was unsettling. The inside of the wagon was like an old tin breadbox, only with a tin bench to sit down on along each side. A small fan set in the roof made a lot of noise, but offered no circulation. With the door closed behind us, all I could smell was stale tobacco, sweat, and foot odour.

All I could think about was being helpless to turn back the clock. I'd made my bed the moment I agreed to work with my brother, and now I was lying in it. I took a breath and moved on in my mind. The wagon arrived at the jail and I was ushered into a long range, just past the admitting desk. All the handcuffs were removed. The cops left.

One by one, we were let out of the range to approach the desk for processing. Then we were lead to a large room where our clothing was taken. Our other property (wallets, rings, gold chains, watches, et cetera) had been taken at the desk. I was given a set of jailhouse "blues" — a loose, baggy, long-sleeved button-down shirt, baggy button-up pants, and one-dollar running shoes. Every article had been worn by a hundred people before me. Socks and underwear came in the bedroll consisting of two sheets and a towel. I had grown a good five inches over the previous year and was now nearly six feet tall, but still only weighed 120 pounds.

I was escorted up a few flights of iron stairs by the guards. They left me with a surly guard on one of the many landings. The Don Jail, old side, was filthy, gothic-looking, grey. Two ranges sat on each landing, one at each end. A heavy metal-barred black grille led onto an eighty-foot-long hall of narrow, barred cells on one side of a seven-foot-wide corridor. One toilet and sink sat at the end. The guard I was left with stood in front of a portable classroom chalkboard filled with the surnames of the occupants of both ranges. Young adults like myself.

"I don't know where I can put you," he lamented.

"I do," one youth yelled out. "Put him in a fucking broom closet."

There were a few seconds of laughter from inside the range, and then another youth yelled, "Put him in here, and we'll kill him."

The guard looked back at his board. "Now I really don't know where I'm going to put you."

"I do," I said, looking him right in the eye and pointing to the range that held my antagonists. "Right in there."

"Okay," he said, and unlocked the grille.

I walked past the thirty or so prisoners, down to the back of the filthy, dusty range. I turned to face the crowd. A younger teen from Regent Park came up to me. "Hi," he said. "I thought that was you. Don't worry about these assholes. You'll be alright."

I relaxed and sat down to talk with him. His nickname was Bugeye. I knew his older brothers. Most of the "kids" on this range were serving sentences between seven and ninety days for minor offences. They were mostly products of broken homes, foster homes, group homes, or training schools. They had definitely lacked positive "role models" or proper supervision. Very few, if any, had had a good start in life. Very few had good hygiene, either.

A couple of guys approached me to inquire about my charges. I didn't feel like talking to them, so I just said selling pot. That night, I had to sleep on an old grey army blanket over a bed of metal springs, no mattress, the frame held off the floor by short wooden benches that ran along the corridor. These bed frames extended through most of the range, as there were only so many cells, and way too many bodies. I didn't sleep much, and spent a lot of the night watching the huge, dark rats scurrying up and down the wooden floors searching for food. The odd person would get bitten, but not on this night. I slept eventually.

I awoke in the morning with a group of teens my age surrounding my bed. "You're a fucking liar," one kid spat out as I sat up and put my feet on the floor. "You're not in here for selling pot," another kid said as I slid on my runners.

"No?" I queried.

"No, you're here for conspiracy to traffic methamphetamine," he answered.

"So?" I said.

Another youth asked, "What is that?"

Right then I knew they had no idea. They all would know what speed was, but the clinical name escaped their knowledge. I stood up. "It's pot. Now, is there a problem here?"

They looked at each other. "I'll find out," their leader said, glaring at me. "We have to go to work, but we'll be back."

"I'll be here," I said.

When they returned, I was on my way off the range for bail release. Gray, the leader, said, "You'd better not come back."

I smiled. "Look me up when you get out. I'd like that."

I was taken down to an area at the front of the jail. A justice of the peace sat behind a desk. On the other side stood my brother and a couple who I didn't know. I went toward my brother, but the older woman grabbed me in a hug and whispered in my ear.

The JP barked at the guard to separate us and have me stand beside him. He eyed me suspiciously. "Do you know these people?"

"Yes."

"How?" he queried.

"They've been friends of my family for years."

"What are their names?"

"Uncle Bob and Aunt Edith," I said.

"Where do they live? Where are they from?"

"Toronto," I answered. That didn't seem to satisfy him, so I added, "Downsview, to be exact."

The JP was still hesitant.

My brother stepped forward in his new pinstriped suit. "Can I have your name, please?" he asked politely but sternly.

"Why?" said the JP.

"Judge Wilson saw fit to grant this young man bail. His sureties are present. If you deny him his freedom, I'll do my best to have you before Judge Wilson this very afternoon," my brother answered.

The JP wasn't the only one ever to mistake my brother for a lawyer. I left the Don Jail ten minutes later.

卌

That summer, I met a girl at a party. She'd call me to her parents' home whenever they were out. She knew I was on bail, but she was alright with that. She told me that her brother, Gray, was in the Don Jail. The day he arrived home, I was sitting on their couch. "Hello," I said. He froze. Although it was obvious he recognized me, he never said a word. After a while, I left. I didn't date her after that, although she called. I'd made my point.

Now that my brother and I had been arrested, one would think that we'd retire from "the game." Quite the contrary. My brother was determined to accumulate a nest egg for when he was in prison. I just wanted to have a good time.

No longer an unknown commodity, I came out of the shadows and into the bars and nightclubs: "The scene." I enjoyed the pleasure of alcohol, soft drugs, and women. And there were a lot of women. It was amazing how many were attracted to drug dealers — the "bad boys." It was also amazing how beautiful they looked when I was high compared to when I was straight. But then, most of them were with me because they had their own abuse issues.

My brother was all business. I rarely saw him during the summer. He employed a lot of criminal associates who were very adept at distribution. I remet the Row Boat at this time. I'd met him in Regent Park years earlier. I'd sat with his sister in one of my high school classes. It was his reputation in the Park that caused me to help him out one day.

I was relaxing on a grassy area near the three-store strip mall in South Regent. I watched as the Row Boat raced his car down into the parking lot beside me, a police cruiser in hot pursuit. He stopped, jumped out of his vehicle, tossed an open bottle of beer away, and ran into the restaurant. The police flew out of their car and pursued him. They came out of the restaurant a couple of minutes later with him in handcuffs and stood him beside his car as they searched it. Finding nothing, they took their handcuffs back and left the area. The Row Boat stood there, looking around, scratching his head.

"Are you thirsty?" I yelled over to him.

"What?" he yelled back.

"I said, are you thirsty?" pointing to an open case of beer over by a parked car. I'd taken it out of the back seat while he was in the restaurant being accosted and handcuffed.

He walked over to me. "Anything else?"

"Yeah, the plastic bag under the driver's seat is in the beer case, too," I added.

He smiled. "Who are you, kid?"

I told him.

"I've met your brother," he said.

"I took three beers," I informed him.

He laughed. "Do you do speed?"

"No, I just smoke weed," I said.

"I have that, too. Come by my apartment later, and I'll hook you up for free," he said, sauntering off.

I dropped by later and he gave me a small bag. I stayed for the beer he offered. While I was there, two guys I knew from Regent stopped by to get some dope. He was nice. They gave him money. He gave them a bag. And then he picked up a wooden club and split one of their heads open. They left. He thought that was hilarious. I thought he was not well-grounded. I left after my beer, which I drank very fast. And I never ever went back.

Now, here he was, standing in front of me. The Row Boat was the main "street dealer" for one of my brother's closest friends. Since most of my brother's "crew" were his age, some thirteen years older than me, the Row Boat, being only seven years my senior, was closest to my age. We'd constantly cross paths in the bars around Regent and in the downtown clubs. He always ensured I had a good time. He'd stop by my apartment just to have a beer and shoot the breeze. His wife had grown up on the next block over from me in Regent. Her older sisters had dated my brothers, and the younger one had been infatuated with me for years. Now, with her being old enough to date and overly experienced, I dated her. That relationship brought the Row Boat and me closer.

At that time, my brother had made his contacts with a chemistry wiz he called Brainiac, and a number of business investors. They worked on a project while I partied. One night, at an after-hours club, I sat with the Row Boat and a few of the crew. My brother was there with his girl, but they sat far back of us. We gave them their space. But I noticed as they stood to leave that a couple of men near the exit stood up and left, too. I knew them by sight. One was the president of a local outlaw motorcycle gang, the other a "psycho," not long released from Millhaven maximum-security penitentiary. After my brother and his girl left the club, I waited five seconds or so, then said my good nights to the guys. I followed them out the laneway door, quietly. No one heard the door open or close. Both men had their backs to me in the darkened laneway, facing my brother, who had his girl behind him, nearer the well-lit street. "Now is not the time," I heard my brother say, as he saw me quietly approaching.

"Now is exactly the right time," the psycho answered.

Standing directly behind, but between the two large men, in the dark, I asked, "Is there a fucking problem here?"

Startled, they both jumped sideways, away from each other. I continued to stand still, with a full-bladed buck knife in my right hand. "Well?" I asked.

They looked at my brother. After a couple of seconds, the biker said that they would talk another time. My brother motioned me toward him. I stepped between the two, turned, and smiled as I folded the blade back into its handle. His girl got the car and I jumped in the back seat as he took the front passenger. Then he turned around, angry. "Are you fucking crazy? Don't you know who they are?"

I assured him I knew exactly who they were, and I told him I saw them planning to waylay him in the alley. His girlfriend turned on him. I'd never seen her so mad. "You might try thanking him instead of being an asshole!" she said. "If it wasn't for him, I'd be driving you to either the hospital or the morgue right now."

He looked at her, then back at me. "You did good. You're stupid, but you did good." That was as big a compliment as I'd ever get from my oldest brother.

Later, he was able to mediate a truce with the biker. The psychopath faded away fast, after finding out people were interested in seeing him. He was in serious danger.

||||
†|||

A week or so later, I was in my apartment when the phone rang. It was my brother. "Phone the guys. Tell them I said to hit the mattresses."

"What do you mean?" I asked.

"Just do it!" he screamed.

"Alright," I said and hung up. *Geez, what the hell is his problem now?* I wondered. But still, I went out to the pay phone a couple of blocks away and began making calls. When I returned home, I ran into two of the men at my front door.

"What's going on?" one asked once we were inside.

"Beats me," I said, putting the kettle on.

"What do you mean? You called us and said to hit the mattresses," the other guy said.

"Yeah, well, my brother called. Said to tell everyone that, so I did."

That's when I noticed the duffle bag one of the guys had with him. He plopped it on my kitchen table and unzipped it. Inside were all kinds of handguns, shotgun shells, and boxes of ammunition.

There was a knock at the door. Three more of my brother's friends came walking in. Two had trench coats on. From underneath, they produced a shotgun and an automatic machine gun. All three had handguns holstered in front, on their sides, and on their backs. There was another knock on the door. Within a half hour, my apartment held twelve to fifteen well-established criminals and a small arsenal of weaponry. *So*, I told myself, *this is "hitting the mattresses."* None of the men looked overly worried. They seemed more irritated than anything. A couple of hours later, my brother strode in and talked to the crew. The leader of the West End speed dealers had his car blown about fifteen feet into the air, and he believed the people in my apartment had done it. My brother, along with a mediator, the Crab, went to his apartment to reassure him that if it had been any of the East End crew the leader would have been in the car when it blew up. As it turned out, while this meeting was still going on, information came in that the explosion had been caused by two older, disgruntled West End boys who wanted to make a point with their own leader. Everything returned to normal in the East End.

Although I had a few girlfriends at this time, I always stayed with my favourite girlfriend at night or when I wasn't out running on the roads or sitting in clubs. She lived with her sister at the Row Boat's house, a ground-floor condo in Mississauga, just west of Toronto. One morning, as we prepared to leave, I noticed a shadow crossing the curtained back glass wall. I got up and went to the back door. Suddenly, there was a knock at the front door and the Row Boat went to answer. I moved a piece of the curtain sideways and there was a bearded man standing there, smiling. He pumped the shotgun in his hands. Just then, the front door flew open, knocking the Row Boat halfway across the room.

The narcs filled the apartment. "Don't move! Get your hands up high on the wall!" I complied but was hit in the back of the head with the butt of a shotgun and knocked to the floor. The cops handcuffed me as they stood on my legs, head, and spine. Then they pulled me onto my feet. The Row

Boat was getting the same treatment. We were driven in separate cars downtown to 52 Division. In the hallway, a number of narcs were already there, cheering on their comrades. Four cops took me into a main washroom at the end of the hall. There, they informed me that my brother and his friends were being arrested up north at some clandestine drug lab. I told them I knew nothing about any lab, and they proceeded to assault me for the next few minutes. When they took a break, I told two of the narcs who'd arrested me before with my brother, "Look, I know nothing about a lab. You have the wrong guy. I don't even have a brother." I smiled. The assault was back on, with my head being banged against the porcelain base of the toilets.

When they finally stopped, they took me down the hall to a large classroom-like area with a bunch of chairs. The Row Boat and a few other people I knew were there, as well as some I didn't know at all. A big, bearded detective sat beside me and removed my handcuffs. "Kid," he said, "you're in a lot of trouble. You're going to prison for at least five years."

I remained solemn.

"Your brother won't be going with you, though. My guys are going to kill him up on that farm. It really is too bad." He shrugged.

"How much time could I get?" I inquired.

"Oh, we could see you get ten years," he volunteered.

"You'd better give me that then, if my brother doesn't walk in here," I swore. "It'll give you fuckers another five to live."

That was it. I was lifted off the chair and dragged back to the washroom.

The next morning, as the Toronto tabloids screamed with news of a major drug bust worth millions of dollars, we were all being arraigned at Old City Hall on charges of conspiracy to traffic in methamphetamine. While most made bail immediately, my brother and I had already exhausted our options and were held in custody and sent to the Don Jail. This time, though, because of the seriousness of the offences, I would not be placed on the "kiddie" range on the old side. Instead, I went with my brother to the newer side, which housed women offenders and the most dangerous of the males. Unlike the old side, it was clean. The cell doors and barriers were automated, save for the landing doors on each of the five floors. Each range had eighteen cells with open, barred doors on one side, a ten-foot-wide corridor down its length.

And so I settled in with my oldest brother and sixteen other men. Being a detention centre, the turnover rate of the range population (of the entire jail, actually) was very high. Few remained for any length of time, either being released on bail or transferred at the conclusion of their trials.

It was the fall of 1975, I was nineteen years old, and for the next two years I would be mentored to the nth degree in the criminal lifestyle. Men busied themselves discussing past and future crimes, playing cards, or poring over court transcripts. Many would pace for hours in the back area of the range, alone in their thoughts. One did not whistle in jail. Whistling cuts like a knife into the minds of troubled men; and being incarcerated, these men were troubled. Whistling was also seen as a sign of a happy and carefree person and one of the men was always quick to change that mood, most often with a punch in the teeth. At mealtime, I learned never ever to reach over another man's food. I saw quite a number of fights break out over that.

Some of the men would exercise daily, but most just paced, during the one hour of yard per day or at the back of the range.

The Don also had a steady stream of drugs pouring in. There were just too many avenues for that not to occur. Guards and jail staff were susceptible to greed and other vices. Holes to the outside world were made in the building. Prisoners came in daily from the street. The Don is where I learned about secreting vials, or substances packed in rubber sheaths like balloons or condoms. These could be inserted into body cavities like a suppository, or swallowed, to be retrieved later during a bowel movement. It was crude, but effective.

The Don was a place where criminals who held grudges might encounter each other on the normal ranges. If not, they might meet in the court cell ranges (ranges designed to group together offenders who had court appearances scheduled for the following morning). Some men would schedule their court dates to coincide with those of their enemies; or conversely to avoid them. The court cell ranges were no picnic. The "code blue" alarm sounded throughout the jail most every court day. Sometimes several times. Bullies would try to take what they liked off other men. Some new guy would whistle or lean over food; sometimes, someone just didn't like the look of someone else. It was that simple. And frequent. Still, the court cell ranges paled in comparison to the Old City Hall bullpen when it came to violence.

The bullpen was a fifty-square-foot cage with heavy metal bars on two sides, flat walls on the others, and one toilet. This was the holding area for men waiting to be taken either to one of the many courtrooms in the building or to a police paddy wagon to take them back to their designated jails after. Plain wooden benches lined all four sides. Most every weekday, the bullpen would be packed to capacity from seven or eight in the morning until four or five o'clock at night. Wagons would arrive from jails or police stations en masse.

During our first few weekly remands, I was leg-shackled to my brother. We were considered flight risks. The odd time a prisoner would attempt to cut in between us and would be met with elbows and scowls. My brother and I stayed out of the intermingling crowds for the most part. He'd always chide me for being a "loon" magnet, though. For some strange reason, if there was a nutcase in the crowd, he'd find me. Different men would come up and initiate a conversation with me, then with themselves, and finally with an imaginary friend or creature. I even met my first real-life cannibal in the bullpen. I did have a few fights in this place. Thankfully, it was after we were relieved of our leg shackles. Men would try to take my cigarettes, my lunch, or my coffee, but not too often.

One early morning, my brother and I arrived on the first wagonload from the Don. We each bought a coffee and he went off to converse with one of the men who'd come in with us. The bullpen was empty. I went to the other side and sat on a bench. I was staring at my coffee, and the floor, when the next transport came in from a local police precinct. I was really tired, and having a hard time waking up that morning. When the men from the cop shop were let into the bullpen, I paid no nevermind. I was just too tired. Suddenly, a man stood before me. "Move!" he screamed. I looked up into the eyes of a huge, enraged black man. "Excuse me?" I said.

"You're in my seat. Fucking move!" he ordered. I glanced at the empty benches to my left, and then to my right. In fact, most every bench in the bullpen was empty. "Fucking move!" he threatened again.

"Take it easy," I said calmly. "I didn't know this was your seat." I stood up with my coffee and lightly wiped the seat where I had been sitting with my other hand. "Have a seat," I told him. He did as I took a step away. After two steps, I set my coffee down on the bullpen floor. Then I turned and, like kicking in a door, I drove my foot into the man's face, driving the back of his head into the thick steel bar behind him. He went unconscious immediately and fell bleeding onto the floor. I dragged him by his coat collar over to the bullpen door. Then I went back, picked up my coffee, and sat down in the same place.

"Starting early today, aren't you, kid?" the court officer quipped.

"Where the fuck do you guys find these people? Jesus Christ," I answered.

My brother then came across the bullpen to find out what had happened. "I was in his seat," I said. He laughed, shook his head, and said, "You are definitely a loon magnet." I wasn't laughing.

I had to knock a few people out in the bullpen. I would have to say, in all my days, with all the terrible places I've been, the Old City Hall bullpen, while not the most dangerous, was definitely the most violent. And the most congested.

卌

Those first two years I spent at the Don, I met a lot of charismatic people, but none so much as John the Hat. He was a character right out of a Mickey Spillane novel. The Hat was a hustler. He was a card shark, a pool shark, and a grifter. And he was damn good at it. He'd been brought into the Don on charges similar to my own: drug conspiracy. He and my brother sat down to play gin for one hundred dollars a game. The Hat dealt and won the first hand handily. My brother dealt the second hand. As the Hat picked up his cards as they were dealt, they ran from the deuce to the Queen, all in the same suit, all in consecutive order. He looked up at my brother.

"Now, do you want to keep cheating, or do you want to play gin?" my brother said. The Hat started laughing, realizing he wasn't the only card shark on the range. "New game," he said. After that, they got along famously. At least until the Hat got sentenced and shipped out. He arrived back from court the last day, totally distraught. "How much time?" men asked. "Six months solid," the Hat answered. The entire range was laughing.

While the others' trials were ending, my first was just beginning. I'd plea bargained the oil and stash house conspiracies to a three-year provincial term. There was no chance of acquittals on either case. The drug lab case was different. The trial judge, the Crown attorneys, the lawyers, jurors, cops, not even us, could have predicted this one trial would last for a year and three weeks. Every workday of every week was filled with courtroom drama. I was young and resilient, so I know everyone else must have found this trial painstakingly arduous, as I did.

My brother and I were awoken every morning around five. We were given a small bowl of cereal, hard toast, and a cup of jailhouse coffee for breakfast. We then dressed and were taken in the first paddy wagon to the bullpen beneath the Superior Court building. We'd sit there until court commenced at either nine or ten o'clock. At lunch, we'd be given either a roast beef or chicken salad sandwich on white, with a small coffee. Every day. Then back to the courtroom for the afternoon session. All day, we sat on hard plastic chairs in the prisoners' box. After four p.m., sometimes five, we were taken back down to the bullpen to await transport back to the Don. We'd arrive back there around six-thirty or seven — well after the four o'clock supper feeding — and be offered cold leftovers. We'd be back on our range in time to take a shower and get locked in our cells for the night. In the morning, the routine would begin again.

After two months of this, we went on a hunger strike. A couple of weeks into it, the trial judge ordered his staff to provide us with a hot lunch each day of the trial. We rarely ate anything at the Don Jail, other than the chocolate bars we were allowed to purchase. After six months of trial, we arrived back at the Don one day, changed into our blues, and headed up the old side's iron stairs to the range that led onto the new side and our range. Halfway up, a couple of guards asked us politely to step into a side bullpen. We were locked in and then the entire landing filled up with guard staff. Three lieutenants opened the bullpen door. "You first," they said to me. I walked out into the crowd of uniforms and was led up the next flight and across the landing. A wooden barrier was moved to expose a heavy barred grille that led to a short range containing four cells. At the end of the corridor was a small, one-man shower. In the middle of the corridor sat a small table and two chairs.

This was 1976. Capital punishment had just been abolished in Canada, and the Don Jail's last remaining prisoner facing the hangman's noose had been transferred to a Quebec penitentiary. And I was to be the first occupant of 9 Holding, a new name for the old death row at the Don. I was barely twenty years old.

Each cell had a heavy bed anchored to the wall, with thick, linked chains of steel on each end. The open-faced cells had thick sets of bars, while the ceiling and walls were steel on steel on steel plates. A metal toilet sat at the back of each cell.

I was locked in on the range. My brother followed shortly thereafter, protesting our situation. Once inside, I told him, "Look at this place. There's blood and shit everywhere." And there was. On the walls, the bars, even the ceiling.

My brother yelled until the guards came back. "You either give us what we need to clean up this place, or the first guard coming in here to lock us up will be getting knocked out. Every time." He was fuming.

They left, and came back with buckets, pails, mops, rags, cleansers, disinfectants — the works. We sterilized the entire range. When we were done, we gave them their cleaning supplies back. We didn't speak to them again for weeks. We also never took any food or liquids from them.

After two weeks, they slid in a small portable radio. Two weeks after that, they brought in a black-and-white television. Two weeks after that, we had a visit from the lieutenant. He spoke to my brother. "We put you guys in here because you create too much unity. Every prisoner in this jail knows either you or your brother, or both. We had to show them that we run this jail." We sat silent. "This range is supposed to be for punishment, but I have a list of at least fifty prisoners on the new side demanding transfer to this range to be with you guys. What do you think of that?" he asked.

"Fuck you," my brother told him.

"Listen, I'll make you a deal. I'll let you two look at the list; you can pick two guys to move in here with you. I'll have my staff leave the cell doors open so you have access on the range from six a.m. to midnight. Maybe watch a late show movie once in a while."

"Sounds good," I said.

The lieutenant looked at my brother. "I can't put anyone up here while you two keep refusing food and drink."

"Fuck you," my brother repeated.

"Look," the lieutenant said. "You can probably keep this up for a while, but your brother weighs what, a hundred pounds. You know, we all know, he won't eat until you say so. Is that what you want?"

Now it was my turn. "Fuck you," I told him.

A week later, my brother told me we'd achieved all that we could hope to in death row. He was going to get two of his crew to move in to the remaining cells. But we had to start eating again. I looked at him. "Because of me?"

"No," he assured me.

"Good. And it's about time." I smiled. "What's for supper?"

He laughed.

I'd remain on death row for seven months. Finally, our trial ended and the jury had spoken. My brother, Brainiac, and four others were convicted of the conspiracy. I was acquitted, along with three others. The main evidence against me had been the testimony of one narc who swore he'd seen me acting as a lookout at the lab in Barry's Bay, Ontario, with a shotgun and two-way radio. But I had my lawyer point to the wiretap, which had me speaking on the phone in Mississauga, some two hundred miles away, the same day, almost to the exact minute. The jury had concluded, and rightly so, that the cop had to be mistaken, if not outright lying. He couldn't have seen me. I wasn't there. Yet I had spent the last two years of my life in the Don Jail because of this charge.

After court was done, I was taken out of the death cells and transferred to a provincial assessment centre in Brampton. It was very clear to everyone that I was not the same kid who'd entered the Don two years earlier. I'd met murderers, bank robbers, hit men, biker enforcers. I'd met Vic Cotroni and Paolo Violi, the two alleged Mafia bosses of Montreal crime families. I'd met the entire gauntlet of acceptable criminals and received a full education in how to act as a "bad guy," a "rounder." And now here I was in a reformatory with young men my own age, or first-time offenders.

The case officers brought me into a side room with two other prisoners from the institution. "If you have any questions while you're here, feel free to ask. If anyone bothers you, and you don't feel at liberty to talk to us, you can talk to these two guys. They are your inmate committee."

I looked at the case officers as if they were crazy. "If I have a problem, I'll deal with it myself," I said.

"Oh, you're the one from the Don," the guard said. "We were warned about you." The meeting was over.

That night at seven, the guards handed out juice and cookies to each man in line. I waited until I thought the line was full, then stood at the back. Two men my age came out of one of the dorms to stand in the line behind me. "You see that?" one meathead said to the other. "A new kid comes in, and butts in the line right in front of us. Maybe he doesn't know who we are?"

I turned and looked at the one speaking. "I know who you are. You're a fucking asshole. And if you have something to say to me, say it to my face." I waited for an answer, but with none coming, I turned back around. I waited for the attack to begin, but it never came.

Three weeks later, I was transferred to Maplehurst Reformatory, a minimum-security institution. My first night there, I was at the billiard table, shooting pool when a tall, blond, buxom female guard entered the room. "Oh," she said, smiling at me. "Give me your cue," she told my opponent, "I want to play with him." I set my cue on the table. "I don't play with coppers," I said, and left.

The next day I was summoned to a boardroom and a panel of the Ontario Parole Services. "We've been trying to locate you for almost a year. Where have you been?" one of the men asked.

"The Don Jail," I answered.

"We asked for you there, and they said you weren't there," a woman said.

"They lied," I said matter-of-factly.

"Well, where did you serve your sentence?" she continued.

"The Don Jail," I repeated.

"All of it?" she asked, incredulous.

"All except the last three weeks in Brampton," I told her.

"Do you want a parole?" she asked.

"Not really," I answered honestly.

"We'll have you out in two days," she said. She seemed nice.

I'd just read in the newspaper that my brother had received a twelve-year prison term. In my mind, at that time, that was like a death sentence. No one could do twelve years. I had to see him. I had to help him get out. "I'll take the parole if you want to grant it," I said.

Two days later, I walked out of Maplehurst and back into society as a first-time parolee.

On provincial parole, my first day, I visited my mother and other family members in the morning. In the afternoon, I went and saw my girlfriend — at least, the girl who had been looking after my clothing and visits since my arrest. She was in the hospital with some form of low blood cell count and would be there for days. She was a beautiful woman, an exotic dancer, actually — a stripper. I then went to see the family of one of my friends who had been convicted alongside my brother. They lived near the reporting centre, so it was there I chose to get hammered on alcohol as the night settled in. Around eight p.m. I left my valuables and money with them and staggered into the reporting centre in Regent Park. "I'm here to report," I told the desk sergeant. Reporting was a condition of my parole release. "Papers?" he asked. I handed him the release papers. He punched my name into the computer. He looked at the monitor, and then went over to the printer. He pushed a button and it began to sing. Just like I knew it would. By the time it finished, I was using the counter to hold myself up.

"You've really been giving us a hard time, haven't you?" he said. "Look at all these tickets you have."

I told him, "Your boys have been giving me a hard time. Look at the tickets. Every one of them is in this division. Everywhere else, no one bothers me."

"Well, you're paying them," he said.

"I ain't paying shit," I informed him.

"You're going to jail then, son." He motioned for another cop to come over. "Lock him up."

"Drunk tank, Sarge?" the rookie asked.

"No, the cells. This one's going to the Don."

Perfect, I thought, listening to the conversation. I smiled at the sarge one last time and said, "Fuck you."

I slept it off in the cells, and the next morning I was taken to the admitting desk at the old Don Jail. The lieutenant eyed the paperwork. "Kid, the death cells are full right now. You can sleep on the range beside it and visit during the day. Obviously, you want to see your brother, or you would have paid these fines?" I nodded. "Okay," he yelled along to the guards, "this one goes to 9 Holding." I changed into blues and led the way.

"What the hell are you doing back here?" My brother could not believe his eyes. "Give me a minute. I have to use your toilet," I said. After I washed my hands and threw a couple of bags of hash and grass on the table, I began. "Okay, how do you want out?" My brother looked at me like I was crazy. "What are you talking about?" he asked. "Listen," I told him, "No one can do twelve years, so just tell me how to get you out, and we'll get it done."

He shook his head. "Just go home, kid. I'll handle this. You're messed up. You need to go home, get a job, and stay out of jail. I can handle the twelve. Trust me on that."

The next morning I was released. All tickets back then ran concurrent to the longest one, and considering the night I reported and the morning I was released, I barely had time to visit my brother.

He was right, though. I was definitely not well-grounded coming out from my two years at the Don. I expected violence at every turn. Every conversation was a potential altercation. The constant daily pressures I had placed on my mind, inside, awaiting violence on so many different levels, and receiving it from prisoners, nutcases, and guard staff. It was etched on my brain. I exploded out onto the streets. I was fighting constantly. I had hardly ever fought before I went to jail.

I assaulted a dealer at a hotel my second night home. One of my friends from Regent had told me he was an informer for the police. As it happened, he was not. He'd assaulted my friend, and it wasn't hard for my friend to sucker me into returning the favour.

One day I got a call from the wife of one of the guys doing time over the lab conspiracy. She was in Regent at his mother's, and there was a major problem. I drove over and came in through the back door. My friend's wife explained the situation. A group of young men my age had thrown a brick through the living-room window and were standing outside, threatening to beat up everyone in the house. I walked into the living room and saw four of my friend's relatives sitting there. All adult males. Roofers. In good shape. I felt confident as I looked out at the gang of youths.

I stepped out the front door; then heard the door being locked behind me. This was not good.

Two young men my age approached me. "Who are you, the heavy?"

"No, I just want to resolve this problem here. What's up?"

The bigger one answered me. "That old hag in there called the cops on my brother and now he's in jail."

"I heard," I said, "but I also heard your brother chased that ninety-pound eighty-year-old woman into her house and was kicking on her bathroom door, threatening to kill her while she was locked inside. What did he expect her to do?"

The other brother, standing off to my right side, sucker-punched me in the face. I knew he was going to do that before he did and I went with the blow sideways, so the impact was minor. I'd had my hand on my motorcycle-chain belt from the start of the conversation, and now the buckle was around my fist, the chain belt snaking through the loops on my blue jeans. I snapped back up and swung. The belt wrapped around the young man's head as I followed through, sending my assailant sprawling to the ground. Then I reefed my belt. The chain links tore across his face as they unravelled to let go of him.

I was still facing his brother and their friends throughout this, but they all stepped back as the one brother writhed in pain on the ground. A few of the others ran up to me. "Put the chain down," they cried. "Go fuck yourselves," I answered. "There's ten of you. I'm not putting nothing down." I was standing my ground. Just like in the Don or the bullpens.

"We'll get weapons, too, then," they shouted.

Picking their friend off the ground, they retreated to their nearby row houses. I looked back at the locked door, then walked over to the neighbourhood restaurant. No one was there, but I could hear music blaring inside. Music meant a party, which meant people. I knocked. Two minutes later, I walked back with several friends to the house where the altercation occurred. After a very brief skirmish, the problem was resolved. The next afternoon, I went back to check on my friend's mother. She was just getting back from grocery shopping, and the young man I'd faced off with the night before was carrying her bags. "I'm sorry," he said. "We didn't know who you were."

"I'm sorry, too," I said, "about your brother. He shouldn't have hit me. As for your other brother, I have a lawyer coming to see the old lady, and she'll drop the charges and get your brother out. But you guys can't be bugging her. Her son's my friend, and he's in the Pen. And I'm keeping an eye on her, okay?"

He smiled and said, "We're cool." That was that.

||||

At the local bar one evening, I ran into Ryan. His mother was one of the Row Boat's customers. Ryan and I had met on a range in the Don Jail, when three other prisoners were attacking him and I jumped in to even the odds. I knew his mom, and I knew who he was. We'd talked after the fight. Ryan was a few years older than I was, but we got along well. He'd been in the penitentiary already. I hadn't. At this point in my life, I looked up to him, as I did to most criminals.

We began to associate. Then we began to do crimes together. I liked break and enters on insured companies. No one got hurt, and it wasn't personal. Other crimes, I liked not so much. I did like to deal drugs. It was something I was used to.

I also liked to party with a crowd, but Ryan was more of a solitary man, and preferred just to get high with his girlfriend in the privacy of their apartment.

One night after deciding to take a friend out to celebrate his birthday, Ryan and I drove to the Beer Store to get a case for after. As Ryan walked in, I noticed a dark car idling on the road that led into the Beer Store parking lot. It was night, and the car's headlights were out. My internal alarm went off. The car I was driving was stolen.

I pulled up sideways to the exit door as Ryan came out. "Don't get in the car. Keep walking. Go. Cops," I told him.

He walked up anyways and opened the passenger door. Throwing the case in the back seat, he plopped down on the front passenger seat. "Fuck them," he said. And then the car headlights came on and sped up through the parking lot right toward us. Three more cars came from the other direction straight at us. Each car had a man hanging out the front passenger window holding either a shotgun or handgun. "Fuck them, eh?" I smiled at

Ryan. "You tell them." I giggled. We were ripped out of the car, thrown to the ground, handcuffed, and placed under arrest.

We appeared in court the following morning for theft auto times six. Apparently, five more stolen vehicles sat adjacent to Ryan's home in a neighbourhood parking lot. And this task force had deemed us responsible. They also thought we were responsible for numerous Beer Store robberies that had been occurring in the city. I fit the description of the robber, which is why they'd jumped us in the first place. There was no evidence to support their theory, though, so no charges were laid. I told Ryan's lawyer to cut a deal, where I would take the time, but he assured me he took no direction from me. Ryan appeared first and was given three months consecutive to his parole. He was very happy. I followed with my lawyer, the Lion. I received three months concurrent to my parole, which was nine months in length, so basically I didn't receive a day. Ryan was not so happy with his lawyer then.

We were both taken to the Don. Ryan was gone within a few days, back to the penitentiary. On the weekend, I received a visit from a very surprising visitor. Her name was Sadie. I'd seen Sadie on occasion, but never really talked to her. Although she was my age, twenty-one, she was hooked up with one of the older rounders in the crew. He was around thirty-five. She told me they'd been split up for a while, and that she'd wanted to get in touch with me but didn't know how until she heard of my arrest. Sadie was a very beautiful young woman. I told her I wasn't getting out for a while. She asked if she could visit, if I thought we could have a chance at a relationship. I told her I needed to check out that I wasn't stepping on the older rounder's toes, but if he truly had no objections, I certainly didn't. I could not believe my good fortune that she was interested in me.

The answer came back from a mutual friend that the older criminal had no objection, and wished us well. Perfect. Sadie was ecstatic when I said she could come see me. She'd visit faithfully over the next six months. I was in love.

Six months in a provincial reformatory to me was easy. I was assessed at the Don to serve my term at Mimico Correctional Centre, just west of Toronto. I arrived there a couple of days later on a bus with other prisoners. The transport guards escorted us, along with a Mimico guard, to the admitting area. The Mimico guard was barking orders like an army drill sergeant.

"You're on my turf now. You keep the line straight, and you, pick up your pace. You, what are you looking at? Eyes straight."

Jesus Christ, I thought, *where'd they find this idiot?*

When the transfer guards began to remove the handcuffs, the Mimico guard shoved his face in front of mine. "You step out of line here, Sonny, and I'll put you back in it," he threatened.

I've never been good with threats. "Not by yourself, you won't," I assured him.

He was shocked, and screamed, "What did you say to me?"

"You heard me," I answered.

"Who the fuck do you think you are?"

I didn't blink.

He looked at the transfer guards. "Get him back on your bus and off my property," he stammered.

And that was that for doing time in Mimico. I was taken back to the Don, and reclassified for the Ontario Reformatory, Guelph.

The ORG had two wings. One building was comprised of dormitory settings, while the other contained cells. Reception for new arrivals was in the dorm on the first floor. I was given my newcomer's issue of clothes, bedding, toiletries, and a metal property box to keep valuables in, such as canteen products and extra clothing. I was assigned a bed. I made up the mattress with the sheets and blanket. I slid the box beneath the bed. I picked up a book off a book cart in the common room, then lay back to enjoy it. I knew how to enter a range without attracting attention.

An hour later, another newcomer arrived, an older man about fifty-five, assigned to the empty bed beside me. He threw his box under the bed, flopped his bedding on top, and left. Two young guys around eighteen years old approached me.

"What's up?" I asked.

"The guy beside you, he's a sex offender," one said.

"Oh, really?"

"Yeah, and we're gonna beat him up," they said.

"Good for you two," I answered.

"We want you to throw a blanket over his head so he doesn't see it's us, okay?" one asked.

"No, it's not okay. If I do that, he'll see *me*, won't he?"

"Yeah, you're right. Forget it," one said, and off they went. Later on that night, as the dorm speakers blared, "Five minutes to lights out," and the older man stood at the foot of his bed flipping his sheets across the expanse of his mattress, the two kids attacked. The first kid smacked the man in the back of the head with the brush end of a large push broom in a pillow case. The force knocked the man over onto the top of his bed. The first kid ran. The second kid began to rain blows down on the man with the stick part of the same broom. Then he ran back to the safety of his bed. But first, he threw the stick out into the hallway, outside of the dorm.

The man began yelling for the guards and ran out of the dorm. Not three seconds later, he come running back with the stick in his hand. He ran over to the second kid's bed and walloped him across the chest. The kid sat up. The second blow from the older man was coming down on the kid's head, but the kid put his arm up. Bone could be heard breaking and the kid screamed in pain. The older man wound up for a third swing. I leapt up and hurdled two beds, landing between the two combatants and grabbing the stick in mid-swing. The man looked at me. "That's enough," I told him.

"They attacked me," he said.

"I don't care. Let go of the stick now and back off."

When six guards came racing around the corner, I was standing there in my white jailhouse briefs, stick in hand. The kid in the bed was crying, with a broken arm. The guards stood me up against a wall while they listened to the sex offender's story. They took him and the kid off the dorm and told me to go to my bed.

I lay back down. For the first time, I was keenly aware of every other man in the dorm staring at me. So much for not attracting attention.

The following morning, I had a lot of visitors — men I knew from the streets and the Don Jail. Word travels fast about who arrives in a place of detention.

The third morning, a man approached me. He lived in the dorm above me on the second floor. Our brothers, I knew, were long-time friends. He told me he had a problem. A group of young Frenchmen on his range didn't like the way he looked, and had let it be known that they were going to beat him up. "I need your help," he pleaded.

"What can I do?" I asked. "I'm not a tough guy. I'm new to this place."

"You can talk to them," he said. "You have friends here. Maybe they'll know that and leave me alone. Please, just talk to them."

Shit, I thought. "Okay, I'll try. If you can get me up on your range."

After lunch, at workup, the guard called me. "You're wanted on the second floor."

Great, I thought, *this is not what I want.*

I went up. Buddy was waiting for me. "Do you play bridge?" he asked.

"Yes," I said, "but I didn't come here to play cards. Where are the French guys?"

"They went to work. They had to sign in, but they'll be back within a half hour. I told the guards I needed you here to play, and we got a game set up, so let's just play until they get back, okay?"

I sat at a card table with Buddy and two opponents I'd never seen before. A half hour later, some men filtered back into the range, into the common room. "Where are you from?" one opponent asked me. "Toronto," I answered. "Oh yeah, you know anyone from the East End?" he asked. "I know a few people," I said. "You know the two brothers busted on that big speed conspiracy?" he continued. I looked at Buddy, wondering if his friend was messing with me. Buddy just shrugged. "What about them?" I asked, wondering where he was going with this conversation.

"Nothing, it's just that I did a lot of business with one of them. I deal a lot of speed. I'd go to Toronto and grab product," he said.

"Oh, that's nice," I reflected. Then using my power of deduction, I said, "You must have dealt with the older one, eh?"

"No," he answered, "I always dealt with the younger one."

I stared at him. Buddy was inching his body and his chair back away from the table. "You know him pretty good, do you?" I continued.

"Oh yeah, I'd pick him up in my Caddy, and we'd go to the bars, and the after—"

He did not get to finish. I was out of my chair and punched him right in the face. He fell back, his chair flying, then came up off the floor swinging. We were both swinging at each other until one man yelled, "Six, six, the guards are coming!" We stopped. He picked his chair back up, but didn't sit. The guards looked around and then left. "What's your problem?" he asked.

"I *am* the younger brother, you fucking asshole."

"Oh," was all he said before he turned and left.

Now I was mad. I turned to Buddy. "Are they back yet, or what?" He turned and looked over at three guys sitting around a table who'd been watching the show. "That's them," he said. "Fine," I answered. I walked over. "Do you guys see that man over there?" I pointed to Buddy. They nodded. "You guys lay one finger on him, and I'll be back up here with some of my friends, and we will beat your skulls in. Do you understand me?" They nodded again. "Good," I said (so much for diplomacy). I turned and left. I never talked with Buddy after that.

I lay around for the next six months, reading and playing cards mostly. I saw very little violence at Guelph. A couple of fist fights between young men on the ball-hockey floor. A couple more fights in my dorm. As jails go, though, in my limited experience, it was pretty tame. The only time I was confronted was by the Native Brotherhood. They surrounded my bed one day as I sat reading Joseph Wambaugh's *The Choirboys*. The book was so hilarious, I did not even notice them until their leader spoke. "Why are you so disrespectful to us?" he said.

I looked at each of the Native guys. They seemed very angry. "Did I do something to offend you?" I asked.

"You don't attend group. You don't follow your heritage, the customs of your people," the leader said. I smiled. "Do you find something funny?" he asked.

"Look at my name on the end of the bed. Does that sound Native to you guys?" They looked. "I have nothing but respect for you, don't worry about that," I continued.

"You're not Native? Not even half?" he asked.

I shook my head no, and they left. I went back to my book.

A few days later, I returned to my dorm and picked up my book. No one else was in the dorm, which was strange, it being just after lunch. But I didn't care. I wanted to read in quiet anyways, so this was a blessing. As I pulled my feet up onto the bed and turned to get comfortable, I noticed a man's body on the floor, lying half under a bed, a pool of blood around him. A heavy sand-filled stand-up ashtray lay on its side nearby. I took my book and went out to the common room. The guard found the man on his next round. He was alive. I went back to my bed and my book.

I spent a lot of time talking with old friends. Hans was there. He was the toughest fighter in his prime that I would ever meet in my life. He was, at one time, an enforcer for the loan sharks in Toronto. His reputation for fighting was unsurpassed. He was also one of the men I met during my days as a runner in the speed business. Now, he and I walked the yard in the Guelph reformatory. I let him know when I was being released. When my time arrived, he pulled me aside for a heart-to-heart talk. "Kid, I need you to do me a favour," he asked.

"What is it, Hans?" There wasn't much he could not ask.

"I have a fairly large cache of speed stashed. I need you to sell it and give the money to my wife, for her and my kids. They really need it, okay?"

I gave it some thought. "Hans, you've met Sadie during our visits here. Her and I got plans. They don't include drugs. I've been in for two and a half years of the last three. I'm only twenty-one. I need a break. I need to go straight for a while. I don't want to lose her," I said. "You have your brother, and other friends. Use one of them."

Hans looked at me. "Kid, I need your help. I can't trust anyone like I can trust you."

I thought about Sadie. "I just can't do it, Hans, I love you like a brother, but I'm sorry."

"Okay." Hans smiled at me and tousled my hair. "Don't worry about it. But if you change your mind, just get a hold of my friend. He knows to give you whatever you ask for, alright?"

"Fair enough." I was so relieved when that conversation ended.

3

The Darkness Cometh

A FEW DAYS LATER, I found out I was getting a five-day pre-release. Sadie sure would be surprised. I arranged for one of the guys to pick me up and drive me to her residence outside Toronto, just to keep the surprise alive. I was happy. I was moving to the sticks. No more cops. Get a job and make love to Sadie all day long. Life was grand.

When we finally arrived, no one was home. Just my luck. Maybe I should have phoned her. We had a cigarette while we waited. After a while, we decided to leave. As we headed to the vehicle, a car pulled off the side road, coming straight up to the house. As it got closer, I could see it was Sadie driving. I could also see her ex-boyfriend sitting beside her — the older rounder. The car pulled up as I stood realizing my shattered dreams.

"Brother!" her ex yelled, jumping out of the car with a big smile. He came up and gave me a hug. "What brings you out here?"

"I heard you were out," I lied. "I didn't have your number, so I came to get it." I could see Sadie still sitting in the car. Tears were streaming down her face. I was stone cold.

"Come on in for a while," her ex offered.

"No, I have to go see Ma. I just got out myself," I said. "What's the number for out here?" He told me, but I didn't have to write it down. I already knew it from memory. I also knew I'd never use it again.

My friend dropped me at my mother's apartment. I spent the afternoon talking with her and a few of my sisters. Sadie called, crying. "He called from the Pen. They wouldn't release him unless it was to my place. What could I do? I couldn't leave him in there. We'll figure this out. It's you I love."

"Sadie," I told her, "don't worry. It's all figured out. You and I were never really together, were we? He's my friend. You two have a good life. We're over. You lied to me, or at best, didn't tell me everything. So, just let it go." I hung up. She called right back, but I had my sister tell her I had just left.

I got changed into some of my nicer clothes, went out for a surf-and-turf supper, and then headed to a familiar bar to pick up a "nice" girl to help me forget about Sadie. It didn't, but the girl sure helped my ego a lot.

I was still focused on "going straight."

Shortly after, I'd gain employment at a loading dock. I didn't like the graveyard shift, but the men were good to work with, and the job was easy enough. After a month, the foreman called me into his office. "Fill out these papers," he told me. "We're going to bond you. You're one hell of a good worker." I stared at the papers. There was no way I could be bonded. I had a criminal record longer than any twenty-one-year-old had a right to possess. *Damn.* I surmised it would be time to find another job. I was right. I told the foreman of my record, and they let me go.

A couple of nights later, the Row Boat showed up at my door. "Get dressed," he said, smiling. "I'm taking you out. Getting you laid, maybe see some of the old friends." I went. I met a "nice" girl at the bar. The Row Boat said, "Let's go to my partner's. He has a nice bedroom. We're not putting out good money on a hotel room, not for the two minutes you're going to be with her." We both laughed.

After my "new friend" left in a taxi, we sat down in the living room with a beer. "Can we talk?" the Row Boat asked.

"Sure, what's up?"

"We're starving out here. We're at the bottom of the food chain, and the other dealers are keeping us there. We get product so cut we can barely make a dime off of it."

"So, you guys are still dealing dope then," I said aloud, but more so to myself.

"Of course. That's where the money is."

"And this has to do with me how?" I asked.

"You've got connections. You can help us." Then his partner spoke up. "Kid, you know I have the wife and kids here. I can barely feed them after I pay the mortgage. I'm already renting out the ground floor. I can't do anything else. Help us, please."

I looked at them. "My connection was my brother. You know that, everyone knows that. And everyone knows where he is now. I can't help you guys. I'm sorry."

The Row Boat drove me home. "You must have met some people," he pressed.

"I don't know anybody," I said, ending the conversation.

I continued to look for a job. The Row Boat would show up most every night to take me out partying, drinking, and spending time with different ladies. One night, being half drunk, I told him, "Stop by tomorrow afternoon. I need to borrow your car. It'll be worth it to you."

He pulled up the next day. "Where are we going?"

"We," I answered, "are going nowhere. I am. You take a cab to your partner's, and I'll meet you there in an hour or two."

He tossed me the keys.

Two hours later, I walked into his partner's home and put a half pound of rock-hard, almost pure methamphetamine, on the table. "I need this much money. Can you guys do that?"

"For an ounce?" his partner asked.

"No, for the whole thing."

They high-fived each other, shouted for joy, and hugged me. Within hours, they had all the money. I left to pay the bill.

The very next afternoon, the Row Boat came to see me. "We need more," he said.

"I gave that to you guys at cost, so you could make some money. I didn't want to get involved. But if you guys want to keep going, I'm going to need to make a profit. I can't do this for nothing." He agreed and said that he'd be my partner, sharing the profits fifty-fifty. His partner could buy off us and work with his other friends. It sounded okay to me. "Okay, I'll meet you in an hour," I told him.

"Do you want me to drive you somewhere?" he asked.

"Really?" I said, looking at him. He knew better. People in the game did not like to meet strangers. They would fold up their tents and leave town, so to speak, when outsiders knew their business. He laughed and left.

And so we began. I would procure the product. We'd cut it together. He'd go out and meet his customers. I would show up where he wanted me to, with whatever amount of product he needed. During this time, I noticed their lifestyle was nothing like I had been told it was during my two-year stay at the Don Jail. Instead of helping each other, friends would lie to each other. They were always trying to cut each other out from financial opportunities. They didn't defend each other. They were even having sex with each other's partners, if the opportunity presented itself. And it did, often.

I pretended not to notice their hypocrisy. Everything was going fine, until one day I was socializing up at the Row Boat's ex-partner's place. I'd begun using speed. Daily. Nightly. All the time. His ex-partner was sitting in the living room with one of his boys, and they were making thousand-dollar piles of money. The Row Boat screeched up outside in his newly acquired, barely used Cadillac. He bounced into the house, gold chains dripping off his neck. "Hey, what's happening?" He smiled at me.

"Just watching these guys count their dough," I answered, "which begs the question, how are we doing?"

"What do you mean?" he asked, no longer smiling.

"How much money have we made?"

"I gave you money," he answered.

"Yes, you did, to pay for the product. But how much profit have we made?"

"Well," he said, thinking, "let me see. The way I figure it, I owe you about four hundred dollars."

"Really?" I said. I was stunned. "Are you serious?"

"Yeah," he answered.

I pointed out I'd spent more than four hundred out of my own pocket on gas, just meeting him. "These guys are cutting up G-notes," I said. "We have six guys like them. We've moved pounds of product. And you're telling me my end is *about four hundred dollars*? Really?"

He bit his lower lip and nodded. I realized he had blown our profits on himself, his family, his friends, and good times. "Okay," I said, "new deal. Me and you are done. You can keep the *about four hundred*. You're going to need it to buy off your friends here. That's if they want to keep dealing with me." I ended the conversation and got up to leave. I looked at his friends. "Just a heads-up. The price of poker just went up, but if you want, you know how to reach me." With that, I left.

The next day they called. So did everyone else. I was in business for myself.

Profits rolled in. I would rent two cars at a time, to keep switching up in case of police surveillance. I rarely stayed at one place at one time. I had a stash house, kept by my friend "the keeper."

I'd see the Row Boat a few times a week, in the bars or the discos, the after-hours clubs. I was having a wild time. The Row Boat was angry and depressed. He hated that I was relatively new to the game, so much younger than him, and he felt I had not earned my way to the top of the drug sub-culture. Many of the older dealers felt that way, too. They were right, but the Row Boat had brought the situation upon himself. He'd screwed me out of my profits. The only thing we had in common now was our daily use of speed and other drugs.

One day, the King of Hearts came to see me. We had a mutual friend with an impending legal problem, and he had to get out of town for a while. He needed money. I told the King of Hearts I'd just paid my bill with my suppliers, my rent, the cars, et cetera, and I was cash light. I asked him to give me a couple of days and I'd help our friend out. "He can't wait. He has to go now," he said frantically. I thought for a second. "Does he know anyone that would flip product for cash? I can give him some product."

"I'm sure he does," the King answered. "How much?"

I told him I could do a half pound. He was elated. I told him to swing by and see the keeper and let him know I said to give that to him. The King of Hearts left.

I then got a call from the Row Boat's ex-partner, and went to visit him. He asked me for more product, and I told him I could do a half pound. He was fine with that, but was upset when I told him he'd have to wait until the following day. "In the morning?" he asked. I agreed.

That night, I went out partying, as usual. The following morning, I showed up at the keeper's house. I went in his bedroom and nudged him awake with my foot. "Get up," I said angrily. "Is something wrong?" he asked. "Yes, something is fucking wrong. Get up and come out to the living room," I barked. He came out, wiping the sleep from his eyes. He looked at the open tool box. "What's wrong?" he said.

"There's only four ounces of 'cut' crap here," I pointed out. "Where's the rest of it?"

He told me the King of Hearts had come by the night before and said I told him to get a half pound for his friend. "That's right. But there was a full pound here yesterday, so where's the rest?"

"He took a half pound for himself, as well. Didn't you tell him to?" the keeper whined. "Shit! He never asked me for anything for himself. Go back to bed," I said. I was angry. The King had pulled a fast one. I shouldn't have sent him to the keeper's. It was my own fault.

In the game, I had learned everyone was always trying to pull fast ones on each other. I knew I'd promised to restock the Row Boat's ex-partner, but now, thanks to the King of Hearts, I had no supply, other than the four ounces the keeper had for his customers. I took that and went over to the ex-partner's house. He was asleep on his La-Z-Boy in the living room. His wife and her girlfriend sat on the couch. There were three other people in the room — some guy and two women from Kingston. One was on the phone. I went across the room to wake the sleeper. I shook him, but he didn't move. "He hasn't slept in days," his wife informed me. "He just went down about two hours ago."

I told her I had to get him up, that he was expecting me. I shook him again. Still no movement. The woman on the phone was saying, "I don't know who he is, George." I looked at her. "Is that George?" I asked. She nodded. I took the phone. "George, who are you looking for?" I asked. "The kid," he answered. "You're talking to him. What's up?" I asked. "Oh my god, I have to see you right away. It's very, very important. I'm at the House of Lords downtown. Come right away," he said, sounding upset.

I looked over at the sleeper. I had my doubts as to whether I could wake him up. Not without beating on him. "Alright, I'm on my way, but I'm loaded," I said, letting him know I had product on me. "No, no, no," he exclaimed, "don't do that. Just come right away. Please."

"Take it easy," I said. "I'm on my way."

I turned the phone over to the woman from Kingston and spoke to the sleeper's wife. "Can you take this bag up to your stash house for me? I have to go out. If he wakes up, let him know I was by, and I'll be right back. Tell him not to touch what's in the bag, because it isn't what I normally have for him, and we have to talk about a price first. That is if he even wants it, okay?" She told me that wouldn't be a problem. On the way out the door, I told her to make sure she took it up to the stash right away. She smiled, nodded, and waved goodbye.

I left with the two women and their male friend. When we arrived, George told me the narcs had kicked in his front door that morning. They'd kicked in a few doors. They were trying to get an address on me, and were swearing to put me in the Pen with my brother. I left George and went straight to the stash house. I had the keeper move all the paraphernalia out, along with the books of who owed what. They were all coded, and couldn't be understood by anyone but me. Still, I knew from experience that they do not read well in the hands of a jury. I went across the street and made a number of calls to different dealers. I couldn't get an answer at the sleeper's. An hour later, after talking with everyone else, I still couldn't get hold of the sleeper or his wife. Then I got a call from one of my guys. The sleeper had been busted by the narcs. His house had been hit, and there were drugs inside.

I spent the afternoon at the home of a couple I knew. I sat on the front porch having a beer. The Row Boat showed up. He was also friends with the same couple. He went inside. I heard loud yelling, and then he came out. He was glaring at me. "You have a problem?" I asked.

"Yeah, I do. The sleeper's busted with your product," he answered. I let him know I had already heard. "I'll bet you did," he said. "It's pretty funny how you go in and drop a bag and the narcs come in just when you leave, eh?" He sneered.

"What are you trying to say?" I asked, the anger rising.

"You set him up, that's what I'm saying," he spat out.

I came off the porch swinging. The couple jumped in the middle. They told the Row Boat to leave. "You are fucked up," the woman told him. "You know the kid wouldn't do that. Now leave my house."

"I'll see you around," he told me.

"No doubt in my mind," I answered.

The sleeper made bail that afternoon, and I phoned that evening to tell him I would be by. He was going to his mother's, he said, and wouldn't be home. I told him I'd see him the next day.

For the next few days, every time I called, he was not going to be available. I was starting to hear rumours that he thought I'd set him up. He had the Row Boat in his ear every day. I ran into one of the boys, and he told me he was invited up to the sleeper's to watch a big boxing event. All the sleeper's adult male friends would be there. His kids would be at his mother's. I waited until that night, and then I crashed the party. When I came down the hall, I saw the Row Boat. "Oh, are the cops here?" he said snidely. I glared at him, and he put his head back down into his drink. The house was packed with drug users and criminals and the sleeper's wife.

The sleeper approached me. "You shouldn't be here," he said.

"We have to talk," I answered. "What is going on with us? I'm hearing you think I set you up."

"Listen, kid, it doesn't look good," he told me. "You made my wife take that bag, and then the cops come in as you left. It doesn't look good. I'd like you to leave my house."

"I made your wife take that bag? The cops come in when I left?" I said. He called his wife over to us. "Tell him what you told me," he said. She looked at me and told me she did not want to take the bag, but that I had forced it on her. Practically threatened her. That she had to take it. And then she did not have a chance to get rid of it after I left before the cops crashed in.

I looked at the sleeper. "And you believe that?" I asked. "She's my wife," he said.

"Then that's that," I said, and turned to leave. I never got two steps before I heard a man yell, "Hold it right there!"

I turned. The man was looking at the sleeper. "Brother," he said, "I'm your cousin. I love you. I don't know this kid from Jack, but I was here that morning. I was right in the room when they spoke. Everything the kid has told you was the truth of what happened." The man looked at the sleeper's wife. "This is serious shit here, and you can't lie. You have to tell your husband the truth." The sleeper looked at his wife. She looked at him and started to speak. "I was afraid of what you would do —" she started.

He backhanded her against the wall. "You fucking bitch," he screamed. He grabbed her by the hair and dragged her into the bedroom.

I looked at the cousin. "I forgot about you," I told him. "Thanks." He nodded.

The sleeper came out of his bedroom. "I am so sorry, kid."

"Not as sorry as me," I told him. "I really thought we were friends. I'm leaving now, but if I was you, I would really thank your cousin here. I would really thank him a lot. You have no idea."

I went out to the stolen car I had parked out front. I got rid of it right after I returned the fully loaded automatic machine gun I had stored in the trunk an hour before.

At that point, I was an angry drug addict who was not well-grounded at all. And no one was getting away with labelling me as a police informant. I don't know what would have happened had the sleeper's cousin not been there. I'm just eternally thankful that he was. I really did like the sleeper, and his family, and his friends. The wife, not so much after this experience; I learned later that she and her girlfriend had gotten into the bag, gotten high, and that the cops had come in a good half hour after I left. A half hour after she was supposed to have taken the bag to safety.

That didn't slow the Row Boat any, though. A few nights later, he appeared in the bar I was at with my kid sister on his arm. He was twenty-nine. She was eighteen. She had no idea of the bad blood between us. I waited until she was off at another table in the bar, and then I approached him. "What the fuck do you think you're doing with her?"

"She's eighteen. She can do what she likes." He smiled. "I kinda like her."

"Really, you think so?" I asked.

"I'm doing whatever I want. It's not your business." He continued smiling.

I looked around the bar. *Not the place.* "I'll see you around," I said, and left.

The next morning, I sat my sister down. "He loves me," she said. "Look at the ring he gave me."

"I get those rings for next to nothing in the drug houses, and so does he," I informed her. "He has a wife and kid. He lives with a hooker that's his old lady. He's only going out with you to piss me off. Now, break it off!"

"No," she cried, "I can do what I want. He really loves me."

"You'll see," I told her, shaking my head in frustration.

Over the next week, he'd show up almost every night with her, wherever I was. I pretended not to notice them, or his malicious smile. One morning, I went to visit my mother. I had a key to her apartment, so I let myself in. No one was in the kitchen. No one was in the living room either, but the room was a disaster — furniture tipped over, ashtrays upside down on the carpet, their contents spilling all over. I knocked at my mother's bedroom door. "Mom, are you home?"

"Is he gone?" she answered.

I opened the door. She was sitting on the foot of her bed, fully clothed.

"Did you have a party here last night?" I asked, smiling.

"No," she said, trembling, "it was the Row Boat. He was drunk or high or something. He broke my knick-knacks."

I could feel the heat rising up through my neck now.

"He hates you," she began to sob. "He scares me."

I smiled again. "Don't worry, Mom, he can't hurt me," I told her, trying to calm her down. I shut her door and opened my sister's bedroom door. She was lying on her bed with her back to me. "That fucking goof doesn't come here again. You hear me?" I growled. "You want to be an idiot and keep dating that cocksucker, that's fine. But you keep him out of Mom's home. You hearing me?" She didn't answer, but I was mad, and I was loud, and I knew she heard me. "Aw, fuck this," I said to myself and I shut her door.

I drove over to the hooker's house, the Row Boat's primary residence. I sat out front in my car for a long time thinking about the past four years, since I agreed to get into the game. Then I went in, letting myself in through the front door. The hooker was in the kitchen doing something. I walked through the living room and headed up the stairs to the bedroom. I'd been there before.

"Where do you think you're going?" the hooker yelled.

"Go fuck yourself," I told her.

When I reached the bedroom door, the Row Boat was sitting up on the side of the bed. I looked around, then pulled over a chair from the vanity table and sat in front of him. "We need to talk," I told him. "I need to talk, you need to listen," I corrected myself. "You can talk when I'm finished. You got me back into this dealing shit when I came out of Guelph, when

I didn't want any part of it. Then you screwed me for the profits. You tried to label me as a rat, or worse. When that didn't work, you start screwing my kid sister to piss me off. When that didn't work for you, you start terrorizing my mother. I'm here to make you a deal, and I'll tell you why. I'm going to clean up what I have left on the streets. Collect my money. Then you won't see me around. No one will. I'll walk away. You get your own supplier, and the streets are yours. I'm done. And now, I'll tell you why. I really don't want to fuck you up. I know your mom, your sister, and a couple of your brothers. You know I can pay a couple of the boys to break every bone in your body. Put you in intensive care for at least six months. I don't want to do that. But if you ever go near my mother or her home again, I will. That is what is going to happen. Now, do you understand me? Do we have a deal?"

He looked across at me, as though I had just bored him to death. "I am going to do whatever the fuck I feel like," he said. "Anyone hurts me, and the minute I'm out of the hospital, I will shoot you dead. Now get the fuck out of my house."

He had not considered me a threat at all. "Fair enough," I warned him. "You just named the game. I'm telling you, stay out of her house."

A few mornings later, I got out of bed. I didn't wake my girlfriend. It was early, especially for late-night partygoers like us. I hadn't seen my mother since she was upset by the Row Boat, so I decided to stop by. First, I went to a grocery store and bought a few large bags of food for her. She loved to cook. I knew it would cheer her up. When I let myself into the apartment, she was seated at the far end of the kitchen table with her hands on her forehead as though she was suffering a migraine. I set the bags down on the counter and said, "Good morning, Mom." She took her hands away from her face. Her eyes were dark and sunken in as though she had cried them out. Her hands were trembling. "I think I'm going to have a nervous breakdown," she sobbed.

I placed my arm across the back of her shoulders and bent down, so my face was beside hers. "What's wrong now, Mom?" I asked. She started to speak, but became all choked up. She pointed to the living room. I stood up and walked into the other room. Her high wooden display case was tilted, leaning kitty-corner into the wall. Her pictures and knick-knacks lay strewn across the floor. The coffee table was on its side. The place looked ransacked. On the couch, fully dressed but shoeless, lay the Row Boat, fast asleep.

I picked up the phone and called for a taxi. I then straightened out the shelf case, the coffee table. I put things back in their normal position. I picked the cigarette butts out of the carpet. Then I gave the Row Boat a slap on the side of his head to wake him up. He didn't stir until I slapped him a second time.

My sister came out of her bedroom. "You leave him alone!" she cried. Then she looked at my face and went back in her room without any further interruption.

"You get up, get your shoes on, and get out of here. I have a taxi on its way for you," I said.

"What?" he asked groggily.

"You heard me, you fucking goof. Now get out. I will be seeing you later." I walked over to the apartment door and held it open until he walked out.

"Later," I assured him.

He went out to the curb until the cab arrived. I then went back into the kitchen and reassured my mother that he had gone, and that he would not be coming back. I stayed until she calmed down, which took a couple of hours.

I then drove around downtown, picking up what monies I could from my customers. I paid off my supplier. Then I went to see my friend Ryan. He was an unknown to my associates in the drug business. He and I had seen each other a few times since our release after the car theft charges. We'd grab a meal together, have a few beers, get high together. But I never brought him around the dealers. I explained everything to him about what had gone down with the Row Boat. He was quite concerned, given the violent history of the Row Boat. I told him I had to take some action, and now. We were both still young, and the Row Boat was not one to mess with. He had shot a couple of guys I knew from the Park and injured many others in his perversions. When he was high and armed, he posed a serious threat. We decided to throw a rope on him, so to speak, and take him for a ride. Maybe that would bring home to him the seriousness of the situation. Either way, I was determined to resolve the conflict. It seemed like a good plan, but then we were higher than kites up in the sky on meth.

‖‖‖

I walked into the bar. At a table in the middle of the room sat the Row Boat and his friends. I walked over. "You got a minute?" I asked.

"What the fuck do you want?" he growled.

"Take it easy," I told him. "I just want to talk to you about something."

He was not afraid of me. I was seven years younger, just turned twenty-two. I only weighed a hundred and forty pounds, and I hadn't begun to shave yet. I was not known to be overly violent. We went out to the lobby. "What?" he asked again.

"I told you I was getting out. Before I give my product to your competition, I thought you might like to buy it," I said.

"I don't have much money, since you cut me out of the business." He scowled.

"Don't worry. I'll give it to you cheap, and on a 'front,' so you can pay me as you sell it."

I could see the wheels turning in his drug-addled brain (*Get the dope, he's out. I pay him nothing*). "Sounds good. Give it to me," he said.

"I'm not bringing that much product into this bar," I told him. "It's in the car if you want it," and I went out the side door into the parking lot. The Row Boat followed.

I opened the back door on the driver's side. He bent down to look in and got hit hard in the back of the head with a gun butt. He staggered up against the car. He was then handcuffed behind his back and pushed into the back seat.

Ryan took the wheel while I kept an eye on our guest from the front passenger seat. We travelled east along the highway, out of Toronto. After a good half hour of driving, I told Ryan he could start turning up north anytime he liked. He looked over at me. I could see he was very uneasy. He didn't want to be in this car, in this position. I turned around and looked at our passenger in the back. I said to the Row Boat, "Okay. What are you going to do if I let you go right now?" And I would have. It shouldn't have been a surprise, given the amount of drugs we each had flowing through our veins and our minds, but his reply was accompanied by a sardonic smile. "Kid," he said, "I knew you didn't have the balls."

"Wrong answer," I told him and swung back around in my seat. "Drive," I told Ryan. He looked at me and I just shrugged helplessly. Ryan looked in the rear-view mirror at the Row Boat, then started slamming one fist on the car's dash. "You have to be the biggest goof I have ever met in my life," he told the Row Boat. "The biggest goof I have ever even heard of. Fuck!"

"Keep driving," I repeated, then added, "Turn north."

None of us knew where we were, or where we were headed. We hadn't thought that far ahead. Once we hit farm country, though, away from the highway's lights, the night became pitch-black. Dead silent. Each of us was alone in his thoughts.

We pulled into a fence-opening of a large field and travelled through. The back fence had an opening that accessed a second field. We stopped at the end along some brush. I told Ryan to pop the trunk, and I got out. I went to the back and took a shovel out, then walked about fifteen feet from the driver's side and began to dig in the soft earth. After fifteen minutes, Ryan walked over and relieved me.

I went to the back door of the car and opened it. "Get out!" I ordered.

"No," the Row Boat protested. "No!"

I grabbed him by the back of his coat and pulled him out. He stood there, facing me. I saw the blood all over the back seat, where he had bled from the laceration he received from the gun butt. I shut the door. "You still think I'm playing with you?" I asked. "You still think you're a smart guy?"

He had no answer, other than "You won't get away with this."

"Do you really think I care?"

He had a point, though. I turned to look at Ryan. We had gone about as far as we were prepared to go. I started to turn back to the Row Boat when he lashed out with his leg and kicked my hand that held the gun. He kicked my hand so hard his shoe come flying off, landing about six yards away. I wasn't watching. I snapped. I came up with my arm and pulled the trigger. The gun roared in the rural silence of the night air. I looked at the Row Boat. He hadn't moved. I fired again, and again, and again, until the revolver was empty. Finally, he went down to the ground, screaming and crying. After the final shot, silence returned to the farmer's field.

I dragged the lifeless body over to the freshly dug hole and tugged it into the bottom. Then I filled the hole in.

All the way out of the fields, Ryan just kept muttering, "This isn't good. This isn't good." I was in shock. I just kept thinking to myself, *What just happened? Why did he kick the gun? Why did he have to be such an asshole right to the end?*

It didn't matter. It was done. There was no turning back.

IIIHt

The sky was black, but it looked a whole lot darker now. We turned onto a road, heading south. Back to the highway that would take us home. Five minutes later, a police cruiser started to follow us. Then he pulled us over. Ryan was panicking, but I gave him a reassuring look. I calmed him down as the cop approached the vehicle. I took the cop through his questioning and we were allowed to continue on our way. Considering he noticed the blood all over the back seat, and had discovered the shovel covered in fresh earth in the trunk of the car, I was amazed he believed any of my answers. What really puzzled me was that he didn't notice my driver's licence and vehicle registration was for a forty-five-year-old Mexican. I'd just turned twenty-two.

IIIHt

The following morning, the farmer who owned the field noticed tire tracks; that night his daughter and a farmhand discovered the new hole and its contents. The police were called immediately.

I was perturbed at my drug associates, who had for months opined that the Row Boat was like a mad dog and had to go. I was the one who had disagreed. Now, they were all in tears. I continued to use speed excessively, even for an addict. I was just waiting for the axe to fall. I was positive that my arrest was inevitable. I'd made no secret of my fallouts with the Row Boat — except the family aspect. Ryan was the only friend privy to that, other than, of course, my mother and the Row Boat.

A few weeks after the murder, I drove my kid sister home from a late-night house party. It was around four in the morning, and she talked me into parking the car and getting a few hours sleep on my mom's couch.

A few hours later, my sleep was interrupted by the sound of heavy footsteps coming across the living-room floor. I awoke slowly, turning toward the sound. Homicide detectives were in the apartment, headed toward me. My mother, who had answered the door, stood off to one side, behind them. "Good morning," one said.

I moved the living-room curtain just a slip, so I could peer out the window. The road in front of the building was filled with marked and unmarked police cruisers. Cops stood out front, and some were lying on the grass, guns drawn. "It doesn't look too good to me," I answered. "That's right," he continued. "You are under arrest for murder," and then he read the standard caution, one I had heard many times before.

I got up and walked past them. They didn't stop me. They knew where I was going. My mother was in shock, grasping her chest. "It's okay, Mom." I hugged her. "It's just a mistake. I'll be home soon." I called for my sister to look after her and to call the lawyer. "Tell him I'm not saying a word to these assholes, and find out where they're taking me."

I was driven to police headquarters in Toronto, then to a jail in Lindsay, Ontario. I had never heard of the town in my life. The first time I appeared in a Lindsay courtroom, I was led in handcuffed to the lead detective of the OPP homicide squad in charge of my case. I stood next to the Crown's table as they prepared to arraign me and George on the charge. I'd glimpsed George on another range when they'd logged me in to their county jail. I knew him well. He was a drug dealer and one of my associates. I was shocked to see him charged with me. In the courtroom, George stood over on the far side of the court, surrounded by uniformed police. I was most curious to discover how he had gotten himself charged. He had absolutely no involvement in the crime.

As soon as court commenced, I asked the judge for an order to have my co-accused and I housed together. He deferred to the cop handcuffed to my wrist. I had never seen a judge do that before. I became upset. "Why?" I asked the judge, "Who is he? Your fucking brother?" With that, I kicked the Crown's table hard, spilling their water pitchers. The police closed tight around me as the lead detective scrambled to uncuff himself from me. I think he was concerned I'd tear his wrist off with the handcuffs. "Where the fuck am I, Green Acres?" I yelled to no one in particular.

The judge arraigned us. I was handcuffed in front and led out the front of the courthouse to the awaiting media circus. We were front-page news in the little town of Lindsay. One reporter scooted in front of me to take a picture of my face for his tabloid. I was handcuffed in front but my legs were still free. His camera went sailing through the air as I kicked it out of his grasp.

Back at the jail, George was again placed on the ground floor while I was taken up to the second on the other side of the building. The following morning, a nurse appeared for urine and blood testing. As is common in any institution, they wanted to ensure no diseases are brought in through the prisoners. She asked if I was an intravenous drug user, if I used syringes. I told her no. When I rolled up my sleeves for her, she gasped. My veins were disgusting. They looked like railroad ties on a road map. "You must donate an awful lot of blood," she observed.

Later on in the day, I was escorted by two guards to the superintendent's office. He was a rather tall, large man. He sat across from me, behind his desk, and ordered me to cease giving his staff a hard time. Since my arrival I had done little but threaten them. I politely told him I was here on a serious charge, and asked that I be placed with my co-accused. He refused. I lunged across the desk, grabbing the lapels of his suit jacket. I pulled his face toward mine and said, "You fucking goof. You are playing with my life, and I will kill you." The two guards pulled me off him and took me back to my range. They all knew I was just a young man withdrawing from substance abuse.

The old Lindsay Jail in 1978, as far as security went, was a joke. Anyone with half a brain and an ounce of determination could have escaped. While the three-and-a-half-storey structure had an updated facade, the interior was still old brick and metal bars. The jail maintained a skeleton staff each shift. The outer yard walls were only twelve feet high. A man did not require outside assistance, but with it, escape was more than a possibility. The next court date, I was returned to the jail ahead of George and placed on his range. A man sitting at a table introduced himself as George's friend and told me George wanted to know why I was charged. I told him the cops thought I knew who committed the murder, but because I wouldn't tell them, I was charged. That was it. Then I began to pace. The man got off the table and walked up beside me as though he were going to join me.

I stopped and glared at him. "Do I know you?" I growled. He returned to his seat. A minute or so later, I was taken back up to my range. George was brought up a couple of hours later. It was the first time we'd had a chance to talk. He told me the cops were saying he was driving the vehicle on the night in question, with me as the passenger. He informed me he was in a holding cell in a police station on the night in question. I told him to keep that information to himself until trial. I also told him I thought his new friend downstairs was an "undercover police officer." He assured me he was not. I remained unconvinced.

George would consistently badger me for the name of my friend that I associated with, but did not bring around the "dealers." I would never talk to George about the murder, or who my friend was. I received an offer from an acquaintance I had met in the Don Jail two years prior. He was an organized crime figure, and he felt he could safely secure my release from the jail, however illegally, and then have me transplanted with a new identity in California. I pondered the offer, but only briefly. I knew what such a debt would entail, especially to a crime syndicate. I was never one to run from my troubles anyways. I sent back a message of "thanks, but no thanks. I'll sit it out."

Six weeks after my arrest, I looked out my range window into the exercise yard. I saw two men walking. I did not recognize the one man, but the second man made me catch my breath. It was Ryan. I hollered out the window to him, but he didn't answer. He didn't even look up. I knew he could hear me. I hollered again. Still no response. I went and sat down at a table. Now I was deeply concerned. With George, I knew the police had no clue. With Ryan, I was not so sure. A few hours later, the two men were brought up to my range. They sat at the table with me. I asked Ryan why he hadn't answered. He informed me that the other man's lawyer had said someone was leaking information, and they weren't too sure it wasn't me.

I looked at Ryan. I was mad. "It is a little late to be second-guessing me, pal," I told him. "When we get to court, we'll find out why you're here."

The second man, Harry, finally piped up. "Yeah, and then we'll deal with it." He sat there glaring, and I just looked back. I had seen this guy once years before in the Don Jail court cell range for maybe one minute, and I had seen him about ten months previous sitting in the front room of a drug house while I spoke to the King of Hearts at the back door. Other than that, I knew him not.

Ryan was a few years my senior, and larger. Harry was ten years my senior, and at least a hundred pounds heavier. I held my anger. It would not be long before court commenced.

A few days after their arrival on the range, another man came on. I was lying near the front of the range, on the floor, as he walked past. I looked down the range and saw a kid sitting on the end table. He was looking at the newcomer, and the kid looked terrified. He looked like he was about to be shot. The newcomer passed him and went to the end of the range. A washroom area was situated just around the corner, out of my sightline, and he entered it. I noticed the kid look over in that direction a few seconds later. After that, he got off the table and entered the washroom. A minute later, the kid came out and returned to his seat at the table. Then the newcomer came out and meandered around the back of the range. A half hour later, the kid came to the front to ask the guard for a request form. The guard left to go get it. The kid had his back to me, as I continued to lie on the floor. "Don't turn around," I said. "Don't look at me. He's a cop, isn't he?" I asked. The kid nodded his head. "You're sure, too, aren't you?" I continued. The kid nodded again. The guard showed back up with the request form. The kid filled it out and then returned to his seat at the back of the range.

I got up after a few minutes and approached the guard. "You might want to take this cop off the range before he gets hurt," I said, indicating the man at the back.

"He's not a cop," he protested.

"Yes," I said, matter-of-factly, "he is."

The guard left and returned with his superior and another guard. They beckoned me to the front grille. "You have my word he is not a cop," the sergeant said.

"And you have my word he is, and my friends and I are going to fuck him up if you don't take him off this range right now," I answered.

The guards took him off.

I talked to the kid. The cop had busted him a year prior on a drug charge. The very next remand, as I entered the courthouse, I came upon the lead detective in deep conversation with the same man. "You owe me one," I told him, "but don't try for two." He didn't.

The preliminary hearing began with George's new friend. Of course he was an "undercover" placed in the Lindsay jail. All he could relay to the court was what George speculated upon, and that speculation was all about me. The second witness was also a cop. He explained how Ryan's buddy Harry lived with an informant for the Toronto homicide police, and she had relayed to them everything Harry had said about Ryan; about what Harry knew, and what Harry had speculated upon. I looked at Ryan and nodded — vindication of my suspicion. Ryan just glared at Harry. He was very, very angry. Ryan would later apologize to me profusely, but I just shrugged it off, saying we had bigger problems ahead. Things were not going well. During the prelim, a man entered the courtroom wearing a long leather coat. He looked like a heavy substance abuser. He approached me at the prisoners' docket and informed me he was an acquaintance of my oldest brother. He leaned in to show me the butt of a six-shot revolver in a shoulder holster. "If you want out, I'll get you out right now." I looked around the courtroom, at the *fifteen* armed police, and I knew that mathematics was not the guy's strong suit. "I'll pass," I said. I would've passed even if there had been only one cop. I was in enough trouble, and just like the cop who had pulled over the car on the night of the murder, I sure as heck wasn't going to shoot anyone I had no beef with, least of all a cop. He left. (I would meet him again in years to come.)

At the conclusion of the preliminary hearing, everyone was committed to trial. We expected no less in a one-horse town with their own circuit judge. A month later a fifth man, another innocent, would be charged alongside us four. Ryan and I were placed on a separate range.

At some point around Christmas 1978, a young local serving a two-month sentence was also placed on our range. Two weeks after New Year's, a guard discovered a security screen on the window had been compromised, and, even worse for them, their window bar had been sawn right through. Anyone could have left the property easily. I told the kid, and Ryan, that the authorities couldn't tell how long the bar was like that, so we couldn't be held responsible. The police talked to the local kid, and he must have given them a story, because Ryan and I were charged for attempted jailbreak. At trial the kid would take ownership of the attempted escape, but no one believed him. He was not serving a lengthy sentence. He said his motive was to be home for Christmas, but when it was pointed out to him the crime occurred after New Year's, he said, "So, I was late." Everybody laughed, except the Crown attorneys and the judge. Regardless, Ryan and I had the jailbreak charges against us withdrawn.

By the time we left Lindsay for our trial in Toronto, I had quit being an "asshole" with the guards. They appreciated the change in my demeanour. I remained an asshole with the upper management there, though, right up to the day I left. In my opinion, they deserved no less.

‖‖‖

Ryan and I arrived at the Don Jail behind the three men charged along with us. We had stayed to appear in court for a remand on the attempted jailbreak. Upon entering the Don, we were taken up to the fifth-floor landing, then placed on the 5C range, south side. The first thing I noticed, other than our co-accused, was the shortness of the range. There were only ten cells. We'd been given our own range. *There's no chance of undercovers being placed here*, I thought. I found out from one of my co-accused that the reason we were not being placed on the pen range was because of my history with an outlaw motorcycle gang president who now resided there. He and I had met in society, when I had pressed a gun under his chin and threatened his life: a friend's sister had told me he raped her. My friend did not want me to retaliate and pleaded with me not to. Shortly afterward, though, the man had phoned my mother's residence asking for my sister. I'd taken the call. I asked where she could reach him, and then I left to meet with him myself. He never phoned or talked to my sister again. I wondered how the guards in the Don would know of this incident, but I couldn't care less. I was content in my new surroundings.

When the trial began, I was the first to enter the courtroom. The judge slightly rose and leaned forward, gripping the front of the bench. His knuckles were white, and he glared at me angrily. He never took his gaze from me as I crossed the floor to my lawyer. The Lion was decked out in the standard High Court attire — a black robe with white tunic. His long red hair flowed over the collar like a lion's mane. I told him, looking at the judge, that this would not be a fair fight. The Lion had always been my lawyer. If he hadn't represented me in court, he'd had someone from his firm act on his behalf. This trial was in the "big leagues," though, and the Lion was now in the arena personally. He was leaving my safety in no one else's hands, and I was more than secure in that knowledge. He was razor sharp, as far as legal minds went.

I was placed in the prisoners' box and moved along to the first chair. Underneath it was a large metal hoop attached to a metal chain that extruded from the floor. The chain from my leg shackles was placed through it, so I was firmly affixed to the floor. I was grounded every time I appeared in the courtroom for this trial. My co-accused sat beside me, in order of their appearance on the indictment (that is, in the order of their importance to the prosecution) — Ryan beside me, then Harry, and then the two innocents. The jury was selected.

During the trial, the Lion had his hands more than full. The murder occurred without any thought or foresight, so I had taken none of the precautions I normally would have when committing any crime. Still, the Lion fought on. He was wedged between the prosecution team and another prosecution team in the form of the innocents' defence team. The Lion would tear down the prosecution and the others would put it back together. They would also dwell on any evidence that pointed to my guilt. On top of being attacked on both sides, the Lion also had the trial judge firing at him with both barrels. The die was cast. Still, he fought on. I felt sorrier for him most days than I did for myself. The trial was a farce. The judge even went as far as placing a camera on a tripod facing us, because he thought the witnesses were being threatened, and he wanted to catch one of us in the act. As it turned out, the witness who told him that was mistaken. The judge had no alternative other than to remove the tripod and camera.

At one point, Ryan, not being grounded, leapt over the dock and told the judge he refused to participate any further. The sergeant of the escort team immediately rushed Ryan from the side. They both stumbled sideways, flying toward the jury box. Ryan landed on top, driving the cop's head into the corner of the box. Blood poured from a cut. The jurors looked on. A second cop had followed his leader at Ryan, but I had caught him around the throat and pulled him into the box. As his legs kicked over the short wall, guns were placed at my head by the rest of their team and I was ordered to let him go. I tossed him back out. When court resumed, the trial judge ruled these events would in no way affect his jury.

What miffed me the most about this farce of a trial was the judge's charge to the jurors. While I am sure it looked appropriate in the court transcript, that would fail to reveal his antics. He told the jurors that they could believe the defence, to which he rolled his head and eyes skyward, as if to say that they would have to be very stupid; or they could believe the prosecution, to which he stuck out his clenched fist, as if to tell them that the prosecution was rock solid. It was their choice, he concluded; he could not legally sway them either way. Sure.

4

Enter the Beast

MEN, BY THEIR VERY NATURE, are social creatures, whether in society or incarcerated. In an institution, each man generally will gravitate to former associates, then to those with common denominators of race, culture, age, religion, or interests. The number of commonalities will usually determine the degree of social interaction. The social geographic history of individuals will also have a bearing on their choice of associations — their home province, hometown, neighbourhood, even their street. Initially, each man is assessed by others through his appearance, intellect, and strength. In time, personalities will override perceptions, defining long-term associations from ostracization.

Millhaven Max, during the late 1970s to mid-1980s, confined a vast array of men from different walks of life from across Canada: psychopaths, sociopaths, murderers, bank robbers, alleged Mafia dons, outlaw motorcycle gang members, escape artists, career criminals, thugs, and drug dealers. It also housed insane men, mentally deficient men, and not least of all, innocent men.

By its very designation, each man housed there was deemed a serious threat to public safety, a violent offender capable of committing grievous harm to others, and hence classified to maximum security. Among the population were those who had regrettably lost control of a situation, and those without regret. There were those whose psychopathy achieved personal satisfaction by causing harm, even death, to others.

Every man entered this environment with little or no hope, but each possessed a will to survive. Although Millhaven Max proved to be a breeding ground for treachery and deceit, leaving dozens dead and in excess of a hundred violent assaults, friendships were formed amongst strangers, camaraderie amongst groups, and it was in those relationships that each man discovered the key to maintaining some sanity, some hope. Contrary to the horror stories about Millhaven, the ominous threat was not so much from "the keepers of man," but from the men themselves. Each month, a few would enter, a few would leave. During my initial time there, most would remain. Allegiances would alter from time to time, but many, whatever the situation, would not abandon their friends and allies.

Being strangers to me, all the men on arrival were monsters and demons.

Off a sideroad just west of Kingston, Ontario, lies a small winding road leading up a middling hill to a fork that channels visitors to one of two places: the federal maximum-security institution known as Millhaven and the minimum-security Bath Institution. Though separated by only a short distance, these two places are worlds apart.

Millhaven Max, being relatively new as prisons go, lacks the imposing archaic effect the older penitentiaries in the Ontario region radiated. But there was little doubt it had been built to house the worst criminals Canada had to offer. Row upon row of intertwining razor wire glistened atop the two forty-foot fences spread twenty-five feet apart. These fences are the outside perimeter of what the media dubbed "the toughest thirteen acres in Canada." At the front entrance gate, a towering pillar of concrete rose to a platform supporting the guards in all their regalia. Fully loaded assault rifles, sidearms, binoculars, and radio transmitters were all made visible to the naked eye of those who entered and those fortunate enough to leave. Similar, albeit not as menacing, were other manned posts strategically placed outside the fencing so as to encompass the full area of the institution. Night and day, dark-tinted security vehicles patrolled, circling. Watching and waiting for any sign of escape.

The prison itself appeared pristine enough, a two-storey structure in most parts, spread across the acreage, joined by long corridors of metal, concrete, and bulletproof glass. Much like the inner "living" units, Millhaven Max from above would have looked like a series of interlocking hubs, each having three concrete spokes. Three long appendages, or corridors, led to the administration building, to the health/recreational area, and to the trade shop/school area. Inside, the cleanliness of the halls and walls was semi-impressive.

It was purely psychological, but, knowing its history, on first experience I wondered if others could smell the underlying odour, if Holocaust victims could smell it as they entered the extermination camps. Death was in the air of these corridors. Every inner sense warned of danger. As a new prisoner arriving at Millhaven Max, with no alternative, you raised your head, and with bated breath stepped forward into the abyss that would serve as your new world.

川卌

Fresh off the Kingston Penitentiary riot, Millhaven's "christening" prisoners had been relieved to shrug off the upheavals of a lockdown and the segregations in their previous filthy, grey, dungeonesque environment. As they were led into the brand-new institution, each felt it was a new beginning, even though they still wore the leg shackles and handcuffs placed on them prior to transfer. One by one, they were escorted to the start of a long corridor, and there their relief ended. Before them stood a human gauntlet of baton-wielding prison guards, massive in stature, stretching all the way down to their eventual holding cells. Each, ambling as fast as he could in the leg restraints while protecting his head with manacled hands, was forced along in an onslaught of blows from clubs, fists, and steel-toed boots.

Welcome to Millhaven Max.

Story upon story would filter down through the Ontario prison system, into the city jails, and ultimately out into the criminal underworld. Men, alone in their cells, day or night, without provocation, were being set upon and beaten by groups of guards. Attack dogs were set on the men in their cells, purely for the guards' entertainment. Men were being individually maced. The cell ranges were being constantly bombarded with tear gas canisters, the gas seeping into each cell, forcing men to scurry to breathe into any air pocket they could find. For hours, for days on end. Any sign of resistance or mention of mistreatment brought severe consequence to the prisoner. In their disparity, prisoners fortified themselves in their hatred of the guards and a penal system that could ignore the atrocities. They persevered through their hope of eventual transfer or release.

Over the course of a number of years, events occurred within and around Millhaven Max that caught the public's attention. Aside from the continual complaints by convicts' families and by ex-cons, ex–prison staff began reporting on a group of guards who allegedly had attacked them and their property when they voiced their displeasure about the cruel and unusual punishment being heaped upon the prisoners. It was reported that this group had a stranglehold on the institution, from the warden on down. It was widely believed the one mass prison escape through the fences in 1973 was ignored, and therefore allowed to happen, in order to get the warden replaced, or at the very least have him fall in line with their direction.

Finally, an investigation was launched into the situation at the prison to determine whether there was any validity to the numerous complaints. Amidst their cries denying any wrongdoing, none could, or would, explain the horrendous physical condition some prisoners were in. Most important to the team of investigators was the lack of accountability for all the tear gas and mace that had been ordered, paid for, and delivered to the prison. No one could explain where the vast amounts of chemicals were, but it was obvious. All three of the living units reeked of gas. It had soaked into the walls.

The team was finally introduced to the offending parties — a group of garrulous, surly, redneck behemoths and sadistic malcontents. The team was shocked to find such a group within a prison, a group that prided themselves on being called "the Millhaven Mafia." But these were not prisoners. They were in uniform. Armed. Unrepentant.

Being a part of, and therefore supported by, one of the country's most powerful unions, and in lieu of little, if any, co-operating or reputable witnesses, society reluctantly acknowledged that there was no way to legally eradicate this cancer. No way other than attrition. Slowly but surely, the men of the Millhaven Mafia would die or retire. Most every prisoner prayed for the former.

Despite being aware society neither approved of nor condoned their actions or methods, the Millhaven Mafia were secure in the knowledge that they'd survived the spotlight. Although they de-escalated their acts of depravity, every now and again a new story would filter on down to add credence to the belief that they still lived. To experience Millhaven Max was to experience a living hell.

~~~~ |||||

The jury had spoken. After enduring a lengthy three-month trial in a plush courtroom at Toronto's Supreme Court of Ontario, the panel had concluded the only reasonable verdict they believed possible, given the evidence and instructions before them: guilty as charged.

The trial judge thanked and then dismissed them. He then set his sights on me. He, too, had endured the testimonies of dozens of witnesses, most of whom had failed to tell the whole truth, if any truth at all. This particular trial had not only insulted his intelligence, but demeaned the dignity and the integrity of his courtroom. Still, he held one consolation. The pathologist had told the truth — the victim was, indeed, dead, and "His Honour" had the privilege of bestowing sentence upon those deemed responsible.

"Stand up," the judge spat at me.

Knowing the penalty to be imposed was a mandatory life sentence, as necessitated by the verdict, I declined. I sat and watched as he trembled and shook with anger, spewing a litany of words I paid little, if any, attention to. I was transfixed by the realization that I felt no emotion at all. I had long expected and accepted this fate, even prior to the crime occurring. And definitely with greater certainty after. I had not wanted to be in this position, events had escalated, and I had lost control, and this was the result. I still believed the victim played a huge role in his own demise, just as I had in mine. I didn't like the jury convicting my friend Ryan, now sitting next to me in the dock, but I understood their decision. The third and last conviction for the same murder, Harry's, came as a complete shock to most everyone. Especially Harry. As he was sentenced, he stood and cried, professing his innocence to the judge to no avail. Although I sympathized with his plight, I had been angry with his refusal to plea bargain earlier in the proceedings, a move that would have taken these life sentences out of the equation. Harry was shocked-white. As our eyes met, I asked, "How does the deal sound now?"

Court was over, at least for this trial. The appeals were sure to follow. But there was no doubt I was headed to the penitentiary, and not just any prison, but Millhaven Max.

I had served time in local jails and reformatories, but I knew Millhaven would be a totally different experience. There was no shortage of horror stories. Even the toughest of men I had met in the criminal underworld wanted no part of that institution. I was twenty-two years of age. Although I was six feet tall, I still weighed only 150 pounds. I didn't even shave yet. But I was on my way to the Max.

|||†††

Immediately after my conviction, I was placed in an empty cell at Toronto's Don Jail, one of a few cells that made up the "holes." A seven-foot concrete cube with an eight-inch-diameter metal pipe set flush in the middle of the floor. It would spurt water around its rim every hour or so, to provide the only toilet one would find in this dank dungeon. My co-accused had been transferred to the Toronto East Detention Centre, awaiting transport to Kingston Penitentiary's assessment unit. I had to be returned to court in a few days to be sentenced by the same judge for a contempt of court charge I had accrued during the trial.

When I finally appeared, and was asked if I had anything to say before sentencing, I respectfully asked my counsel, the Lion, to take his chair. I knew I would be a while. I proceeded to tell "His Honour" exactly what I thought of him and the way he had conducted my trial. I assured him I had every confidence his pronouncements upon me and my co-accused would be overturned by a higher court. Then I allowed myself a vehement, rage-spitting diatribe that easily warranted a few more contempt charges. I was sentenced to three years concurrent, which in my case meant nothing.

I was then transferred from the hole at the Don to the East Detention, and subsequently off to Kingston Pen. After a brief stint there, I was classified and transferred to Millhaven Max.

On the bus ride there, one could hear a pin drop. Total silence. We could see the fear in each other's eyes. We had all heard the stories. And then we were there.

We were ushered in through the front doors of the institution. Once inside, we were placed in an anteroom and had our shackles and handcuffs removed. A couple of prison guards escorted us to the end of a long corridor. The large metal grille barrier slid sideways to allow access down the hall. The corridor was very clean. Black rubber covered the floor. Windows on both walls extended its length. As we walked, I could see outside on either side. There were small cloistered areas of green, well-manicured lawns surrounded by a swept margin of asphalt and concrete, all within the building's outer walls. Although the sun shone through the window slats, and the anxiety about coming here was over, the reality of actually being here was, to say the least, unnerving. At the end, a grilled barrier whirred, sliding open. We were now standing in a dome-like area, centred by a gun tower that controlled the barriers to the corridors and the three living units. A few guards milled around a small table, set directly behind a walk-through metal detector. They paid us little heed. Another corridor barrier whirred and slid open, and we followed the guard down that corridor's length. There was no barrier at the end, but rather the inner walls of the "back end" — an adjoining building that housed the school, library, and trade and vocational shops. At the T sat a separate security post, but on this day we didn't have to proceed that far.

The institutional stores were located at the end of the corridor. Serving windows were encased in the concrete walls and the metal shutters were open, as our arrival was expected. Each of us was issued bedding: two sheets, a blanket, and pillow with case. A face cloth and towels. We also received institutional clothing issues of shirts, pants, socks, and briefs. A jacket, shoes, slippers, and T-shirts.

Then we were escorted back to the domed area, which I'd come to know as N Area. I was then led into A Unit, a normal population living unit consisting of five ranges, double-decked so as to be D2, C1, C2, B1, and B2, the 2s being the upper-floor ranges. D2 was above the food server. The second-floor ranges all ran off stairwells that sat directly in front of the unit's control tower, operated by armed prison guards. They had electronic control of all doors and barriers within the unit, as well as control of their shotguns and side arms. I was placed on C2.

Every range had some fifteen cells on each side. Between the ranges, at the front of the stairwells, were common-room areas. The front wall of each common room had the same bulletproof glass as the control tower. I stood in front of my assigned cell with my bag and box of new possessions. The door whirred and then slid open with a bang. I entered my new cell and the door promptly slid closed.

About five feet up, in the centre of the door, was a small, unbreakable observation window. With the door locked, a thin slit ran down one side, while another narrow space appeared between the floor and the bottom. The side aperture allowed one to partially see up or down the range, depending which way the door closed. The bottom space was utilized to pass items of minimal thickness, such as magazines. During lockdowns, men would "fish" between cells, passing cigarettes, lighters, dry coffee, sugar, notes, and the like. Whatever would fit through those cracks. Lines made of string would criss-cross the hallway floor, sometimes allowing a man in the last cell to receive a confidential note from the man in the first cell. That would take time, but time was the one thing every man here had a lot of.

The cell walls themselves were composed of concrete cinder blocks. The back wall housed a four-by three-foot window made of unbreakable slats resting on thick horizontal metal bars. By turning a hard plastic knob at the base, the slats could be opened, if only a few inches. Along one side, extending from the back wall, three feet off the floor, was a strong metal sheet, six feet long by three feet wide. This served as the base for one's mattress. Along the other wall were a desk and a thin metal, stand-up locker. Just inside the cell door, off to one side, was a toilet and small sink with a tiny glazed mirror above it. Mounted in the wall above the desk was a metal plate that housed a pre-selected six-station radio. Beside it was a light switch that controlled the two long fluorescent tubes encased in a box that ran along the top of one wall. The night light was controlled by a switch outside the cell or by a main switch in the control tower. This was used by guards during their nightly counts or walks down the ranges. These cells were every prisoner's private refuge from the rest of the world. At least, that is, when the doors were locked.

I no sooner had the bed made and clothing sorted into different compartments when the motor on the door whirred again and the cell door slid wide open. All of the cells slammed open at the same time. I sat on the foot of the bed and watched as different men in prison clothing, the odd one in sweats, meandered past. Some were talking to each other, some not. Some quickly glanced my way, but most not. I had learned long ago that looking into a cell was deeply frowned upon by the prison population, and staring at a man you didn't know was usually interpreted as a challenge. Either action has caused many a man to be assaulted in these environments.

Ten minutes later, the doors slammed shut. Every man in his assigned cell. Minutes later, a guard's face appeared at the door-window, then moved on. Fifteen minutes after that, all the cell doors slammed open again, and everybody was heading off the range, past the common room, and down the stairs. I followed.

At the front of the living unit, on the main floor, was the food server. From behind a wall on one side that had two slots in it, food or beverages were dispensed in single servings to each man as he passed. I stood at the back of the line, and after being passed my portions, immediately returned to my cell. No one had spoken to me. They looked, but never acknowledged me. After a couple of minutes, all the cell doors slammed shut again. They opened a half hour later to allow men to drop off their food trays and go to work or school. Ten minutes later, they closed again. The same exercise occurred hours later when the men returned, got counted, and had supper.

Stepping out onto a prison range for the first time amongst strange men is similar to entering a new classroom where everybody knows everybody else, but no one knows you. They all stare, however briefly. Some mutter a few indiscernible comments to each other, but all show a total disinterest in your arrival. Standing for the first time in the food line allowed me my first noteworthy visual of my new neighbours. They were all well older than me. Some were overly muscular, some were just plain huge. A couple of them appeared insane, but most seemed much the same as other men in the other jails I had been in. I accepted their disinterest in me. I knew it wasn't personal. It was actually very common. I knew that, by suppertime, through the prison grapevine, each of them would know my name, my crime, and my sentence. Those more curious would probably know my criminal record, my past associations, my hometown, and, if they pushed it, my favourite movie. There are few secrets in prison. I knew I would learn about each of them, as well, but for the time being I was just concerned with not doing anything to disrespect any of them.

I didn't want any new friends right away. I knew, at my age, those showing interest would be the "chicken hawks" — homosexual men looking for companionship, offering gifts and protection in exchange for sex. I also knew not to converse with the guards. Prisoners, particularly in max, were paranoid of jailhouse rats, snitches, informers. Talking to guards could get you murdered. Easy. The prison code had few rules, but they were firm. Non-negotiable. Over the years, hundreds of men would break them, but in Millhaven Max in those days, no one dared. Each man prided himself on carrying out the code to the letter. To their death, if need be. They had little else.

"Yard up."

Exercise time.

Anyone could go to the gym or yard when this time was announced. I had been looking forward to it since I arrived. I would get to see Ryan. Not only was he a few years older, but he had been in federal custody before. He'd know people here, and more importantly, he knew me. (Harry had left Millhaven almost as fast as he had arrived. He had secured a job as an "orderly" at Kingston Pen's Regional Treatment Centre.) I was also nervous of going out to the yard, as I had heard from many men on my way through to Millhaven that I had an enemy here I had yet to meet — a well-known, fully grown psycho serving his second term for murder, this one a triple homicide.

I went out to the yard. I was not walking the track that circled the yard along the inner fenceline for long before Ryan appeared. He was as happy to see me as I was him. We continued to walk, with him explaining the routine of the prison, the dos and don'ts, when I stopped suddenly. I recognized a man sitting with a group of men over at the outside weight pit. It was not my psycho, but he was watching us, and more specifically, Ryan. I mentioned this to Ryan and he shrugged it off. The man was not going to be a problem, Ryan assured me.

I had met Dwayne as a teenager. At that time, I had no comparable reference, and still hadn't at this point in my life, of anyone like him. I would come to experience like-minded men, but would never understand their penchant for physical violence. At a time when the national news was following the Watergate hearings of U.S. president Richard Nixon, I had taken a case of beer to a friend's house just south of Regent Park. We were drinking when Dwayne showed up. He was my friend's cousin. He was older, larger, and definitely talked a lot faster. He was very muscular, in a defined "I just got out of jail" kind of way. When the conversation turned to cannabis, I offered to get a small bag in Regent. Dwayne insisted he escort me, and his cousin, my friend, encouraged me to take him along. I relented. Halfway there, in the middle of my neighbourhood, Dwayne dropped down on the concrete sidewalk and started doing push-ups. I glanced at the people staring, somewhat embarrassed. Finally, he leapt back up, produced a comb out of his pocket and started running it through his hair. "I'm ready now," he said. "Nobody better mess with us, you know what I mean, kid?"

"Sure," I replied, wondering what the hell he was talking about, and secondly, what was up with those push-ups.

When we returned to my friend's house, Dwayne was upset I hadn't let him see where I purchased the marijuana. "If he wasn't so small ..." he told his cousin over and over. Later that day, we went to a birthday party my friend and I were invited to for an older teen in my neighbourhood, with Dwayne in tow. We were welcomed and each given a beer, and I sat on a couch between Dwayne and his cousin. This was a great party. Everyone having a great time — music, dancing, laughing. After a short time, Dwayne got up and approached a group of the older teens. "Which one is the birthday boy?" he asked. Frank, the teen whose house we were in, smiled and sheepishly nodded to Dwayne that it was him. "I have a present for you," Dwayne said. Then he punched Frank as hard as he could right in the face. The other teens were on Dwayne immediately, beating the tar off him. Then they threw him out onto the street. I looked at my friend and asked him, "Really?"

"He's my cousin," he answered, as though that explained everything. Then we were told to leave, as well, the consequence of bringing the nutcase in with us.

Six years later, while in custody at the Don Jail, I ran into Dwayne again. He'd been arrested for breaking into lockers in the basements of high-rise buildings. I'd committed the same crime myself as a young teen. But he was around twenty-eight then. He was furious at his partner. Although his fingerprints had been found on scene, he was sure his partner had snitched to the police; otherwise, Dwayne reasoned, his partner would be charged with him. As it turned out, his partner wore gloves. Dwayne didn't care, and continued to slander his partner. He made bail, but failed to appear at his court date, so a warrant went out, and he was picked up at his girlfriend's place and returned to the Don.

Ryan had been asleep on the couch when the cops picked Dwayne up. He was dating Dwayne's girlfriend's sister, who lived there, as well. Because the police hadn't arrested Ryan, in Dwayne's mind, Ryan was now a snitch, too. Dwayne, as everyone knew, loved to fight. He'd fight almost anyone, save those he knew were much, much tougher. He'd fight all the time.

Now, here we were, in the yard at Millhaven, Ryan beside me; Dwayne across the way. In my mind, this was not a good situation. Still, Ryan gave it no never mind, so we continued to walk and talk.

Another man I knew from the Don Jail years approached us. He was a committee member now at Millhaven, well known and well respected. "How are you, kid?" he asked. I told him of my concern about the psycho I had yet to meet. He rubbed me on my head, laughing. "It's your lucky day," he said. "That guy's in Quebec. He tried to escape, so they shipped him out."

I drew a sigh of relief. I wouldn't have to deal with that, at least not now.

Ryan told me he was employed as a barber there. It was a great place to work, he assured me. He arranged an interview for me with his instructor. I told him I'd think about it and do the interview. What harm could it do?

My second day began locked in my cell in the morning, as I was unemployed. At lunch, I picked up my food tray and returned upstairs to my range. As I passed the common room area, a man who lived on my range told me I didn't have to eat in my cell, but could sit at a table in the common room and watch TV. Being confined all morning, the idea sounded good to me. I went in and sat down at a table in the middle of the room, facing the TV. The cell doors on my range banged shut, and then I heard the next range's doors open. My eyes left the TV as I noticed another prisoner come hurriedly through one door. He turned and flung the door to close it, but it bounced back open. He looked terrified. Then he raced across the common room, passing my table, and out the other door. My gaze followed him out of sight. Then I turned back to the first door. A huge man had come into the common room. He was naked save for a calfskin loincloth and some smears of different-coloured paints on his face and chest. This was a big, big man, and the knife-shaped piece of metal in his hand was big, as well. He looked quickly around the common room. Then the Native man went racing out the other door in search of his prey. I just sat there, open-mouthed. Two things were certain to me at that moment. One, I had lost my appetite, and two, I wasn't going to survive this place. I ate my supper in my cell.

The daily routine of Millhaven Max seldom changed unless there was a lockdown or a full-scale disruption by prisoners. A lockdown, which sees each man confined in his cell, occurs after a violent event such as a murder, attempted murder, or gang fight. Prison breaks or attempted escapes also precipitate lockdowns. These can last hours or weeks, the duration dependent upon the length of the ensuing investigations. Major disruptions see prisoners blocking cell doors, range barriers, common room doors. Generally, this would give prisoners access throughout the entire living unit. This seldom occurred, except when prisoners felt their rights en masse were being violated or ranges were being unnecessarily tear-gassed. These disruptions would last a few days at most. Sit-downs in the gym or yard, with prisoners refusing to return to their cells, were again a form of protest against administrative actions. (This also disabled guards from obtaining an accurate head count in the course of attempted escapes.)

The third day, I was told to proceed to the barbershop. After passing through the walk-through metal detector in the dome, or N Area (one always had to pass through it, if a prisoner), a barrier was opened and I went down the corridor, passing the store windows and the guards standing watch in the trade shop hallway. They looked at the pass — a piece of paper that had been handed to me in my unit — and then one guard led me to the barbershop door. He let me in with his key. Ryan was there. He introduced me to the instructor. After talking, reassuring him that I could handle the theoretical part of his course, the textbook part, and that I had adequate hand-eye coordination, he agreed to hire me as a trainee. I informed him I was not as confident in finding a talent or flair for the business. I remained at the shop the rest of the morning. It was quite impressive: sterile and very well lit. Huge mirrors adorned the walls over the counters that contained sinks. On one side was a huge tub sink with a reclining black leather chair, used for shampooing and rinsing. Down the same side, spaced evenly apart, were three old-fashioned barber chairs. Each station before them had an ultraviolet sterilizer on the counter, a glass disinfectant jar for hand tools, and a hair dryer. Each barber had his own tool kit, dispensed from the office, when he arrived at work. There were scissors, old-fashioned straight razors, brushes, combs, clips, the works. Three more chairs ran along the back wall. On the other side of the shop was one chair with a small counter. That area was occupied by the most experienced barber, who would work on both staff and prisoners. Directly behind that chair was the shop cleaner's chair and a table that held the huge hot-water urn, coffee, sugar, and whitener. The music was tuned to easy listening. Ryan introduced me to his co-workers. They all were friendly enough. I was sure I'd enjoy the experience of becoming a hairstylist.

A few days later, I was approved to start work there by the institution's work board. I watched the others as they performed several different styled cuts, perms, hair straightenings, facials, and old-fashioned shaves, day in and day out. I soon realized a lot of the prisoners just came in to relax and take a break from school or the jobs. The barbers didn't seem to mind most of the time.

During my first week of training, I missed a half hour of work for an intake assessment interview with the prison psychologist. I was taken to an office and told to sit in a chair across the desk from him. He looked me in the eye and said earnestly, "Son, you're serving a life sentence." I nodded. "Do you think you can make it?" he asked. "Doc," I answered, "not a chance." He smiled and replied, "Well then, there is nothing wrong with you mentally. So, have a good day." That was it. Interview over.

5

The Razor's Edge

THE FOLLOWING WEEK, my instructor gave me a pass to attend health care once again. This time I had to see the institutional doctor for a mandatory intake checkup. That took as long as my psych interview. When I returned to the shop, everything appeared normal. Ryan was by his chair, honing his razor. Another barber was giving a prisoner a facial. A couple others were giving haircuts. I gave my pass slip to the instructor and headed down the shop, toward my chair at the back.

"Hey, kid, how are you doing? Remember me?"

I glanced to my left. It was Dwayne. He was sitting in the lone barber chair on the far side. That barber had taken the day off.

"What's up?" I nodded to Dwayne, and went to keep walking.

"Come here, I want to talk to you for a minute," he said.

I walked over and leaned against the counter, facing him sitting in the chair.

"Grab a coffee, the water's hot," he offered.

I went to the table behind him and made one, then went back to the counter and listened to him talk. He still talked faster than anyone I had ever met. "You remember me, right?" he asked again.

"Sure, you're Buzzard's cousin. Kevin's brother."

"Yeah," he said. "You know the Row Boat tried to kill my brother. Shot him right in the chest?"

"I heard." Actually, the Row Boat had hid out in my apartment after that event, until he was sure Kevin hadn't exposed him to the police. But I was not about to tell Dwayne that.

"I was going to kill him myself, soon as I got out," Dwayne continued. "You know that, right, kid?"

"Sure, Dwayne," I said, not believing anything.

And on and on Dwayne went about Regent Park, his cousin and brother, how tough he was. I just leaned on the counter, listening.

I saw Ryan coming up to the coffee table with his mug in one hand. In a flash, Ryan was standing behind Dwayne, pulling his head back by the hair. Dwayne smiled until he saw it was Ryan. By then, it was too late. Ryan's arm had already swept across his neck and back across. Dwayne was cut deep across his throat, one ear to the other. Ryan stepped back. I sidestepped out of the area. Due to the sharpness of the straight razor, the cut itself had not bled immediately. Not until Dwayne leapt out of the chair. He turned to face Ryan and they began to fight. Fists and kicks flew between them. The blood from Dwayne's neck wound flew everywhere. It was pouring out. They landed on another barber chair, Ryan on top, Dwayne weak from blood loss. The barber instructor had been pounding his panic button alarm since the fight broke out, and now the guards were pouring in, separating the two combatants. Dwayne was stretchered out first, with towels clamped down around his throat. Ryan was stripped naked on the spot, then escorted down to the "hole" by a throng of guards. The rest of us in the shop were sent back to our cells. When we did eventually return back to work, we found the days of old-fashioned straight razors were over. Not a razor in sight.

Dwayne made it, by a thread. Ryan pled to wounding and was shipped out west after serving two years in the special handling unit. I was told later on by the other barbers that Dwayne had come into the shop while I was at the doctor's appointment and had been threatening Ryan. And then he turned his back on him. I never said Dwayne was smart; just another nutcase who loved to start trouble and fight.

The morning after the barbershop incident, my cell door opened and the guard yelled for me to go to the Keeper's Hall. I went out to N Area and was told where that was. I followed the corridor up to where I had first entered

Millhaven. The control tower opened a side door. "In there," the guard barked. I walked down a short hallway of offices that led to a large room. Guards milled about the area. A couple of older guards in more decorated uniforms called me over. "We have to speak with you," one began. "You know Dwayne has been here for a while, and that he has a lot of friends?" I just shrugged. "There's a lot of information coming to us from different sources that you're going to be murdered in retaliation for what happened to him, do you understand that?" the keeper continued. "Okay," I answered. Then he added, "We want to help you out. We want to lock you up in a protective custody environment. You'll be transferred to another institution." My mind was racing. The other keeper spoke: "Look, these guys in here, some of them, they have nothing to lose. They're going to stick you to the wall, and we're going to get stuck cleaning up the mess. So, just agree to lock-up, and we'll get you moved."

I looked at the gruff old keeper. (*So, Ryan, Dwayne is not going to be a problem, eh? Shit!*) I looked around the room, at all the guards looking at me. I could tell they expected me to run. They'd expected me to "check in." Any sane person in my position most likely would. But I hadn't expected to come so far, and I certainly didn't expect I'd survive anyways, Dwayne or not. "I'm sorry if you have a mess to clean up, but I am not voluntarily agreeing to any lock-up," I told the gruff keeper. Then I turned to the other one: "If you want to do me a favour, just tell the cops investigating the barbershop incident that I have nothing to say, so don't bother calling me out."

"Fair enough," the second keeper said. "Go back to your cell."

For two weeks, not one prisoner spoke to me.

I followed my same routine. No one sat in my common room if I sat out there for meals. I would glimpse some of Dwayne's friends looking in and glaring, but they never approached me. No one came near my barber chair, so I did a lot of reading. And, definitely, no one approached as I walked the yard each night. I'd always see Dwayne's friends in a group, huddled off to the side, whispering and glaring at me. A couple of them were huge men, the rest weather-beaten and evil-looking. One day, my cell door opened on the range and the guard yelled for me to pack up my belongings. I was being moved from A Unit over to J Unit. There really was no difference. Although all Dwayne's friends were with me in A Unit, both units intermingled at yard and at work.

The only thing different from my range on C2 to my new range, M2, was that one man actually talked to me. "Do you play gin?" he asked. "Sure," I answered. "We'll play sometime," he said, walking away.

I still went to work at the barbershop and walked the yard every day. Every moment since the keepers talked to me, I expected the assault that would end my life.

Cheech and Chong's *Up in Smoke* was being shown in the gym one night. Being a fairly recent hit, the vast majority of the prison population went down to watch it. Chairs were set out across the entire gym floor. When I entered, I saw an empty chair. "Is this chair taken?" I asked the guy sitting next to it politely. He looked at me, and then looked around. "You can have it," he said, "but don't sit near me. I don't want your blood all over my clothes."

"Thanks," I said. I left the chair and went to lean up against the back wall. The lights went out. I watched the entire movie, listening to everyone laughing out loud, but I never cracked a smile. The lights came back on at the end, and everyone, including me, left to go back to their cells for the night. This had become my favourite time. It was a time when I could be alone with my thoughts and not look over my shoulder for trouble.

A few days later, as I walked the yard, Dwayne's crew approached me. I steeled myself. The biggest man, some 270 pounds, obviously the chosen leader, spoke: "Kid, you had nothing to do with what happened to Dwayne?"

"No," was all I said.

"We're going to let you slide on this, okay?"

"Sure," I said, not believing a word.

"You know, you don't have any friends here, so if you want to hang with us, you can."

"I'm okay," I answered, "but thanks just the same." I eyed them all warily. They walked away. I walked the other way. Nothing had changed. I didn't trust them, and continued to watch whenever any of them were in my vicinity.

The next day, the man I knew on the committee stopped by my cell to chat. He'd been absent around me the last few weeks. Waiting, like everyone else, I suppose, to see what happened. "How are you, kid?" he asked. I shrugged. "I was the one that got you moved to J Unit, away from that other crew," he volunteered.

"Thanks," I said, not really thankful, not seeing how that was helpful. I could have used a friend.

"The French crew are the ones that talked to those guys, though, you know," he said. I asked why. "Well, they said they were going to do this and that, and everyone was getting sick of the waiting, the drama, and their bullshit, so the French guys just went and told them what everyone knew. The pigs wanted to lock you up, and you wouldn't go. That says a lot. That, and you walking the yard and everything. Not running, you know?" I nodded. "The French crew said if you had been involved, their friend would not have made it out of the chair. They told them to either stop talking or do something."

Dwayne's crew must have decided I was not important enough to risk the time. Either way, it was over for now.

The next day, the other barbers chatted me up, as though the last few weeks never happened. Other men would nod to me as we crossed paths. I guess not running had earned me some small degree of respect, since it didn't get me killed. I still knew I could count on no one but myself. As I became acquainted with the men on my new range, I asked about the gin player. I had to pass his cell to get to or from my own cell, and each time he would ask me about playing a game. He was an odd but insistent fellow. The other men laughed. That "fellow" believed he was a woman trapped in a man's body, and he was dying to be my new girlfriend. Knowing this, I finally sat down for a chat and let him make his pitch. I assured him that if I ever felt the urge to go off the straight life, he would be my girl. He wasn't happy, but at least he quit harassing me to play gin.

I met another prisoner, close to my age, up on my new range. Ken was from Hamilton, and was also just beginning to serve a life sentence. He'd arrived a year or so ahead of me. Ken was a very quiet, reserved kind of guy, a loner, more or less. He spent a lot of his time drawing. Art seemed to be a passion for him. One day he informed me he'd purchased, through the institution's black market, a homemade tattoo gun and some different-coloured inks. He wondered if I would be interested in having him give me a tattoo. He was very eager. I never had any tattoos. After some thought, I figured I would let him hone his skill on my upper right arm. That seemed to lift his spirits.

Not long after he completed his work on me, Ken fell victim to his depression and took his own life. Prison life was not for him and he could see no way out. He was not the first nor the last of the men I would meet who would kill themselves.

卌 |||

Every prisoner was assigned a parole officer (PO) in charge of his case. They were seen as the frontline decision-makers, although the warden and his senior administration held the ultimate power within the institution. If a man requested a private family visit, a prison transfer, a transfer of funds, or even to get married, he would have to apply through his PO. Back in 1979, phone calls were only permitted once every few months, from the PO's office, with the parole officer present.

My PO called me in shortly after I arrived in Millhaven. He put me on the phone with a professor of law, a lawyer from Toronto. "Your trial lawyer has asked me to represent you at your appeal. Is that okay with you?" the lawyer asked.

I'd never met the man. Had never even heard of him. If the Lion had recommended him, though, that was good enough for me. "Of course," I answered. "I only have one request." I told him I didn't want to be bothered with a million questions; I just wanted to be told when the appeal was over. He laughed, saying, "You took the words right out of my mouth. I'll call you then."

I hung up, and never gave the appeal a second thought after that.

My first visitor at Millhaven came about a month and a half after I arrived. Notified that someone was there to see me, I went down the corridor leading to the visiting room. Before entering, each prisoner is searched, his possessions documented. The front wall of the visiting room is mostly clear bulletproof glass. On the other side is the guards' room, and they have a clear and easy sightline of everything that transpires during a visit. The other walls are brick. With as few as ten tables, spaced out, and a few vending machines near the front door, the room provides little privacy.

My older sister, the third-oldest, arrived with her husband and my mother. After a brief hug, kiss, and handshake, we took chairs around the table and began to chat. My sister asked how things were. "Just fine," I said, smiling. "The food is good. There is a big yard, and gym. I'm learning to be a barber. Everyone treats me okay. And how are you?" I said, changing the subject. "How are the kids?"

"Oh, the girls are fine," she said, and she started into a lengthy accounting of her life.

I kept looking at my mother, but she averted her eyes. She hadn't said a word. Finally, I interrupted my sister and I turned to my mother. "Mom, what's wrong?" I asked, concerned. "You're wearing an earring," she choked out. I felt the gold stud in my left earlobe. "Yes, I am, Mom. So?"

"Well, doesn't that mean you're queer now? Are these men here making you have sex with them?" She was almost in tears.

I was stunned for a second, and then I began to laugh. And then I really laughed hard.

"What's funny about that?" she asked, still serious.

"Mom," I told her, "if you ever see me wearing earrings in both ears and carrying a purse, then you can start to worry." I assured her I was not gay, that I was not being forced into sex. The last incident I had heard of like that was when prisoners had come from Millhaven to Toronto to testify in defence of a man accused of murdering a jailhouse rapist behind the handball walls. The deceased had upwards of fifty holes through his body.

My mother relaxed and joined the conversation. "How is Ryan doing?" my sister asked. "Oh, never better," I lied. "I'll tell him you said hello." (Ryan was at that point in the hole facing wounding charges for the barbershop incident.)

When my family left that day, they had no idea of the danger I had just come through or the reality of the environment I now resided in.

My oldest brother, serving his twelve years one penitentiary over, was my next visitor. He had gained permission, and the guards from Collins Bay Institution had brought him over to the visiting room. "Are you alright? Do you need me to transfer over here?" he asked. I looked at him much like he had looked at me two years previous in the Don Jail. "Just go, brother," I said. "It's bad enough for Mom just having one of us here in this hell. Just go. I'll handle it." And that was that. His twelve years I had thought no one could serve now looked like an easy sentence to me.

I laughed. There's nothing like a life sentence to put everything into perspective. He went back to the Bay. I went back to my cell.

For the most part, Millhaven was an exceptionally quiet institution. The constant clanging of the cells opening or closing was the only major offender. While men tolerated normal decibel levels of each other's idle chatter passing before their cell doors, it was common knowledge that noise almost always precipitated an act of violence. The exception was the verbal communications during lockdowns — conversations between men from cell to cell, or yelling through the windows to the other living units.

One night, as I sat listening to the radio, I could hear two men conversing between units by using numbers only. It was a pre-arranged code to avoid eavesdroppers. Later on, that same evening, I could hear shouts and loud bangs emanating from E Unit. That was the living unit that confined the men in either the special handling unit or administrative segregation. After a couple of hours, silence fell over the institution. The night took hold. Everyone slept.

The following morning, after breakfast, when the cell doors opened for work, a shout came down the range. "Everyone into the common room!"

The men in the prisoners' committee were present, and so, to a man, we followed the direction. Being relatively new there and as such devoid of opinion on any issue, I leaned against the back wall and listened. Everyone was told to block their cells and all barriers in the living unit. We were in a protest. No guards were allowed on the unit save those in the control tower, who were now glaring at everyone. A few prisoners, senior in the time they had served at Millhaven, requested clarification on the requested action. One tall black fellow, who appeared none too enthused about the proposed action, spoke up. "What's the point? As soon as the guards or the army show up, what do you think the new guys are going to do? Run under their beds and hide like women." He was staring right at me, and I was acutely aware that so was everyone else. I could feel the anger rising in my neck.

"Are you talking to me?" I asked.

"You'll do," he chided.

"Okay, I'll tell you what I'm going to do. As soon as a squad of guards show up, or army, or whoever comes through those doors, I'm going to find you. And you and me are going to be the front line. You have my word on that," I answered, staring at him icily.

The committee member who had known me shook his head at the tall Black. "You fucked up, pal. Believe me; the kid will come for you." Now, I was not the one feeling uneasy.

Then to everyone, the committee chairman yelled, "This is not a fucking debate! Block the doors."

Everyone left the common room. No one worked, and for the two-day standoff, my antagonist remained invisible. We never spoke again, although we lived in the same unit for years. The major disruption was a response to the "unnecessary" tear-gassing of one of the E Unit ranges. At least the committee had deemed it so.

A week or so later, on a hot, sunny summer afternoon, I went out to the yard for my usual weekend walk. It felt good, but it sure was lonely, not having any friends to talk to … or any strangers, for that matter. After about an hour of my walking "donuts" on the oval path that wound around the yard, I saw my committee associate approaching me. He asked what I was doing. "Just walking," I said.

"Well, if you're not busy, I was wondering if you could help me out with something."

"What is it?"

He motioned me to walk with him along the path. We got to an area between the tennis court fence and the tall fencing that cordoned off the yard. The path had a small rise to it in that spot — not drastic, but a small hill just the same. In the middle of the rise was a circular three-foot heavy metal lid that rested over a concrete sleeve, extending down into the ground. On the tennis court side of the rise, the ground had been removed to bare the concrete a few feet wide by a few feet deep. "Do you think, if I got you a sledgehammer, that you could knock that concrete out?" he asked.

"I don't know," I answered honestly. "I don't know how thick that is. But if you want, I'll give it a try."

He smiled. "Okay, just walk another lap and I'll meet you back here," he said. He took off toward the gym.

I walked the lap, thinking it was too nice a day to be working. However, this was a good way to ingratiate myself and make a friend. Being committee, he probably had a few of these projects on the go, as well as having to look after all the internal problems within the institution. As I came around the path to the rise, he'd already returned with the sledge. "Thanks a lot, kid. I'll be back," he said, handing me the hammer.

And so I stood on the lid and slowly swung away at the concrete. I was not physically fit at all, being very thin, and so it took quite a few minutes and a lot of swings before the concrete began to chip and crack. Then it began to break up in pieces. After a half hour or so, I had a hole the size of the dug-out area. I slowly knocked off the rough edges, making the hole look nice. My friend came back and took a look. "That's perfect, thanks a lot," he said, taking back his sledgehammer.

"If you don't mind my asking, what exactly do you need this hole for?" I asked.

"Oh," he answered, "we're leaving."

I didn't understand. "What do you mean?"

"My friend and I are going in there. We're following the pipe all the way past the fences where it comes out, and we're gone." He started to chuckle. He had watched as my jaw dropped and my eyes widened.

"You are kidding me," I said.

"No. No, I'm not. I can't take you with us, but if the guards don't find this hole, feel free to use it," he answered seriously.

"Sure," I said, still taking in the situation. I had just stood in plain view of everyone in the yard making this hole, and not one person had paid any mind. Not even the guards in their towers. Holy smoke.

I went back to my unit on the next changeover. I never did see anyone go down into the hole, but at supper count, two men were missing. From my cell window, I could see the yard, and more specifically, the rise in the path. Guards combed over the yard with their attack dogs. Finally, one of the dogs walking over the rise started pawing at the loose ground. Then he started pawing faster. The guard pulled the dog away, bent down, and then called to the other guards. They were staring at the hole. A few minutes later, they opened another metal lid farther down, and closer to the fenceline. They began firing rifle shots into that hole — the drainage system pipes.

I lay back on my bed and listened to the radio. Good tunes. A few hours later, our doors opened. The institution had resumed normal movement.

The two captured men were released from the hole — segregation — about a month later. Upon seeing me, my committee friend said, "That fucking pipe never went anywhere but to a bunch of smaller pipes a hamster couldn't fit through." And then he shrugged, smiling. I took it as a lesson learned. I wasn't mad at him, although I did feel sheepishly stupid. I never did anything for anyone in there again. Not without first asking why. Both of those men would eventually successfully escape, though only one from Millhaven Max.

Every week for the next few years was exactly the same routine. Monday to Friday, work, exercise, sports, shower, and sleep. The food menu also recycled itself. Saturday and Sunday meant more exercise time in the gym and yard with a couple of hours of TV in the common room.

My sister and brother-in-law would visit each month. I had two lady friends who would (without knowing it) alternate weekend visits. Every night of every day, I would lie on the hard bed and stare up at the ceiling. I never wallowed in self-pity, nor fantasized about escaping to some remote Garden of Eden. I just simply endured. Each day, I got a little older, and a lot stronger.

The barbershop served my first year at Millhaven well. Not only did I acquire the skills and knowledge that would eventually earn me a hairstylist certificate, but I was able to rest my body each day in the soft chairs after hours of weight training the night before. The only thing I was focused on since the straight razor ordeal was getting myself into a physical condition to adequately defend myself. Every day I would consume copious amounts of bread, potatoes, peanut butter, milk, raw eggs, and any other weight-gaining proteins or carbohydrates I could obtain.

Moose, a friend of Ryan's, had arrived in Millhaven. He was, as his name implied, a big, broad-shouldered man, though not much older than I was. We'd met once in Toronto, in a bar where he'd been solicited by the Row Boat's friends to intimidate, or better yet, assault me. I had recognized the direction our acquaintance was headed and had a friend call Ryan, who lived just across the street, to join us with a weapon. Ryan came, and I was surprised when Moose called him over to the table; but Moose was more surprised to learn his friend was my partner.

Now, Moose and I were in the weight pit together every day, training hard. Moose knew quite a few of the men, having been at Millhaven before. (This was his second time in for manslaughter; he'd hit too hard, and men would die.) Saul was a friend of Moose's, and he joined our training. I began to show some weight gain, some progress from my anorexic beginnings. I met another man, Corky, who had come in from Collins Bay. He was a decade older, but we had mutual friends. I had him sit at my table in the common room. He was in great shape for his age. A dedicated weightlifter. Corky, though vain and bad-tempered, had a great sense of humour. Not long after his arrival, he had an altercation with one of the bikers. That same afternoon, I was approached by the biker and one of his sidekicks. "Don't go to the yard tonight," they told me. "Corky is going to get hurt."

"Is it one on one?" I asked.

"No, just don't go out," I was warned.

"Well, knowing what I know now, I have to go out," I told them.

"You will get yours, too," they threatened.

"That's fine," I said, asking, "Would you leave your friend?"

Before the supper count, the biker came back. Corky and he had reconciled their differences, each man apologizing.

The incident stayed with me on account of Willy. He occupied the next cell to me, and having overheard my conversation with the two men earlier, he approached me. "Good for you, kid. I'll be going out to the yard with you," he promised. I had never really gotten to know Willy. Through the prison grapevine, and his hometown boys from Hamilton, I knew he was a feared fighter. I really appreciated his gesture of support, and Willy and I spoke more frequently after that. One night, after lock-up, high on pills, Willy kept conversing with one of his buddies across and four cells down the hall. While that action was frowned upon, no one seemed to pay any heed. I slept in the following morning.

Willy's voice woke me up. He sounded alarmed. I rolled out of bed into my pants and shoes. Then I walked out on the range, looking up and down. Everything looked usual. Men were going to and from the food server with their breakfast trays. I went back in my cell and washed my face. Then I went over to see Willy. He was inside his cell, but near the door, down on one knee. His left arm on the toilet seat seemed to be supporting his weight. His eyes were wide open but unseeing. He had a massive gouge right through the centre of his naked chest. Willy was gone, dead, and there wasn't anything anyone could do about it.

Saul pulled me away. He lived across the range from me. I'd hear different stories of why it happened, but I would forever believe a crazy psychopath didn't like being kept awake that night. That was a bad reason to end such a good life. Willy was my friend, and I never slept in again at Millhaven Max.

I increased my workout regimen. Not long after that, Sal came into the "Haven." He was a big, strapping farm boy, much like Moose. We'd met briefly at the Don Jail. On one occasion, during my stay on death row there, Sal had been brought in to occupy the one empty cell. He'd told me he couldn't handle the claustrophobic atmosphere and asked if I could help him get off the short range. When the guard did his "range check" at the front grille, I approached him. I told him, in no uncertain terms, to move Sal before he got hurt. I feigned a lot of anger. After the guard left to speak to his superior, Sal came out of his cell. "You want to fight?" he asked. He was twice my size at this time, and I had no reason to fight him. "What are you talking about?" I said. "I heard what you said to the guard, I'm kicking your ass," he threatened. "Hold on," I said. "You asked me to get you off this range, and that's what I was doing." Taking off his shirt, Sal said, "You sounded too serious to me."

"Well, if I didn't ..." I speculated.

Sarge, another prisoner at the time in the death row cells, came out of his. He was the same size as Sal, and Sarge loved to fight. He'd been lying on his bed, listening to the whole exchange. "You want a fight?" he asked Sal.

No reply.

I interjected. "Sarge, he just can't handle being locked in here. Sal, you weren't really going to beat me up, were you?" Sal shook his head no.

Sarge told him, "If the kid doesn't get you moved by suppertime, I am kicking your face in." Then Sarge went back in his cell. We all went into our own cells.

An hour later, the lieutenant showed up. "Sal, get your stuff. We're putting you back on the pen range, but any more of your shit and you'll be coming right back here." Sal could not leave fast enough, and he never came back.

Now he was here at Millhaven, in my unit, on the very next range. We nodded at each other in passing. That was the extent of our interaction. Sal noticed one day when a man passed me a small roll. I walked into Moose's common room and spoke with him and two friends. Then I exited, walking right into Sal. "What did that guy give you?" he asked. "I seen the play."

Not really knowing why, I explained that the other prisoner had owed me money and given me some pills to square up his debt. I told Sal I'd split them already four ways with Moose and his friends, and only had mine left. "I want them," he demanded. "I want yours."

I told him there were only a few left. "I don't care, get them, I want them." He began posturing like he was going to start fighting. "Relax," I said. "Give me a couple of minutes. I'll go get them for you. What cell are you in?" I asked timidly. He told me, and I left.

I walked into my common room and made a hot coffee. Then I fished in my pocket for the remaining pills and I ate them all. I swallowed the hot coffee behind them to speed up their effect. Then I went down to my range and changed clothing. I put on a loose hockey sweater, track pants, and steel-toed boots. On the way back up the range, I grabbed a large shank — a piece of heavy thick metal shaped like a carving knife. I sat back down in my common room until I felt the pills start to take effect, and then I marched down Sal's range to his cell. He had company. One of the guys from the Hamilton crew that knew him was there. He also knew me. "Would you mind stepping outside the cell?" I asked the Hamiltonian.

"No, please. He doesn't know you. He doesn't understand this place," his visitor pleaded. "Oh, he knows me, alright. Don't you, Sal?" I growled. "Get out," I told his friend. Sal was no longer posturing, but up on the back of his bed, trying to fade into the corner of the cell walls.

"You asshole. You want something from me? Because I have something for you, if you want it," I growled again.

"No, I'm sorry, I'm sorry," he repeated.

I exposed the shank from under my sweater. Sal's eyes began to tear up. "You couldn't muscle me years ago, and you sure as hell aren't muscling me now. You are damn lucky your friend was here. Don't ever get in my face again, as long as you're here," I warned him. Then I left the cell and turned right into Moose and his friends. They had been standing just outside and to the right of the cell door. "Is everything okay?" Moose asked.

"Never better," I answered and went to walk away.

"Hold on," Moose said. "You have to tell us when you got problems, you know. We're your friends."

"Okay," I answered.

They'd seen me from their common room, noticed the change in my attire, and made the right assumption that there was trouble.

Months later, Sal would run. He would check himself into protective custody, even though no one was after him. Sal was a bully, but with little backbone. He was not well-grounded.

Corky would later involve me in yet another of his dramas. One weekend morning, he went to the gym. On discovering the rubber ripped off one of the Ping-Pong paddles, a game he liked to play, he proceeded to rant and rave, saying the guilty party must be a "goof" — not a well accepted term in prison. Actually, it was one of the worst. It was certainly not a word to be used when the offender is standing nearby with his three buddies. The Native man was a 240-pounder who could fight like hell, and Corky did not fare well. Actually, when I entered the gym to work out with Moose and Saul, Corky was still panting hard. He had a small cut over his left eye. "What happened to you?" I asked. "They jumped me," he said, pointing to the four men.

We approached them while Corky stood back. The Native guy said, "He called me a goof." I responded, trying to pick a fight, "Well, you are. Now, get up." His buddy, who I had had some interaction with previously, said, "Kid, we don't want to fight."

"You should have thought about that before you jumped my friend," I shot back. He shook his head. "We didn't do that. I know he's your friend. We just pulled our friend off him. I swear." I looked at Corky. Someone was not telling me the truth, and I was pretty sure I knew who. "Corky, your call," I said. I could see the wheels turning in his mind. This was a very serious situation. He had blown up over a stupid paddle, and used the "goof" word. That was a huge no-no. People died for a lot less, especially in

Millhaven. Maybe he misinterpreted the actions of the three men separating the fight. "Screw it," Corky said. "Forget it."

It was over. But I was more careful now in my association with Corky. He made bad decisions, and in Millhaven those could cost you heavily. Still, we remained friends until he was released.

$$\mathbf{||||}$$

The Rocket arrived six months or so after me. We'd met briefly in the Lindsay jail, when I was going through my preliminary hearing on the murder charge and he and some of his "brothers" had come in on their murder charge. I'd felt it necessary to introduce myself, to warn him of the danger of undercover police being planted in the jail as prisoners to obtain evidence against them. This had occurred twice in my case while I was there. I cautioned him to talk to no one, including myself. I asked him to pass a message on to his one co-accused that I knew. The message was simply "The cops have nothing on me." The Rocket informed me he was in the same situation. They had nothing on him either. Now, a year later, I sat in the stairwell at the front of J Unit server, watching him stroll in with two of his five co-accused. The others convicted with him were housed in A Unit. As soon as he saw me, we both started laughing. "They don't have anything on us," we said, almost in unison.

The Rocket went to his assigned cell on M2. I showed him an empty table and chairs in the common room they could sit at to watch TV and socialize. He was an outlaw motorcycle gang member. Hence, the "brothers" were not related, but club members. Even with his long hair, and knowing him for years to come, I could never see the Rocket in my depiction of a "biker." And I met dozens of them, inside and outside. Still, he was loyal to the club, to his brothers, to a fault. I respected that. In sports, we were always on opposing teams. And we actually shared the same birthdate, though he was some years older. Moose also had the same birthday.

The Rocket was determined to get in shape and educate himself while in prison. The man exceeded all expectations in the academic field, graduating university with a BA in the social sciences, I believe. His weight training was a more arduous journey.

After a few weeks in the Haven, the Rocket coaxed me into watching him bench-press a new maximum power lift for him. I went down to the gym and stood behind the bench to spot him. He lifted the bar, with all the weights on he wanted, off its cradle. He brought it down to his chest and bounced it off. The bar came back up, straight backward, and right onto his throat. As it touched his Adam's apple, I had my hands around the middle of the bar, and pulling up, lifted it back onto its cradle on the bench. We looked at each other. We were both white as ghosts. He'd say it was a good lift. I'd say he was damn lucky I was paying attention.

I always liked the Rocket, and the bikers I met through him. Others not so much.

When the Rocket's friend Alex arrived, he was also beginning a life sentence. Like the Rocket and I, he began weight training right away. After he was there a week or so, he came storming into the common room and took a seat beside us. The Rocket asked him if something was wrong. "Yeah," Alex said, "some asshole is trying to pick me up as his kid. Do I look queer to you guys?" We shook our heads no. We could see he was fuming. The Rocket asked, "Did someone say something to you?"

"No," he answered, "but when I got back from my workout just now, there was a pile of clothes on my bed, stacked neat and clean. And you guys know what that means."

Alex glared at me: "What's so funny?" The Rocket was staring at me, too, because I was in hysterics. Finally, I calmed down enough to tell Alex he was too ugly to be anyone's kid. I noticed he had no workout clothes, wearing only institutional clothes all day and night, and because he was the Rocket's friend, I'd dropped off some of my extra sweats. The Rocket burst out laughing. Finally, Alex smiled. "Well, thanks," he said. "I can use them." Then all three of us laughed. We became great friends, and worked together at different times in the recreation and canteen areas. Alex and I were even on the committee together for a short time.

Whenever I exercised in the weight area, I always had a partner or two. It was an unwritten rule never to go in a man's space when he was lifting. With Moose and Saul, we had an understanding that if our area was breached, the "spotter" would grab the weights, leaving the "lifter" to deal with the interloper. It seemed to work on the rare occasion our space was violated. Once both men had been released from Millhaven, I agreed to train with a huge black fellow named Terry. I explained my system. Two nights later, as I lay on the bench pressing weights, Terry called over another huge weightlifter named Bruiser, and they began discussing exercises. As they stood off to one side chatting, I put the bar down on its cradle and sat up. I stared at Terry, then glared at Bruiser. Bruiser knew better than to violate another lifter's space. He walked away. "What are you doing?" I asked Terry. "I just wanted to ask him something about training," he answered. "Well, do it on your own time. If you're training with me, you don't have people around the bench," I admonished him. "Don't you like Bruiser?" he asked. "That's not the point, and no, I don't, but I don't care who it is," I replied. Terry looked across the gym to where Bruiser was picking up his curl bar. As Bruiser leaned over a stand-up preacher bench to do some arm curls, he was stabbed repeatedly in the back and through his side by another prisoner. Terry looked back at me. I just shook my head. "Spot me," I said, as I lay back down to continue our workout. Terry never again had people hanging around our workouts.

Over the course of my first year and a half, my training took me from a 150-pound, six-foot beanpole to 220 pounds of proportionate muscle. I took up jogging a few miles each day. I didn't want to be bulky, just big enough to deter enemies.

Around the same time, I had a special visitor come to see me at work in the barbershop. It was my psycho — the man I had dreaded seeing upon my arrival at Millhaven. He was an average-sized man, but his reputation preceded him. He was not uncomfortable at all with stabbing a person he took offence with, and he took offence often. As soon as he introduced himself, I placed myself between him and the many sharp implements in the barbershop. When I confronted him with the story he'd told men about killing me, he denied it. I told him flat out he was lying. Too many people with no knowledge of each other had warned me with the same story. The psycho said he had no reason to attack me, and on that we agreed. Still, I assured him he would never get behind my back. But we could coexist in Millhaven. If my sense of danger had waned since my arrival, it had just been fully recharged. I kept my eyes and ears open, checking out his routine, his associates, their associates, et cetera. I waited for any token of aggression in my direction. The psycho did not take long in getting offended by another prisoner, but not by anyone associated with me. It was not my business.

During my time at Millhaven, a few men from my past found themselves there, as well. From my old neighbourhood, old schools, from the streets, jails, or institutions, they appeared one by one. Without exception, being established somewhat, I would offer each my friendship. I found they "grounded" me. They reminded me of better days. They kept my spirit alive. I would do my best to ensure they stayed alive, as well.

Ron showed up shortly after the psycho returned. His case eerily reflected my own, except for the motive. He had grave concerns his victim's friends had reached out with a bounty on his head. He was correct. I assured him I would keep a close eye on him. The bikers were the first to voice negativity in his direction, though not for monetary reasons. Their one "brother" in society was a close friend of Ron's victim. I met with a few of the bikers. I opined that all our victims had friends, and if we were to start taking each other out based on that, Millhaven would be a pretty empty facility. They understood, and agreed not to take action against Ron.

The next challenge over Ron was a cop killer and his sidekick. They'd attempt to instigate others to attack Ron, but everyone could see he travelled nowhere in the place where I was not far behind. And I had developed into a serious threat. I, of course, noticed the psycho's interest. He, too, was an associate of the biker outside, and the cop killer inside. One day, Ron and the psycho were locked up in administrative segregation. I had the committee check out what the problem was. Ron was in danger of being killed, the psycho for suspicion of being the weapon. Two days later, both were released back out into the population. They were back amongst us. The psycho did not take long in approaching me, now that he knew I knew. He asked what my interest was in Ron. I simply told him he was my friend, and if anyone were to kill him, they'd be joining him. And that was that. Still, I watched.

The boys from Regent, like Joey, Bullethead, Buzzard (Dwayne's cousin), and Roddy would all come in without conflict, the way most of my friends would. Rod would come in with the same baggage I had on arrival. The psycho was threatening his life to anyone who'd listen. And it had gotten back to Rod, just as it had me. Rod was no first-timer, nor was he a very young man. He was a rounder, somewhat of a street legend in my neighbourhood. We'd met in the East End bars, and behind bars, as well, in the Don. I was just a punk kid compared to him years earlier, but he knew my older brother. I knew his sister, his daughters, and his girl. Rod knew the psycho, and he knew his character.

Upon entering the gym area his first day, Rod spotted me. "Kid, I need a weapon," he said.

"I can't help you out there," I answered.

He walked away and sat at a weight skid in the far corner, talking with Will, another prisoner I knew. Will came over. "Rod is upset with you, very disappointed," he said. "Why?" I asked. "You know what the psycho has been saying, and you won't help him." Will seemed confused, so I cleared things up for him. "Listen, Will," I explained, "Rod can be upset and disappointed all he wants to be in me. Rod is serving four years this time, right?" Will nodded. I continued, "I'm serving life. I know his problem, and when it gets here, I'm going to be the one to deal with it. Not him. He's going home at the end of his four years if I have any say in the matter. And that's that." Will smiled and walked back to the corner. Rod was not so confident.

The psycho entered the gym. As he approached Rod, I approached him. Rod asked why he was telling people he was going to stab him. The psycho denied it, just like he had done with me. I started to laugh in the psycho's ear. He turned to see me there for the first time. "You're full of shit," I told him. "You've told half this place that alone." He looked back at Rod. "Okay, I was mad at you, I shouldn't have said those things. I apologize. I am really glad to see you now though, okay." Rod said, "Sure, forget it." As the psycho turned to leave, I tapped him on the shoulder. He looked at me. "Is it forgotten?" I asked, tapping the weapon I had concealed under my hockey jersey. "My word," he answered.

Rod looked at me. "You've grown up in here, eh, kid?"

I just smiled and walked away.

Of course, this incident did little to ingratiate me with the psycho, but then we would never be friends. Ever. I'd never trust him behind me, and he'd continue to make my stay at Millhaven interesting.

Lovely Larry came in on an involuntary transfer from Collins Bay. He was one of my oldest brother's friends, and a more polite and courteous fellow than one could hope for. He was fastidious in his appearance, with long wavy hair (hence the "lovely"). He also weight trained every day. He was a bit shorter than most prisoners, but, pound for pound, he could out-lift anyone in the weight pit. And in Millhaven, in those times when there was little else for men to do, that was saying a lot.

I noticed right away that he seemed to know the psycho. They'd chat whenever their paths would cross. I warned him, but I was not his babysitter. They knew each other's people in society, so I said no more. Larry was a short-timer, due to be released within four months. One afternoon, I sat in my common room, watching a football game. Larry came in on a changeover — the ten-minute period where all the cells were open and one could go to or from the gym and yard. Larry was shock-white as he sat beside me. He was very afraid. He explained quickly how he had been at the gym training, and the psycho had yelled to everyone there that Larry, although he lifted heavy weights, was nothing more than a "goof." That was a wrong choice of words. Larry had punched him in the face, sending him sprawling. The psycho had run out to the yard, with Larry in pursuit. Larry'd caught his self-control before he caught the psycho, and went back into the gym to await changeover. "I warned you about him," I said, "so, what's the problem now?"

"The psycho is going to kill me," Larry rambled. "All the way back into the gym, he was asking guys for a shank. I'm not a murderer. I'm not going to kill him. I have four months left. But I'm not checking in either. I won't go into protective custody. He's going to kill me, I know it."

I looked at my friend. "Alright," I said, getting up, "here's what you do. Go put on your workboots, the steel toes, and meet me in front of the server. We're going back down to the gym." He left, and I went and got ready. He met me, and we went into N area. I had him walk ahead of me through the metal detector. It beeped, its red lights going off. The guards jumped up quickly and surrounded Larry. I just kept going down the corridor. When I arrived in the gym, I found out the psycho had also returned to his unit — A Unit. He was not in the gym. My associates informed me, though, that four of his friends were huddled in one of the side rooms in the gym, and looked like they were up to no good. I looked through the room's window, and saw them. I entered, locking the door behind me, and asked innocently, "What are you guys up to?" The four looked at each other. There was

Jughead, the leader and main instigator of what he called "the east coast crew"; the Vulture, best friend to Dwayne, my old enemy from the barbershop incident; Johnny, the only other psycho that compared to his best friend, my psycho; and lastly, a little Charlie Manson–looking moron who did all the stabbing for Jughead.

Jughead spoke first. "We're waiting on your friend, Larry. We're going to kill him, if you must know."

"Why?" I asked, already knowing the answer. "He attacked our friend, and we're killing him," Johnny answered.

"Your friend is lucky it was Larry and not I," I said. "I'd still be beating him."

Jughead started to stir in his chair. "You could be dead right now, if we want," he growled. Then he pulled a large knife out from under his sweater and set it on a small table.

"You're right," I answered, flipping up my own sweater, exposing my weight belt and taking out the two long metal shanks that had been tucked between it and my stomach. "But two of you are coming with me." The four exchanged glances. Each was motioning to the other to strike first. None were moving. I broke the ice. "Your friend got high on pills. He came down here and called my friend a goof in front of the whole joint. My friend didn't do anything that any one of you wouldn't have done in the same situation. So, if you want to die over that, then make your move," I threatened. They looked again at each other. Jughead spoke up. "We didn't know the psycho did that. He just said Larry attacked him."

"You know Larry," I answered. "Would he do that for no reason?"

"So, are we doing this, or what?" I asked, getting impatient

"No," said Jughead, "I want to ask my friends if that's what happened, and if you're telling the truth, Larry is okay."

I unlocked the door and went back out into the gym. Now with my own associates, I watched as the four went around talking to different men they associated with. Jughead walked over to me. "You were right, it's over."

"Nobody touches Larry," I emphasized.

"No," he said. "Word."

I had a friend put away my weapons. I couldn't take them back through N area with me. The next changeover, I went back to J Unit, back to my common room. Larry was waiting at my table. "What's up?" he asked. "Not much," I said. "He wasn't down there, so you'll have to see your 'friend' later. I wouldn't worry about it though."

"Not worry? The guy's gonna stab me. He has friends here," Larry rambled off nervously. "Those guys are nuts."

"Look, I talked to his friends. You're okay. Just talk to the psycho when he comes out, okay. I'll be around," I assured him.

"You told me to put on those steel toes. You didn't think that machine would go off? The guards stripped me naked. The guard in the tower had a shotgun on me." Larry was rambling again. "Larry, please," I said, "shut the fuck up." I sat down in my chair, mentally drained. That was so close down in the gym. Too close.

The psycho had flipped out on the guards when he'd gone back to A Unit, and they had put him in the hole. It would be three days before Larry and he got together out in the yard and talked. Both shook hands and hugged. I stood four feet away. "Everything is good," Larry said, smiling as he walked up to me. "Yes," I said, thinking *until the next time the psycho gets his hands on some pills.* "Everything is good, Larry."

I kept my eyes on Larry until he was released a few months later. Everyone else stayed, forgetting nothing.

⊦⊦⊦⊦

Sports in Millhaven dominated the activities of the men housed within, even more so than weightlifting. At a time where the only electronic thing in your cell was a six-station radio, and no phones were available, recreation time was a valued privilege. If men didn't play sports themselves, they became avid fans.

During the summer, seven ball teams were fielded. Four designated as "the minors," for those less adept, and three "major" teams. The best at each position in the majors would comprise the joint's all-star team. They'd play any outside team. Those games were very infrequent at Millhaven, for obvious reasons. Nobody voluntarily wanted to be there. Meanwhile, teams in the two divisions would play within their respective ranking.

I hadn't played since I was very young, and not very often then. Once I took the field, everyone else knew I didn't play either. Hitting a lobbed ball pitched underhand was not so hard, but fielding one on the run would take some practise. I made it up to the majors the second year, with the opposite problem. I could catch a ball on the dead run, but fastball pitching seemed to always elude my swings with the bat. The third year, I was able to combine both hitting and fielding to be an average player, at best.

Flag football. That was a different story altogether. We had to wear a thin belt around our waists, a flag Velcroed to each side, the idea being once the flag was pulled off, the play ended. At least that was the concept explained to us by the recreational staff. Once a game started, though, they were no longer visible, and the hitting began. I was tall, lanky, and agile enough to get around defenders. I'd block a lot of passes from the quarterbacks, if I wasn't dumping them on their behinds. If the quarterback handed off the ball, I could usually run down and sack the runner. Of course, men got their noses, cheekbones, and the odd leg broken, but we played every night we could. Rain or not.

Then came ice hockey. I was the worst player ever in the history of worst players. I spent my first winter at Millhaven pushing a chair around on my ankles, on the ice on the pleasure rink, just to learn balance. I joined a team the following year, on its fourth line, and of the three teams' fourth-line players, I was the worst. But I was having a great time playing. I was being accepted. The following year, I'd made great strides in skating, skill, and size. I could pass the puck tape to tape, on the fly, and I hit hard, real hard. I was used to screen a goalie's view mostly, and surprisingly I could fight on skates. And I would. I was also very fortunate to be on a "stacked" team each year (teams that had better players than the other two teams). Some of the other teams' players were as good as my own, but line for line, I was always on the dominant team, fighting, hitting, and screening goalies.

Every sport was taken seriously, and if you were on the field, or on the ice, each man was expected to give his all, on every play. In a place like Millhaven, one would expect tempers to flare and fights to occur, and they often did. But the bad feelings at those moments never left the game. During one hockey game, my good friend the Rocket left his wing at the blue line to come racing in to clear me out from the front of his goal. I was a little intoxicated, but I saw him coming all the way. I was sure he wouldn't hit me. I was wrong. His check knocked me sliding half the width of the rink and into the boards. I came up helmetless. Throwing my gloves off, I went after him. When I caught up to him, a crowd of players had gathered between us. His captain yelled at me, trying to hold me away. "For Christ's sake, he's your friend."

"You're right," I agreed, so I punched the captain in the face. The skirmish was then broken up.

‖‖‖

Moonshine, white lightning, booze.

Whatever one would call the concocted alcoholic beverages made in a prison, they were a constant. Other substances like hash, grass, or pills would come and go. Hard drugs like heroin or cocaine rarely surfaced during these times at Millhaven. Though security would wreak havoc searching for booze or pills, they never seemed overly concerned with the men having a few tokes of pot. All we did was sit around and laugh at each other, and maybe eat a lot. The other stuff seemed to predicate violence.

"Who's winning?" I was sitting on the second from top row of the "major" bleachers. It was a nice, hot summer day. Two of the teams had been playing each other for almost an hour. I turned my head to the right and came eyeball to eyeball with Big Red. I hadn't even noticed him walking up from behind, and here he was, standing right beside me. He had both feet on the ground. "Red team," I answered.

Big Red had been at Millhaven long before me. He was definitely the most visible of all prisoners, standing around six feet eight and weighing three hundred pounds. He was not fat. Big Red was a big, big man. He was the most respected, and most feared. In his case, it is important to note the difference. He was respected because he told the truth as he knew it, regardless of whose feelings might be hurt. He was respected because of his intolerance to bullying — physical or psychological. He was feared because of his size and his temper. Big Red, once riled, took a lot of time (and distance, if one was smart) to cool down.

"What's the score?" he asked.

"Not sure," I answered. "Can I ask you a question, Big Red?"

"Shoot," he said tersely.

"I've been here over a year and a half now, and this is the first time you ever spoke to me. Why?"

"Yeah," Big Red offered, "I like to check people out first, you know. See what they're made of." I paused for a few seconds, reflecting on that. "You're a pretty slow read, eh, Big Red?" I observed. "How'd you like a punch in the head?" he retorted, smiling. "No thanks," I answered and turned my head back to watch the game.

That was our first conversation, but it broke the ice. Every game I played in, regardless of the sport, I could always count on hearing Big Red's voice yelling, "You're a bum, you suck!" At every sports banquet or social, Big Red would emcee, presenting the trophies. Each time he'd call me up from my table, I'd be sure to ask him in front of everyone, "Me? Are you sure? Check the list. Come on, check it again." He'd just growl like a big old bear and shove the trophies at me. All but one, that is. He thoroughly enjoyed the one year he got to call me up to present me with an enormous pink baby pacifier mounted on a wooden base. The plaque read: "Whiner of the Year." He told the crowd, "I checked the list, checked it twice. It's him." I took the trophy in kind. After all, I did argue every call in every sport I played. I have to say, save football, all my other trophies were representative of the teams I was on, and not my individual skills. Although, in the final ice hockey playoff game, Big Red confessed to me that I did my job on the team well.

6

Monsters Deep

ONCE OR TWICE A YEAR, Millhaven Max received prisoners on interprovincial transfers. Men came in from other provinces, be it New Brunswick, Quebec, Manitoba, Alberta, or British Columbia. Without fanfare, these men would settle in amongst the other prisoners. Usually. Of course, a few brought "baggage" with them, mostly past conflicts with other prisoners. Upon recognition, their adversaries would strike quickly and strike hard.

I had just entered the gym one evening and noticed a newcomer from the East Coast sitting on one of the chairs. I knew where he was from because he had come into the barbershop upon his arrival, and the instructor had assigned me to cut his hair. On his way out, he'd promised me a can of kippers as a gratuity. The other barbers were laughing at his meagreness, and at my lack of knowledge as to what exactly a kipper was. Anyways, the man now looked across the gym floor, and seeing me, he smiled. The man standing directly to his right then drove a sharp metal shank into the right side of his neck. It exited out the left side. His assailant then pulled the knife back out. The man sitting now slumped over onto the floor. A huge pool of thick dark blood began to form. I walked out into the yard. I never saw that East Coaster again. I heard he had raped a young newcomer down east, and that youth had matured into an adult at Millhaven. Prison justice.

About a year later, Millhaven received an influx of about twelve "unmanageable" prisoners. For some reason, they decided to establish their presence right away. The wrong way. Word filtered around fast that they had muscled an older, established prisoner out of his common room table, threatening him not to return. The old guy had been sitting in that room for years without incident. Days later, I came out of my cell onto the range one morning. I saw two of them talking with Louis, one of the barbers I worked with. The two were coercing him into the small sink room at the front of the range. Louis seemed hesitant, but he walked out of my sightline with the one man close behind. The second man had stopped and was watching me. He had his one hand across his waistband. A sweater hung loose over top. Not a good sign. I started to walk toward him. I heard the sound of flesh meeting flesh from the sink room. A fight.

"Stay back," the armed man said to me. "Go fuck yourself," I answered, continuing my approach. He started to back off the range, calling for his friend. As I came up to the sink room, his friend exited. He looked at me, and then they both hurried away. Louis came out almost immediately, shaking his head. He was fine, and after having viewed both combatants, I knew Louis had given as good as he had received. He looked at me. "Thank God you were around. Those two were going to kill me," he said. "Take it easy, Lou," I said, and asked him what it was all about. "They asked me days ago to front them some hash, and so I did, as a favour. Then, when they're supposed to pay me, they get me in the sink room and call me a 'joint merchant'" (a person taking advantage of another's needs and overpricing their product). "Are you going to be okay?" I asked. "Oh yeah, I'm going to see my friends right now. We'll be keeping an eye on these fuckers," he said. And off he went. Louis was French, and as such, was a part of the French crew. In Millhaven, this crew was deemed very, very dangerous.

Not long after, there was a movie night in the gym. When the lights went on, everyone noticed that the new group, along with their new friends — men who had preceded them into Millhaven — were all drunk. That was fine. However, they'd sloshed the mash from their brew bags all over the gym floor. The recreation crew — prisoners employed to maintain the area — were none too pleased. Moose, my friend, was one of them, and he had no problem voicing his displeasure. Everyone returned to their units. I went and sat at my table in my common room. Minutes later, Mack came walking in. He was a 280-pound bearded East Coaster. He ripped off his jacket, handing it to another man. "Hold on to this," he growled, "I'll handle this fucker." And with that, they both exited out the other door. I got up and followed, interested in seeing just who the target of Mack's aggression was. They walked into the next common room, me right beside them. There were about eight men in the room, but Mack went straight to Moose's table. "You want to fight, fucker?" Mack challenged Moose.

"No. No, I don't. I just want you guys to clean up your own mess. I'm not your bitch, and neither are my friends."

"Well, we're going to fight right now," Mack insisted.

"You're drunk. Go lay down and we'll talk in the morning. I don't want to fight you, Mack," Moose said.

Mack was smiling now. He was sure Moose was afraid of him. "Well, if you're not going to get up and fight, I'll hit you sitting down," he snarled.

The men on each side of Moose at the table got up and moved aside as Moose rose out of his chair. "Okay, Mack, you want to fight, let's go."

Mack advanced, throwing a punch. Moose ducked, then came up hitting, catching Mack flush on his jawline, lifting him off his feet and onto his backside. Moose was a big man, too, but unlike Mack, he was all muscle. Growling, Mack picked himself off the floor and went at Moose, swinging wildly. Back step, back step, side step, then bang, bang. Moose fired off two punches, both landing, one to the bridge of Mack's nose, the other to his temple. Mack stumbled to his knees, then tried to use a table to pull himself up. In this, he laboured. Blood was pouring out of the gash in his forehead, caused by the temple blow.

Moose told him, "Go lay down, you've had enough."

Mack continued to try to get to his feet. I'd threatened his friend with the jacket not to move one inch once Mack had begun his challenge to my friend, and the man hadn't moved. Now, I told him, "Go get your friend. Take him home." So he did, and they left. I went back to my common room.

The following morning, I could hear loud arguing coming off of Mack's range from where I sat in the common room. As it ended, Moose and some of the other men from the recreation "gang" walked through my room.

Moose stopped and looked at me. He looked downhearted. "Kid, these guys are going to be big trouble."

"I know," I said sadly, shrugging. Personally, I was still of the opinion that there was no way I was leaving Millhaven alive anyways, so any problem was fine by me, if someone wanted to bring one.

The following day was a weekend. The sun was shining. It was very warm outside as I entered the yard. A lot of men had the same idea as me that afternoon. Get some sun, breathe some fresh air. It was really nice. I saw two black men who worked in the barbershop with me down past the tennis courts, so I sauntered over to talk with them. Shortly into our conversation, Moose came by with Saul and a couple of men I had met from Hamilton. "I need to talk to you," Moose said. I excused myself from my two friends. "What's up?" I asked.

"Those guys are spoiling for a fight," he said, nodding toward a group of men lying on the grassy ball field. I hadn't paid the group much heed walking past them minutes earlier.

"Yeah, so?" I asked.

"Everyone has had enough. We're going to accommodate them," he answered.

"Well, you let me know when," I said.

Moose and his group went over to the small outside weight pit. I walked over to rejoin my black friends, who'd gone over behind the ball diamond. I apprised them of the situation, and told them they might not want to be around when this melee broke out. One of them, Cleveland, asked me, "Well, when is this going to happen?"

"I have no idea," I answered honestly. Moose and his group were passing by us just then. "Are you coming?" Moose asked. I looked at my two friends. "Right now," I said. "Go inside the gym."

I left them and walked out onto the ball field. Homemade knives, iron bars, and aluminum baseball bats glistened in the afternoon sun as they were swung amongst the grunts and groans of embattled men. The minutes ticked by. Gunshots began to ring out from the guard towers. One bullet kicked at my foot, as I pursued the leader of my adversaries toward the tall perimeter fencing under the tower. I looked up at the guard looking down at me and I stopped. Everyone had stopped. Adversaries either lay on the ground, or were up against the perimeter fencing, under the protection of the armed guards from the towers and patrol vehicles. Some had fled back into the gym, into their units.

At least four ambulances rolled out of Millhaven that afternoon. No one died, but quite a few men were wounded in the attempts. The institution was placed on lockdown.

When the cell doors reopened and normal routine resumed, there were still men angry their friends were injured, or just paranoid, thinking that the fight had stemmed from these men being from a different region. Of the latter, they were assured that men had come to Millhaven from all over for years without any trouble, and would continue to do so. As for those injured, one was our own, Saul, and another was with the group socializing, unaware of the conflict, and should not have been injured. Besides their friends, no one regretted what happened to the rest of them. They'd pushed for a fight, and they got a fight. Later that evening, when the cell doors were opened, I stepped out. Two men were at the entrance to the range, and I knew right away something was wrong. They wore shin guards, elbow pads, and loose sweaters that looked tight with padding. I slowly walked down to Moose's cell. The men began to walk down the range. Moose was asleep. "You had better get up," I warned him, "there's trouble."

"Where?" he asked groggily. Both men were now standing in his doorway. "Right here." As Moose swung out of bed and into his pants, I stayed in front of the doorway, in front of the two men. "We're not here for you," one said, "we're here for him." I looked over my shoulder. Moose was at the sink, splashing water on his face. I continued to block the doorway until Moose put his hand on my shoulder and eased me out into the hallway. He stepped out beside me. The two men began yelling at Moose, taking fighting stances, but Moose remained silent, unmoving. As they continued their harangue, other men were exiting their cells. There were a lot of dangerous, violent men on this range, and the two were becoming increasingly uneasy. When they finished yelling, everyone knew the crux of their anger was their friend getting hurt. Moose told them he understood. Their friend was set upon by men who did not know he was a non-combatant. He was in the wrong place at the wrong time. Everyone felt bad about that. I believe that was the only reason the two were allowed to leave the range in one piece.

The next afternoon, another prisoner rushed into my common room. "Big Red's in trouble on L2," he shouted.

"Not again," I moaned.

Five or six other men who'd been watching TV followed as we raced to L2. I saw Big Red down the range. There was no immediate violence, just one man raising his voice to Big Red. Everyone who lived on the range was outside their cells, watching and listening. I looked around at the men I had come with. We all silently nodded to each other, then took a slow approach, mingling amidst the inhabitants. It wasn't hard at all to identify Big Red's would-be assailants. They were all with the new group. They all had a hand under their sweaters.

Big Red looked nervous as he stood listening to this man tell him how things were changing. How his friends were the new power. I'd heard enough. I walked up behind Big Red and slapped my hand down on his huge shoulder. Startled, he turned his head. As his eyes met mine, I smiled. "How are you, Big Red?" Then turning to his adversary, I said, "And how are you? What's going on here? You guys having a party, and you forgot to invite me?" I was raging inside.

The main antagonist took a step back. Big Red was looking around the range now, and noticing that his friends were there, and that his would-be assailants were now targeted. He put his big mitt on my shoulder, clutching, as if holding me back. He half-whispered, "I am really glad to see you."

Now I was mad. I barked at the bigmouth, who, up until then, had a lot to say. "Is this what's happening? You guys want to keep pushing it here? Let's do this. Come on. Please," I urged him.

"No. No. It's over," he responded.

"It had better be. The next time will be the last. Do you understand me?" I growled.

"Yes. It's over," he said.

Big Red put his arm around my shoulders. "Let's go home."

The shock and surprise on the opposition's faces was priceless as they saw the men behind them they didn't know were behind them break cover and walk off the range with Big Red and me. All of us except Big Red looked back at them with knowing glances. *Don't mess with our friends, not in this institution. Not anywhere.* We each knew anyone could be killed in this place. That realization settled in with experience. Our advantage was we could not have cared less about dying. We just cared about each other.

The following week, I was placed in the hole. I'd had an outstanding institutional charge for quite some time. I had attempted to smuggle painkillers to Moose when he was locked up in the health care cells, but the guard had discovered them in his canteen bag — a bag that I personally had handed to the guard. I was given fifteen days in the hole.

Each cell in the hole was an empty eight-foot-by-eight-foot space with a sliding solid-steel door. A thin mattress, rock-hard, was thrown in late each night and taken out early each morning. In the hot summer months, as it was then, the cell was like a sauna. It was very hard to breathe. The aperture at the bottom of the door became my best friend. A few days into my sentence, I was told I had an outside visitor, one of my two girlfriends.

I was escorted through the back door into the range that housed administrative segregation prisoners — those deemed "unmanageable" in the population. Halfway down, I heard a prisoner yell from inside his cell, "Look out your doors." Then a few men were yelling. "You're in the hole now, eh, asshole? We're coming down there to kill you. We got you now."

It did not take a genius to figure out these were the men from the yard melee, as well as a couple off L2, from the episode with Big Red. I wondered why they were threatening me in front of the guard. (*Just come on down, tough guys*, I was thinking.) On the way back from my visit, the guard took me through the disciplinary courtroom instead of the range. I guess he'd heard enough.

The following morning, I heard some noise out in the hallway in front of my cell. One of the men had made his way down. He saw me looking out of my cell and mouthed, "Yard." I nodded. At yard time, I went out first, as my cell was closest to the door. I walked over and leaned against the far wall. I'd seen this guy fight a couple of times. He was fairly tough, but I liked my chances. Besides, I had no choice. I waited, but he never came out. When yard was over, I looked in the cell I'd seen them place him in. It was empty. I never saw him again, or any of his friends. I heard a year or so later the main antagonist had gotten released. He went to Hamilton looking for a couple of men who'd been involved in the fight against him. He found someone that knew them and had offered him a ride to see them.

But when he looked at them, it was from the trunk of a stolen car. He was in very bad shape. His driver happened to be the men's partner, the one who liked wearing war paint and calfskin loincloths. The antagonist was not heard from again. People assume he left the country. Perhaps rightly so.

Saul had been injured in the yard melee that day, stabbed in his left buttock. When he arrived back among us, he was the butt of many of our jokes. He was reminded time and time again: in a fight, do not lead with your ass.

As much as I enjoyed the atmosphere of Millhaven's barbershop, when the opportunity arose to work in the recreation department, I took it. My instructor was upset. He was just setting up my test to get my hairstylist licence. I was grateful for his tutelage, for his kindness toward me. I thanked him profusely, and explained that, with my sentence, a licence meant nothing because I'd never get the opportunity to use it. Rec offered me more time and space to concentrate on my physical goals. I jogged every morning, lifted weights in the afternoon, and played sports at night. I incorporated stretching exercises, as well as pounding the heavy bag when I felt like it. I was not the toughest man in Millhaven, nor was I the most intelligent, but, combined, I ranked among the best the institution had to offer in those times.

After a while, I transferred into the canteen area. It afforded me the same opportunities without the responsibilities of preparing the ball diamond or the ice rinks. After a brief stint there, I was asked by Big Red and others to represent them on the prisoners' committee.

I had mistakenly assumed, upon arrival, that this group was the prison hierarchy. They were not. They were simply men who had served considerable time in Millhaven and had garnered the trust of the men. Each conveyed understanding and compassion when dealing with issues that arose amongst the men, whether as a group or individually. That's what got a person into office. Their length of term was often determined by their strength of character and intelligence. There were always those men who wanted to riot, or protest, because the ice cream was too hard or too soft, depending on how they felt that day. They thrived on unrest. It was a job keeping them in check while pursuing what was best for all the men.

One of my first experiences as a committee member came as I sat in the canteen area one night with a few of my associates. Another member came in. His hand was bleeding. "What happened to you?" I asked. "A few men are drunk up on M2, and they smashed the glass on the barrier. When the keeper got me to go talk to them, I accidently cut my hand," he said. "So, what's going on now?" I asked. "Well, I have to go to health care —" he started. "Not about your hand, who cares about that. What's going on with M2?" I said. "Oh, I don't know. Maybe you should go see the keeper in J Unit," he answered. "I think I will," I said, more so to myself than anyone else.

As soon as the living unit barrier of J Unit was opened, I could see the area in front of the servery was packed with armed guards in riot gear — vests, shields, shotguns, side arms, tear gas launchers, the works. Remnants of the Millhaven Mafia were present. They weren't hard to distinguish. They had engorged eyes and were drooling. They welcomed the opportunity to knock some heads.

I approached the keeper. "What can we do to resolve this?"

"What do you suggest?"

A couple of the Mafia were yelling to quit wasting time with me and just give them the order to go, to turn them loose on the drunks. To his credit, the keeper listened to what I had to say. He had a concession. He wanted a man slated for release the following morning to be taken off the range, in case the drunks persisted and the range had to be gassed. Otherwise, the man would not be released and the institution might be accountable.

I took the proposal to the drunks, who I obviously knew — I'd served months of time with them. I told them I'd arranged to escort them, one at a time, down to the administrative seg range so the guards couldn't beat on them. They'd have to sleep off their drunk, but they'd be released back to their normal cells in the morning. Granted, they'd be charged and have to face disciplinary court, but as deals go, this was a "sweetheart." The alternative was the guards gassing the range and then beating their skulls in with batons.

"Fuck them," one drunk said. "Let them come. We'll kill them." The others joined in.

"Sure you guys will," I said, shaking my head. "Well, I need the guy out of cell twelve. He's getting out tomorrow, and I have to have him off of here, in case they gas."

One drunk went and looked in cell twelve. He yelled back at me, "Fuck that, he's a fuckin' nigger. He comes out, I'll kill him."

I coaxed the drunk over and spoke clearly and softly into his ear. Then I had the control tower open cell twelve. The man came out. I motioned for him to come to the barrier. The drunks stayed far away. The barrier opened and I left with the black man. Down the stairs, we ran into the keeper. He thanked me for getting the man out and asked what the drunks had decided. His men were itching to go. I told him they were thinking on it. As the black man went into a temporary cell in health care, I turned back into the canteen.

I no sooner sat down in my chair when the barrier to the disciplinary court whirred open and four guards came around the corner carrying one of the drunks, one appendage of the drunk in each guard's hands. The man was unconscious. A guard went to rap on the solid-steel door. He was stopped by one of the Millhaven Mafia. "I got this," he said, and then he took the drunk's unconscious head and began to pound it on the door. The door opened, and in they went. The next drunk came around the corner in the same shape, and also went through the door, and so on, until they were all in seg. When I returned to J Unit that night, I could smell tear gas everywhere.

I resigned from the committee after just a few months. My friend Alex resigned with me and the others a few hours later. I'd submitted various proposals over my tenure, all of which were denied by the administration, save one that a small drinking fountain be placed in the gym area. I'd asked for a Christmas social for the population and family and friends, but was informed by the deputy warden that the commissioner of Penitentiaries had denied my request. In the New Year, I was told we had a meeting with the commissioner, his deputy, the warden, and his senior administration. I drew up a new list of proposals. When I confronted the commissioner on his Christmas social decision, he was confused. He'd approved my request, he said. The deputy warden, noting that Christmas had passed, told me to move on with the meeting. "I don't think so," I told him. "You're a fucking liar. You told me he denied the social. I will not deal with liars.... No offence, Mr. Commissioner, but I resign as of right now.... I'm getting something out of this meeting, though." And with that, I picked up the classy coffee mug that had been provided for the commissioner as I exited the room — hot coffee still in it. I had that mug for a few months.

I returned to my job in recreation. As another spring fell upon Millhaven, we began practising for the upcoming ball season. On the field one day, the public address system paged me to report to my parole officer. I continued to practise, and they continued to page me. I had no reason to see my PO. I hadn't seen him in years.

Big Red finally walked over. "They're going to keep calling you until you go. Just see what the asshole wants. We'll still be here when you get back."

I set my ball glove down on the bleachers and sauntered off to administration.

The PO sat behind his desk. He handed me the phone. "You have to call that appeal lawyer," he said.

The lawyer told me the appeal was over. The Supreme Court of Canada had ordered our convictions quashed. There'd be a new trial. I was no longer serving a life sentence. Neither was Ryan or Harry. The authorities had thirty days to return me to the Don Jail.

Oh my God, I thought. The room was spinning. *I may actually be leaving this place alive, after all.*

But by then, the institution was no longer hell to me. It was simply concrete and steel. And the men were no longer the monsters and demons I had envisioned upon my arrival, but friends and associates, normal human beings, made of flesh and bone. They laughed and cried. They had families, relatives, and friends they loved.

I would leave in thirty days, dressed in prison-issue clothing. My personal clothing I had left at the admitting area no longer fit. I was no longer the tall, skinny weakling; I was 230 pounds of pure muscle and stamina.

When I arrived back at the Don Jail, I could see the shocked look on everyone's faces, both guards and prisoners. I was no longer just another prisoner, another human being in their eyes. I was a monster and a demon from Millhaven Max.

7

Blue Boys

AFTER THE TRANSPORT BUS ARRIVED at the Don Jail admitting area, my green penitentiary attire was exchanged for jailhouse blues. A few of the old guards were present; the same ones who, three and a half years ago, had said goodbye to a young, anorexic-looking man on his way to the Pen for the first time. Nobody expected my return. Everyone, except a couple of my family members, was certain I couldn't survive. But as I stood before them now, I was not being called "kid," but "mister" or "sir." The younger guards were taking their lead from the more experienced. They'd expected our arrival; they had not expected the threat I now posed. The lieutenant told me Harry and I would be placed on the pen range. That was fine. He also told me that he didn't want any trouble from me. That was fine, too.

I liked the Don. The food wasn't bad (though it was far from good). I also liked the fact that there were no windows to look out on the new side. You couldn't hear the traffic either, unless you were in the exercise yard. Staring at life passing you by in the form of people walking freely and cars heading off in various directions can be very depressing. At least I felt that way. I didn't like to think of everything I was missing. I'd just concentrate on the trouble I was facing.

Four guards led us up to the fourth floor to the 4C range. As soon as we entered, I heard my name. I looked into the crowd of men walking toward us. On the south side were a couple of men I knew from Regent, a few I knew from the streets, and some others from different jails and institutions. They were all asking the guard to place me on their range. There were no vacancies, but he assured them when one became available, he'd move me. For now, Harry and I were placed on the north side.

As we walked past the strangers to our assigned cells, all eyes were upon us. I recognized the look. I'd once had the same look on my face. Now it was very disconcerting. I felt less than human. They believed they were staring at a threat to their own well-being. They believed me a monster.

We stored our effects, then paced up and down at the back end of the range (a thirty-foot stretch between the back wall and the end table), talking. Although Harry had spent all but one year of my time at Millhaven with me, we'd had little interaction. Harry was at least ten years older that I, and our personalities, our characters, were miles apart. The only thing that joined us was our criminal charge. I never knew Harry before he was charged with me, and everything involving him since only caused me to have great disdain for the man. Ryan had known him, and since Harry was the reason for both their arrests and our convictions by jury, he hated Harry with a passion. Until court was settled, though, I was stuck with him.

I was happy when an ex-convict from Millhaven showed up that afternoon. The Dip, an Italian fellow, came in suffering severely from heroin withdrawal. I busied myself tending to his needs. At night, we were each locked separately in the open-door barred cells. I slept, but awoke when I heard my door being slid open. A young man stepped in with a bright yellow food tray. On it sat a plate of "jailhouse" bacon and eggs. Dry toast and a coffee rounded out the contents. "Your friend," he said, "on the other side wanted me to give this to you." Sitting up in the bed, I thanked him. The young man then ran his tongue over his lips. "And he told me to give you anything you want ... anything at all." He smiled. I knew as soon as he spoke, he was a "queen" — a man who believed himself to be a woman. "Put that down," I said angrily, referring to the tray, "and get the hell out of here."

I drank the coffee, then walked out on the range with the tray. The Dip was sitting at a table across from Harry. He had three blankets pulled around his sick body. "Eat this," I said, putting the food in front of him. "I can't," he moaned, "I'm too sick." Harry jumped into the conversation. "I'll eat it," he said. I just glared at him until he looked away. "Dip, you eat it. It'll help. For me. I'm not going anywhere," I reassured him. He ate.

After lunch, the guard called my name. "Get your stuff, you're moving to the south side."

"No, I'm not, but Harry will."

He was happy to go. I stayed for three more days, until Dip was out of any danger.

When I finally entered the south side, it was like old home week. There were only about a half dozen men who I hadn't known previously. One of them was the Beluga, but he was quick to introduce himself. He was definitely the most charismatic in this rogue's gallery. A staunch advocate for the legalization of marijuana, his past involved major cultivations, as well as the importation from other countries, of all things grass and hashish. He was definitely a poster child from the hippie era. He was also a major pain in the Canadian government's rear end. The Beluga introduced me to two of his co-accused. Then he asked me why I had refused his "gift."

"What gift?" I asked.

"That one," he said, pointing to the queen.

"I'm not gay, pal," I answered. Then I excused myself and went to talk to the men I'd known for years.

I found out the Don no longer housed women on the fifth floor. At one time, some of us would flush the water out of the toilets. The women would do the same, and we could talk through the pipes, some for hours each night. Now, the only females at the Don were guards. That was a new concept for me.

One young, tall, well-built, good-looking guard showed an overzealous interest in me. While other prisoners were jealous, I assured her that I had no interest in any woman that wore a uniform. To me, that was crossing a line. The other guys thought I was crazy for turning her down.

I did appreciate the guards who would bring prisoners "packages" from their friends outside, though. I hadn't been on the south side very long when I inadvertently spied a yellow tray holding about a pound of loose sensimilla. The colour of the tray had caught my peripheral vision, and I'd looked without thinking. They noticed I'd seen them. Later that day, one of the men approached me. "You don't smoke weed?" he asked. "Sure, I do," I answered. "We know you saw us earlier. Why didn't you ask? Everyone else has. You can smell it all over the range."

"I'm sorry about that earlier," I told him. "I didn't mean to look in your cell. The tray caught my eye. As for asking, I won't do that. I like to be offered."

"Well, would you like some pot?" he asked, smiling.

"Sure, but I'd much rather have your 'in' so I can get my own."

"You have your friend call my friend, and you'll have any messages within two days. Does that work for you?" We shook hands. He handed me some rolled joints, and I went to smoke one.

The next day, I noticed Harry in deep conversation with two of my associates. I knew from their posture it was not good. I injected myself into their discussion. Harry had a message for these two from a friend at Millhaven, he said. A man was scheduled to arrive who'd testified against the man, and he wanted my two associates to beat him up. "Bullshit!" I said, looking at Harry. They all looked stunned. My two friends had just arrived the week before, and not even they knew they'd be in the Don at this time. Harry tried to clean it up by saying the Millhaven guy wanted any of his friends to do the deed. "He gave you the message, right? And you're his friend?" I told Harry, "You look after it." I told the other two men not to get involved. I had a feeling something stunk.

Coincidentally, the man in question arrived on the north range a couple of hours later. I went over to his range with Harry. As I explained to another associate who lived on the north side why we were there, Harry sucker-punched the man. Before I could pull him away from the fray, he'd hit the man twice, taking any fight out of the stranger. The guard came quickly and placed Harry and I back on our range. I'd discover a year later that no one knew the man, save his wife, whom Harry had designs on. Harry was a real piece of work, and not a good one.

The following day I received a care package from a friend. Hash and oil, enough to last me for months (I read a lot of books and newspapers through a curtain of smoke).

Harry's lawyer was able to get a Supreme Court Justice to grant him bail. That was unbelievable, considering Harry had already been convicted once by a jury. But then, Harry was, indeed, innocent of his charge. We both were called the following day for transport to the Toronto East

Detention Centre. I was not happy. I was comfortable in the Don, with my range, with my neighbours. I knew most of the old guards by name. They all knew me. Plus, I had too much product to conceal. Still, we had to go. It wasn't optional. So, Harry and I "packed away" as much product as humanly possible, and I left the rest for the boys.

When we arrived at our new jail with four other prisoners, we were locked in the first large, barred bullpen. The other men sat while I paced. Just as I reached the front bars for what seemed like the two-hundredth time, a young guard came around the corner carrying a Styrofoam cup of orange-coloured water and a wafer-thin sandwich wrapped in plastic. He set those down on the bars in front of me. "Lunchtime," he yelled loudly.

"Is that all we get?" I asked politely.

"Listen, man," he said, puffing out what little chest he had, "you're lucky to be getting that. Now, do you want yours, or not?"

"What I want is for you to take that sandwich, fold it in half, and shove it up your ass."

He grabbed the cup and the sandwich and left as quickly as he'd appeared. I knew I had overstepped. The guards in "the East" had a reputation for ganging up on a man. I swallowed some Valium I was carrying; no point feeling the beating I'd just brought upon myself.

Soon, the guards began calling out my fellow prisoners for processing. One by one, they left, five minutes apart. After a half hour, I was alone in the bullpen and anticipating the goon squad's arrival at any moment. I was feeling no pain. The pills were kicking my butt. I yelled for the guard.

A senior lieutenant came around the corner. I'd known him from the Don years earlier. "We're not accepting you in this institution," he said. "You're being returned to await your trial from the Don."

"Harry!" I yelled. I wanted to make sure he gave the soft drugs he had stashed of mine to fellow prisoners of "solid" standing. "I'm going back to the Don. You're getting out tomorrow, so make sure you say hi to my friends, okay?"

"Okay," he answered.

"Make sure now. Don't leave without giving them my respect. It doesn't matter who, as long as they're alright. Okay? Make sure they know I said hi, right?" I yelled.

"I understand. Don't worry. I'll be in touch," Harry assured me.

Harry was released on bail the next day from the East Detention, taking everything with him, giving "the boys" there nothing. That was Harry.

Back on the south side of 4C, I watched as men left and new ones arrived. Some I knew, some I didn't. Many had their own monikers. The King of Diamonds showed up with his entourage of heroin dealers, the King of Spades would venture in on some pimping charge. The King of Hearts would be in and out so often I almost believed he needed a turnstile. The King of Clubs stayed free. The Kings of Sting and Pain would be on other ranges.

Not everyone preferred the penitentiary range. Someone there always knew someone who knew someone who knew him. If not, they were moved to the north side or to another range. Case in point was Forehead.

I'd been napping on a thin exercise mat when the quietness of the range disturbed me from my sleep. At the first table, alone, almost beside where I lay, sat a big "plow boy" sort of man. Down the range, at the back, a group of associates were huddled. I got up and, passing the big man, I went down to the back sink to rinse my face. Moose coaxed me over to the crowd. "Do you see that big fucker?" he asked. "Of course. It's kind of hard to miss him. Do you know him?" I asked. "No one does. We think he's a cop," Moose answered. "Really?" I said, more to myself as I looked back up the range. "He didn't get that hairline from baling hay. That's from wearing a cop hat," Downtown offered.

I was looking at the metal squeegees from the mop pails that had been brought in on the range. They had no business being there this time of day, but then, the mop and broom handles really had no business being off their respective ends either. The boys had their hands taped and were ready to attack. "Hold on," I said. I told the range cleaner to grab the push broom and clean around the guard's desk. I wanted him to check the man's file that held all our admitting information. I'd distract the guard.

He got let out to sweep, and five minutes later the deed was done. "He's okay," the cleaner said. "He's here on a murder beef from Lindsay." All eyes stared at me that knew my case. I was there for the same, but only because my case stemmed out of Toronto. The odds were not very good of finding anyone in the same boat, at the same time. Not unless they were undercover.

"Let's get him," Moose said.

"Hang on," I told them. I walked back up to the front, passing the man, and then back again. "You wouldn't think they'd be so obvious," I told the guys, "and something is just telling me he's not a cop."

Downtown piped in again, "Better safe than sorry."

I didn't want to be responsible for this man being assaulted mistakenly, so I went back up and asked the guard to move him off the range. It's usually just that simple. Instead, the guard picked up the internal phone and made a call. Hanging up, he said, "The head of security says he stays on this range. Sorry."

Now I was really suspicious. I walked back down, eyeing the man carefully as I passed. I told the boys what the guard had said. "Okay," Ward said, "he's got to go. I'll hit him first." Ward was a professional boxer, a light heavyweight, over 210 pounds. Between the men there, the newcomer had zero chance of escaping without serious bodily harm. I shook my head no. I was still not convinced he was a "plant."

I went up to the guard one last time. "Move him or lose him," I said. "Your choice."

He got back on the phone. They moved the man.

Forehead was not the only one to enter our range at the Don looking like he could be law enforcement. Rooster fit the bill perfectly, as well. But Rooster had served time before, and he had references. As soon as he came on the range, he came to me and acknowledged his dilemma. I had him checked out. Rooster stayed with us until he finished court and went to the Pen. He was a very nice guy, funny.

I was not the only one to come from Millhaven to the Don for an appeal. A few months after my arrival, the alleged Mafia dons arrived. They arranged residency on 4C south. We coexisted alright at this time. Back in Millhaven, not long after their arrival, they'd approached me, wanting to know why I hadn't tried to ingratiate myself to them as so many others had. I'd answered them bluntly. While they might be good guys, they meant nothing to me. Truthfully, I knew enough to know that if a man wasn't of their bloodline, in their eyes he was expendable, just a tool to be used and discarded. I had my own associates, and none of them belonged to any organization. I was very comfortable with that.

Still, they were on my range now, so I felt compelled to see that they were comfortable. I didn't want to hear any complaints from the guys back in the Pen. About two weeks after they'd landed, one called me over. He said he had a problem with a man over a woman they'd both known while in society. He felt he was about to be beaten up, since the man had just arrived. "Where is he?" I asked. He pointed to the front of the range. Outside the sally port, with the guard, stood one of the biggest, most chiselled black men I'd ever seen.

I knew the man's reputation. He was a rounder from Toronto's West End and a really nice guy. When it came to fighting, though, he was no slouch. *Damn*, I thought, *I am going to get hurt on this one*.

The guard was trying to figure out which range to put the newcomer on. I spoke up. "He comes on this side."

"Your range only has two empties, and you have two coming back from court," the guard advised me. I told him we'd work it out; just send the big man in. He did.

I immediately introduced myself to Joe. I explained to him the position I was in, having to keep an eye on the Italian. He assured me he held no grudge, although he wasn't happy the Italian had messed around with a woman he was dating. But, to use his words, she was a skank anyways. He went down and spoke with the Italian. I stayed a few feet away, my eyes on the situation. I was so relieved when nothing occurred. I was not confident that I could handle the big man. He was back on the streets on bail a few hours later.

Another Italian, a friend of the guys I knew, was also living on the range. I paid him less attention than I did most men. One afternoon there was a big fight on the north side. I saw my friend Downtown come back onto our range. He'd been involved. "What happened?" I asked. "Business," he answered. Later, he explained the Italian had consigned him to beat up his uncle. Apparently, the uncle had sexually molested the man's sister when they were very young. The uncle left the north side on a stretcher, his body and face broken. "He's paying me thirty-five thousand dollars," Downtown told me, smiling. "What would you have done?"

I told him I would've taken the deal, same as he did. A few days later, Downtown was transferred to the Toronto East Detention Centre. About two weeks later, his wife came to visit me. The Italian had not kept his promise. He hadn't sent anyone to put the money in Downtown's account for the job done.

I approached the man on the range and told him I was well aware the agreed-upon price was way over the top, but that he needed to put $7,500 in Downtown's account. He told me he'd do that when he was released from custody. "No. No, you won't. You'll pay him like you agreed upon. Now. You have one week," I told him. He told me to ask the Mafia dons how good his word was. I assured him that didn't matter to me. He either paid my friend, or he and his uncle would look like twins. And I would do it for free. I watched as he approached the other Italians. The following week, one of my guys returned from court with a message from Downtown: a simple "Thank You." The bill had been paid.

One morning, a few of the guards entered hurriedly and disappeared around the corner to the north range. A minute later, they returned escorting a Sikh man. He'd been beaten, his head shoved into a pail of human excrement. There were clumps of feces clinging to his hair and his face. One female guard was in tears. "How can human beings do this to someone?" she wailed.

I've seen worse, I thought.

The next week, a guard posted on our floor brought a young Lebanese man over from the north range. He, too, had been beaten up. "I want to switch him with someone from your side," the guard told me. "Can you find me a volunteer?" I told the guard to leave for a minute while I spoke to the youth. His name was Ali, and the only problem he had next door was that he wasn't white enough for a couple of "rednecks" who seemed to be controlling the range. When the guard came back, I volunteered to change cells with Ali. The guard refused. "I know what you're up to. I'm trying to avoid trouble," he said. "Fine. Give me a minute," I told him. I talked to a stranger who had just come on our range, and he agreed to the switch. It was done.

Fifteen minutes later, the two rednecks were at the front of the range, calling for the guard to bring Ali back. The stranger had identified and beaten the crap out of both of them that fast. Ali went back to the north side without any further problems.

The stranger, now back with us, began to reminisce with me about old times together. We'd played on the same hockey team, on the same line in Millhaven. I knew he could more than hold his own in a fight. However, in the Don Jail, racism and prejudice ran rampant in all cultures, and the only thing it needed to thrive was for bad men to watch and do nothing.

‖‖‖

Dwayne arrived one day and was placed in 4C north. I hadn't seen him since he had his throat slashed in Millhaven's barbershop. We paid little heed to each other.

Moose came down the range one afternoon, just after lunch. He was walking all off-kilter, as though he had lost his equilibrium. He was also holding his jaw with one hand. "What's up?" I asked.

"Dwayne just suckered me for no reason. Then he jumped on me and tried to gouge my eyes out."

"You kidding me? Where?"

Moose had gone over to the north side, he said, and was conversing with a friend when Dwayne had blindsided him. "He wants to finish it at yard. I got to lay down first," he said.

I agreed. He was in no condition to be fighting. Just then, the guard yelled yard time. Moose looked at me. "Go lay down, I'll talk to him. You can fight later," I told him.

I went to the front with the other men who were taking yard time. The north side was let out first. Dwayne came around the corner with the men from his range and exited onto the landing. A minute later, we were let out. Walking into the yard, I saw Dwayne near the back wall in conversation with a mutual acquaintance. But his eyes were on us. He had his shirt off, hands on his waist. He was ready to fight.

I approached. "Moose said he was over talking to a guy and you attacked him."

"That's right," Dwayne answered matter-of-factly.

"I've known you since I was a kid, right?"

"That's right," Dwayne said.

"And for as long as I've known you, you're always calling guys rats and goofs and suckering them."

"Yeah, that's right," Dwayne answered.

"And they always seem to be friends of mine."

"Yeah, so?"

I hit him so hard in the left temple that he wobbled sideways, half walking, fading down to his knees until the wall offered him some support. "So," I asked, "how do you like it?" I turned to our mutual acquaintance. "Don't even think about jumping into this fight," I threatened. He backed off with his hands held high.

I turned back, only to see Mousey, a diminutive but tough little scrapper from the East End, racing along the back wall toward us. "I got you now, fucker!" he yelled as he jumped on Dwayne. He got off one punch before I tore him off. "Back off," I growled. "You don't understand," Mousey pleaded. "He beat me up twice. Once so bad I was in the hospital." I told him I didn't care and continued to back him away from Dwayne. "This is my fight."

Dwayne came off the back wall, having regained his composure. "I'll fight anyone in this yard," he yelled.

"That would be me," I answered.

Dwayne took two steps toward me, and for each one he was sucker-punched by a different young man. He went down. "Jesus," I screamed, "one more guy hits him and I'll beat the shit out of you!"

The guards began racing into the yard. They cleared everyone out, back to their ranges. Except for Dwayne; they carried him to health care.

Both kids apologized sheepishly once we were back on the range. Ali, the Lebanese kid, said, "But he said anyone, and I was the closest."

"Ali, where I'm from, you do not interfere, no matter what, okay?"

"Okay." He smiled.

I tousled his hair and told him to get lost.

Moose awoke about an hour later. "Did you see Dwayne? Are we on for tomorrow?" he asked. I explained what happened. I wasn't happy; it was unfinished business. That was the last I'd see of Dwayne while I was in the Don, but it would not be the last time I'd see him.

A month or so later, a man named Benny came on the range. He knew a few of my associates and was an avid boxer. He'd use the back area for push-ups, sit-ups, and bag work. Benny had a strict regimen. Me, I read a lot. Benny was also cut from the same cloth as Dwayne. He firmly believed that if a man did not fight, he was a goof. At least that's what he imparted to me shortly after we met. He asked me at one time if I could fight. My reply was simple: "I'm from Regent, not Rosedale." (Rosedale being an "upper crust" society section of the city, and one where no fighter had come from that I ever heard of.)

Benny continued his training. I continued my reading. Reading, for me, was my escape from the bars that surrounded me.

One afternoon, as Benny trained and I sat at my usual seat on the end table, an old frail-looking man of about sixty-five came on the range and sat across from me. He was just sitting, taking in his new surroundings and thinking about God knows what when Benny came up on him from the side. "What's your name?" he asked. Old Joe, the man told him.

I looked up from my book. I knew the name. Joe was a safe-cracker from the 1950s, and a friend of my oldest brother.

"Oh yeah," Benny said. "Well, fuck you, Old Joe." He was leaning into the poor old guy, intimidating him.

I put my book down. "Is there a fucking problem here?" I asked.

"Mind your own business," Benny snapped.

"I'm making it my fucking business," I said, getting out of my seat.

"You want to go?" Benny asked, putting up his fists.

I didn't answer. I just started to walk around the table. A few of the men who knew us jumped in between and talked me down while holding him back. "You don't stand a chance against me," Benny stated as he walked away.

I told him, "I'm from Regent, and I'm telling you, don't bother the old man again."

Old Joe had remained sitting through it all. Now, as I sat back and picked up my reading material, he thanked me. He was shaken. "Relax," I told him, "the guy's an asshole."

He asked who I was. "I know your oldest brother," he offered. I told him I knew that as soon as I heard his name. I reassured him he was alright to be living on this range. He'd heard of me, and he knew he was safe. He relaxed. He would go to court in a couple of weeks, get sentenced, and leave for the penitentiary.

Benny stayed. Benny trained.

Surprisingly, after a few months, the Beluga was brought in from Collins Bay. He had more criminal charges to deal with. He brought with him a good many well wishes for me from the guys in the Pen. He also brought some pills they'd sent. He gave each guy living on the range five each, but not before I'd agreed to accept, and had eaten, ten of them. A half hour later, I was feeling no pain. A half hour after that, the Beluga told me he was sorry, but he had to move off the range. "Why?" I asked, incredulous. He said Benny was threatening to hurt him if he didn't give him more pills. The Beluga was not a fighter at all; he was one of the most non-violent people I'd ever met.

I was not.

I went directly to Benny's cell. I suggested he move to the north side, or to a different range. He declined, but offered up that he had waited months for an excuse to punch my head off my shoulders. I told him today was his lucky day. I told him to get up off his bed, get ready, and meet me at the back of the range.

I went to the back and unhooked the heavy bag that hung in the middle, tossed it in the shower area. Then I leaned against the bars and waited. Benny came out of his cell and was pacing between the three tables, shadowboxing, warming up. After a couple of minutes, I grew tired of waiting: "Benny, are you just about ready, or what?"

Down to the back he came.

The man could box; I'll give him that. I also gave him a beating. I broke his nose, cracked his ribs, and banged him all over the back end before the guards came rushing down. We stopped fighting just before they got to us. Benny went off to health care. One guard, seeing me covered in blood, smiled. "It's about time you got yours," he sneered. "Hold that thought for a moment," I told him. I walked to the sink at the back and washed off. I didn't have a scratch to show him when I walked back.

The Beluga stayed. Benny returned from health care two days later. His eyes were black and his nose puffy. He approached me at the end table as I sat reading. "I want a rematch," he said. I looked at him. "Let me know whenever you're ready," I answered, totally disinterested. "I'm only joking," he chuckled. "You surprised the hell out of me." I put down my book and looked him in the eyes. "Benny," I said, "I've kept telling you I'm from Regent. I've been fighting half my life."

I really felt sorry for Benny. He loved fighting — boxing, anyhow. Me, I hated it. To me, Benny was okay. I understood his mindset. He was just not well-grounded. He stopped his aggression toward others on the range after that, but maintained his training. I never had to worry about Benny attacking me. That would have been out of character. He respected fighters. We parted ways with mutual respect.

I knew I had to go to court sometime when they brought me back to Toronto. Obviously, I didn't want to appear in prison attire, which was all I had that fit me, now that I had grown. So, I called my sister and asked her to visit, then sent her out a cheque from my account. She showed up the following weekend with my mother in tow. She'd seen me once a year since my sentence had begun, so she wasn't surprised by my growth. I told her my new sizes and what I wanted her to buy me.

My mother kept staring at a person a few phones down from me. "Who is she staring at?" I asked my sister. She turned to look, then said to me in a half whisper. "We were shocked when we came in. We didn't know the Don Jail was coed."

I got up and took a look and started laughing. "It isn't," I said.

"But that's a young woman three phones down."

"Take a good look," I said. "I'll give you a hint. You used to go to school with him.... It's Lou from Regent."

"Get out!" she said, and took another look. "Oh my God! But ... but ... he has breasts!"

I laughed. "Pretty big ones, too."

She turned and whispered to my mom. My mother shook her head no. Just then, Lou's mother came in. My mom knew her. She was speechless.

"Ask mom how she likes my gold stud earring now. Better than boobs, eh?"

My sister roared with laughter.

She returned about ten days later to drop off my new clothing. She was on her way to work and had a co-worker with her, a twenty-year-old, hard-bodied woman with jet black hair and green eyes, skin as white as snow. She never reminded me of Sadie at the time, although in retrospect they were very close in appearance. Her name was Cher, and she was beautiful.

I had a phone in each hand, so I could talk to both of them. My sister did all the talking. Finally, I asked Cher to take a couple of steps back from the glass and turn around. She had on thin, form-fitting jeans. She turned back, blushing, after a few seconds. My sister's laughter had given away the reason for my request. Cher was "smoking hot."

A few weeks later, I got the lieutenant to allow me a call home (phones on ranges did not exist at this time). I told my sister the clothes fit. She told me Cher wanted to visit me again — alone. I reminded her of the two visits per week I was allowed. I was already seeing Mandy and Mary each week, and had to bump one of them every so often to see family as it was. "Can you just see her, ask for a special visit? She bugs me every day. The girl is driving me crazy." I told her I'd ask the lieutenant. He approved it, and not long after Cher came to see me. She'd been sending me letters and cards since we met. "I'm serving a life sentence," I told her. "You're young and gorgeous. The last thing you need in your life is to get mixed up with me. I already have a girlfriend — two, as a matter of fact. Just run."

"But I want to get to know you. I want to help you," she implored.

I flexed my bicep. "Do I look like I need help? I'm telling you, run. You don't need me in your life."

"I want to keep writing you. I want to keep seeing you," she pleaded.

"You can write and I'll answer," I told her, "but my visits are already taken. I'm sorry."

She nodded her disappointment. "Okay, but I'll write until you get out, or until there's a time when I can visit. Promise me you'll tell me if I can, okay?"

I agreed. She smiled. She was gorgeous. She wouldn't turn around for me this time, but I did look hard through the glass as she left.

After the Crown's appeal of the Supreme Court decision, which they lost, the lawyers began interviewing us, getting set for a new trial. A plea bargain was offered, with all three of us taking a life sentence with a ten-year parole eligibility. It wasn't the greatest deal, but I didn't want to put everyone through the whole ordeal again. The lawyers felt that since we had already served five years, with day parole eligibility in three, it was a pretty good deal. I refused to take the deal unless Harry was released, as much as I loathed the man. Actually, I thought he was a piece of crap. But I didn't want him serving a life sentence for something I'd done. Ryan was furious with me; it was Harry's fault Ryan was ever found out. I agreed with Ryan on that. Those were the facts. However, I held steadfast. Harry must be cut loose. The Crown relented.

Ryan and I pled to second-degree. Harry agreed to a six-month sentence on an inclusive charge, so that he could not sue the state for wrongful conviction and imprisonment. Ryan and I would never talk to each other again.

The "deal" my lawyer was so high on was to turn out to be one of the biggest mistakes of my life. I should have taken the trial, and let the real story come out — the real background of each "player."

卌

One thing I learned while in the Don Jail was that the stories that filtered down through the system were not only about the Millhaven Mafia, but also about the men housed there. My own reputation had grown amongst the criminal subculture as a deadly force to be reckoned with, especially if your history was one of violence toward women or children. Prison informers were also wary of my presence. I was perceived to be within the hierarchy of the criminal subculture, regardless of the venue. Common people gave me more than common respect, which I did not appreciate, as I was sure it was out of fear. I didn't want people to fear me. I just wanted them to be respectful.

8

Gladiators

THE FIRST THING I HAD TO DO upon my arrival back to J Unit in Millhaven, aside from dropping off my property in my assigned cell, was to visit Dwayne. I was told he was in the unit the second I set foot in the institution. He was sitting at the back of his cell, near the window. "We didn't get to finish our fight in the Don," I said. "So, where do you want to take it? Or will right here do?"

"I don't want to fight you," he answered. I was quite surprised. Dwayne always fought. "I know you were mad at me. You were protecting your friends. I know you even stuck up for me in the yard. I seen it. I just want to call it even," he said. I looked at him and wondered if I could trust him. I also knew the answer to that question wouldn't come on this day. "That's fine with me," I answered.

"Can I have your word it's over, that I don't have to look over my shoulder?" he asked.

I couldn't believe my ears. "Are you kidding me? I should be the one asking for that!" I said. Dwayne smiled. "Yeah, you're right. You have my word. Do I have yours?" he asked again. "As long as I'm not hearing any bullshit about you coming after me, you have my word." With that, I turned to leave. "You hit pretty hard, you know?" Dwayne smiled again. "Yeah, Regent," I told him. He liked that. He considered himself a Regent Parker as well, at times. Still, he seemed unsure of his safety as I left.

The men I had come to know at Millhaven were happy to see me. Even my old enemies, like the psycho and Jughead, came up to congratulate me on Harry's release, and Ryan and my parole eligibility reductions. It was rare to see an appeal won amongst the men of this population and even rarer to have someone receive a more positive outcome.

As I travelled through J Unit, I saw the suspected undercover from the Don Jail. He was seated beside the Rocket at my old table in my old common room. "You know this guy, Rocket?" I asked. "Of course. For years. He grew up around Alex and me. Why?" I looked at the big plow boy and said, "Now I believe you're not a cop."

"What do you mean?" he asked. I told him the story of waking up in the Don, seeing him there, and the boys planning to kill him. "I wondered why they moved me ranges," he said. The Rocket was laughing. He also knew a few of the guys involved, and knew it could have been deadly serious. We would call the big man "Forehead" for obvious reasons, and we would become close friends during our time together.

Rooster was also there, and Saul was back in, and I hung around with both of them daily. Ron had grown, much as I had, and was now close with the two newly imported members of the "Stopwatch Gang" — Canadians who had run throughout the U.S., committing bank robberies. Big Red, his cousin, and a lot of the same friends and associates had remained while I was gone. It was "old home week" for me, again. I was handed a cold pop. I hadn't had one since I'd left and I couldn't wait for this one. I pressed down on the lid to open it. The liquid burst forth, covering my face and chest with foamy pop bubbles. The can had been well shaken. Everyone laughed. Nothing had changed.

Near the canteen window in the gym Cord approached me. An older, bald fellow who always wore a pair of "hospital scrubs," pants only, pulled up high, halfway between his waist and armpits. "Glad to see you back. I see that asshole Dwayne is here too, eh?" he said. I didn't recall having any conversations with Cord before this, but since I knew his reputation as a "bug," a psychopath, I saw no need to agitate him. "Thanks. Yeah, we're both back," I said.

"You and him had a beef in the Don, didn't you?"

"That's over," I informed him.

"Fuck that," he said. "You can't trust him. When he gets down here and goes to the yard, me and you will take him out. I got the weapons."

"I said it's over. I gave the man my word."

"We can get him, no problem," he persisted.

"Listen, Cord, I don't know how many ways I can tell you this, but my beef with Dwayne is over. What part of 'over' don't you understand?" I was beginning to get very upset. He finally left it alone. Left me, and went out to the yard.

I went back to talking with my friends. A couple of hours later, I noticed Cord on the far side of the gym, conversing with Dwayne. I asked one of my associates what he knew about Cord. "Oh," my associate said, "he's Dwayne's partner. Has been for years."

"Really?" I pondered that new information. Then I waited to catch Cord alone, and meandered up beside him. "Buddy," I told him, "there is no doubt in my mind that Dwayne was not the one you were going to try stabbing if I had gone out to the yard with you. I am going to let you slide, because I know you were just trying to protect your partner. But me and you, we will never be friends. You would do well to stay the fuck away from me at all times. Do you understand me?" Cord nodded, put his head down, and walked away.

A man had to be careful of these pitfalls in Millhaven. Close associates would sometimes divide themselves among adversaries to entrap men in vulnerable positions, and Millhaven housed some of the finest "moles." In this instance, it was a good thing I was a man of my word.

My PO, now that the appeal was over and my parole date had been advanced by fifteen years, had me reclassified. I more than qualified for medium security. Within three months, I was on my way to Collins Bay.

Located in downtown Kingston, Collins Bay was referred to by prisoners as "Disneyland" to outside guests, visitors, and outside volunteers — the high concrete walls stretched between guard towers gave it a castle-like appearance, the gun towers on each corner were capped with red cones. Throughout the federal prison system, though, the prisoners amongst themselves used its more realistic misnomer: "Gladiator School."

While it did not contain the degree of violence that Millhaven did — the murders and the failed attempts — Collins Bay did have a lot of fist fights. Especially in a sport they played there nicknamed "war hockey" (a type of ring hockey, played the same as ball hockey). The games were very combative. Regular-season games saw the odd devastating bodycheck and the usual fights between two men, but when the once-a-year "block tournaments" were held, even the guards would pile into the front end of the gym and find their seats. Both sides of the gym would be lined with prisoners, cheering for one team or another. But mostly, they cheered for blood. The fans would be screaming throughout the entire game, and the players, high on their adrenalin, if not other substances, would feed off the fans' excitement. They would crush each other with bodychecks, legal or not. Everything was legal on the floor. Men would expect, and receive, three or four fights a game. A stretcher was usually brought in to each game to carry a player off to health care at least twice. Getting possession of the ring, and actually scoring a goal, was secondary in the players' minds. It was a crazy experience. I played in three tournaments, and ended up on the winning team each time.

One Block was the primary reception unit and the first block I occupied at Collins Bay. The prisoners there had dubbed this block "Animal House." Rooster, my friend from the Don Jail, was on that range when I arrived. My arrival coincided with the arrival of a large shipment of black hash and Valium. And since I had some time to waste before I was eligible for any passes or paroles, I saw no reason not to "party."

The third morning on One Block, I was awoken around seven by a very loud stereo. I came out of my cell, banging the door on the way. I couldn't tell who the offender was, but I yelled a challenge for everyone to hear. I wanted to fight the early morning music lover. The stereo went down. I looked down to the front of the range and saw a man I knew from Millhaven. He was now the committee chairman at Collins Bay, and he was shaking his head. Suddenly, I felt a little cool. I looked down and realized I was naked. I went in my cell and got dressed for breakfast.

When I returned, the committee told me the guards wanted me to move either to 2A or 2B in Two Block. "What's the difference?" I asked. I was told 2A was the hole. I chose 2B.

In the next ten days, I would come across various men I knew from the street. These were older men. Some of them had chased me out of "their" bars, off "their" streets, and away from "their" customers — usually while giving my 140-pound body a few punches or kicks. I reminded them of these occurrences while I was evening up my old scores. I also invested myself in internal problems my associates were having with other prisoners there. High on Valium, I was like a bull in a china shop. I'd even yell at the prison staff. I lasted about sixteen days at Collins Bay, six of which were served in the hole awaiting the paperwork and transport that would take me back to Millhaven.

Back at the Haven, the guards didn't even know I'd left. They thought I'd just been in their hole for fifteen days. The preventive security officer knew, though, and he cornered me soon after my return. "What happened?" he asked.

"I deserved to be shipped back," I told him. "I would have shipped me, too. I can't complain." He just shook his head. He was one of the few administrators I'd meet over the years who understood the necessity for prisoners to intercede on each other's behalf. A prisoner didn't take certain problems to the staff unless he wanted to be known as an informant. If he did, he lost all respect from the other prisoners, if not his life. The security officer knew that when I injected myself into conflicts, nobody died. He was very, very happy about that. I never had to stab anyone or hit anyone with a metal bar. Any physical conflicts I had were with my fists and boots. Head, elbows, knees. I hit with whatever was necessary to win, but no weapons. Of course, I came into possession of weapons whenever I felt their appearance would deter a volatile situation, and they did deter many. I had occasions to threaten men with their lives. There were some men I had to threaten many times. I knew I would not act on my threats, but that wasn't important; what was important was that they didn't know.

But my penchant for mediating serious situations would become my Achilles heel, my cross to bear, especially in the lower-security institutions. I would be reviled by people on both sides of the bars. On my side, the prisoners' side, the enemies of my friends would hate me because they could not safely attack their prey. They would hate that, deep down, they regarded me as a very serious threat if angered. They feared me. Some prisoners resented the respect I was given from other prisoners. On the other side, the same resentment was occurring. The staff and administration hated me for the respect I garnered from my friends and associates. They ruminated on the idea that I could diffuse situations they had no control of. They hated that prisoners would come to me with their problems instead of running to them. And prisoners would come to my door often, so much so that it caused one security officer to remark that I had my finger on the pulse of the institution. They didn't understand that I didn't want these problems coming to my doorstep, but once they did, I couldn't very well do nothing. I had to live with myself. I had to live with the man in the mirror. I had to live in the environments I was placed in. I did not choose the men I was housed with. I did know I had seen enough people die, like Willy. Back then, I was in no position to intercede, to stop them from being hurt or murdered. So now, I was not against voicing my dissent with friends or foes alike. If I learned they were up to anything harmful to someone who was undeserving, I would step in to stop it. That happened more often than people know. I did not like seeing bullies pushing weaker men around, either, and would put myself in positions of confrontation with them. I apologize for none of my actions while at Millhaven Max. Period.

My first day back, the first thing I did was go to the gym to see my old friends and associates. They were glad to see me, but had wished I would have made it through Collins Bay to lesser security. Big Red pulled me aside once everyone had gotten their salutations out of the way. "You may have a problem," he warned me. "What's that?" I inquired. Jughead and his crew had been telling everyone that I had just made it out of Millhaven in time. That they were going to kill me. "Are you serious?" I said, not really asking. Big Red would not joke about something like that. Nobody would in Millhaven.

I looked across the gym floor and saw the aforementioned parties huddled around one of the weight skids in the far corner. I approached them alone. "Hi, how are you?" Jughead asked. "Cut the crap," I said. "I heard what you guys were saying after I left. Don't even try to deny saying anything either. Do we have a problem?" They looked at each other. Jughead told me they weren't serious. They were just upset I didn't shake any of their hands when I left. And so I was straight with them when I spoke: "I don't like you guys, any of you. Why would I shake your hands? We've been here for years together, and all of you have had lots of chances, if you wanted a problem with me. I hear one more word about this crap — that I'm lucky — and I'll be back and there will be a problem." With that, I strolled back over to my friends. Big Red just smiled at me and shook his head. "Well, you're still as diplomatic as ever, eh?"

This crew loved playing their little mind games with others, though. Not long after, we heard a rumour these guys were going after the Jamaicans housed in Millhaven. They were saying they were going to "stab them up." There were only a few Jamaicans, but they always came out to yard. When Jughead and his crew showed up in the yard to do their deed, they found the Jamaicans in conversation with me and a few of my closest associates. He called me over to ask us to separate from them. I told him I had heard what they were up to and I thought it best for him and his friends to re-think their bias before they got a lengthy trip to the health care unit. They left the yard very unhappy, but unharmed.

They were always up to no good. They preyed on weakness in others, going after those who had no protection. I would hate it each time I would hear about their involvement in another prisoner's demise, but I had my hands full just keeping an eye on my own friends and associates. Besides, for me, Jughead's crew were not the major concern. I'd always hear when they were up to something. They loved to talk. But there were far more dangerous men in Millhaven, and they did not give notice of their intent.

Surprisingly, I didn't have too long to wait for a second chance at Collins Bay. This time, I did not arrive an hour after a huge drug influx. I had a more stable core of associates, and so I thought I was adjusting well to my new environment. The security officer had other plans for me, though. I was still very obnoxious with some of the staff and callous toward the prisoners I did not know, and not long after my arrival, I was placed in the hole. Two men had gotten into a physical altercation in the weight pit in the yard, a simple fist fight. The security officer believed I was somehow responsible. I was released from the hole by the warden once it was determined I knew neither man. Turned out they were co-accused from the street who had simply had a spontaneous disagreement over their weight training.

I was locked up again shortly after for apparently threatening the black population. Once every black man in the institution petitioned the warden for my release, and he discovered they had hung out in my cell every day while I was at work, listening to my tunes with my permission, the warden had me once again released from segregation.

Then I was thrown in the hole again, this time for threatening to kill a black pimp. The deputy warden came down to see me in seg. I denied the accusation. She had me walked to the front of the hole, the "protective custody" unit, and stood in front of the cell that contained the black man. "Is this him?" she asked the pimp. "Yes," he replied. I was taken back to my cell. On the way, I told her he was lying. Ten minutes later, she had me released. (The pimp had been told, upon entering One Block, by two other blacks that once I found out what his crimes were, I would kill him. He ran to the guards and "checked in." I never even saw the man. I was at the back of the range playing cards.)

Finally, the security officer was able to have me transferred back to Millhaven on allegations of assault.

It was good to see some of my old "monsters and demons," but I was not happy with the transfer. I reapplied for medium-security prematurely. I wanted to see the transfer board. When the day came and I presented myself, the board chairman admonished me for "having the nerve to ask for a transfer so soon after being kicked out of Collins Bay." I told him I just wanted to ask one question of the representative from that institution.

The head of the Bay's classification department identified herself and told me to ask away. "Whom did I assault?" It was a simple question. "You didn't assault anyone, but you had friends that did. The friends of the assault victims wouldn't retaliate against your friends, because you were sitting there. So, now you're sitting here." She finished with a smile.

Every other transfer board member was staring at her, dumbfounded. The chairman admonished her. "You can't do that. Not only are you depriving him of his rights, but you're condoning the violence of other prisoners." He turned to me. "Now I know why you came to see us so soon."

I told him I would like to transfer to Joyceville Institution, the other medium penitentiary in the Ontario region. "No, you're going back to Collins Bay immediately," he said. Then he looked at the Collins Bay representative: "And you had better have a damn good reason if you send him back here again, or heads will roll."

And with that I was off for a third time to Collins Bay. Again, I was housed in the "Animal House." I would spend a year there, with the security officer denying my requests for a cell change to either Three or Four Block. I managed fine, though, and eventually would effect my move to Three Block.

My first day there, as I moved into my new cell, I could hear a man growling in the next cell. He was threatening to kill someone. I walked around and looked in. The door being half open, I could see Tweety — one of Jughead's crew from Millhaven. He had a young man by the throat, pressing him up against the wall. He also had a long metal shank pressed against the man's sternum. "Excuse me," I said, "I couldn't help but over-hear you guys." Tweety asked me to close the door. He was not at all con-cerned that I had seen him. He knew I would not say anything to anyone. I told him I had a better idea. I knew from listening, the problem was that Tweety had sold the young man some homemade liquor and that he had not been paid. It was only a matter of a few cartons of cigarettes. I told Tweety I would pay the young man's bill right then. "Why? He's just a goof," Tweety said. I told him I was just moving in, and I didn't want the trouble his stabbing the youth would bring. Tweety agreed, and I paid him. He left. The young man came to my cell to thank me. He asked what he could do to show his gratitude. I told him to simply pay me back what he owed when he could, and if he couldn't, not to worry about it. I told him not to purchase anything in prison anymore, unless he paid cash. "I prom-ise," he said. I never knew his name, but he did repay his debt within the next two months. Tweety would get transferred back to Millhaven after a couple more altercations.

One early afternoon the leader of Toronto's Dirty Tricks gang come into my cell. His group were serving lengthy sentences for a number of bank robberies. Slick was a well-known rounder out of the West End of Toronto. He was a very big man and also a boxer and trainer out of the Lansdowne Boxing Club. He was also black. He told me he needed to talk to me, so I had him take the chair. I was lying on my bed. He informed me he had been involved in racial wars in the past in different institutions.

I said okay, not knowing if there was any truth in that. He said he had no desire to experience another. I asked if someone was starting one now, in this institution. "Yes," he replied, "You."

He told me about a "brother" who had arrived that morning. He had many friends amongst the blacks and he was telling "his people" I had threatened to beat him up after supper because he was black. I explained a few things to Slick. First of all, the brother had ripped off the Beluga in the Don Jail, and he had to account for that. Second of all, the last guy who did that, and was held accountable, was white. Third, I'd hung with Slick's cousins, brothers, and friends on the streets for years, so what would possibly make him think I was racially motivated. I told him if the brother's friends wanted to get involved, so be it. They would be accommodated. Slick was a good friend to the Beluga also, and now that he knew what was going on, he apologized. He went to step out my cell door, but turned back quickly, closing it. I looked at him. "A little help, please?" he said. I got up and opened the door. Three of my lifer friends from Millhaven were on the other side. "Is everything cool?" Alex asked. I nodded. Slick left. Slick had come on the range in a huff, asking which cell was mine, acting as though there was going to be a problem. My friends did not appreciate that, but had directed him toward me while they went and got their weapons.

I went to meet the "new arrival" in the gym after supper, but he had "checked into the hole." Slick had words with him after finding out what the man had done at the Don from the Beluga himself. Slick also told the rest of the black men to quit getting suckered into confrontations that were none of their business.

I obtained my hairstylist licence while there this time. The barber instructor was upset that I had chosen two models I had never seen before to work on in front of the examiners. The other barbers being examined for licences had worked on the same men for weeks in preparation of these exams. I just felt if I could not do the required work on anyone, then I did not deserve a licence. The instructor was relieved when I passed with flying colours. I really had no expectations of being a barber in society, anyways. I held loftier goals at this time in my life.

Each year, the Bay held the Exceptional People's Olympiad. A core of prisoners worked year round on this project, liaising between the various health facilities, raising donations, and coordinating the schedules. This two-day event was participated in by numerous centres for the mentally challenged. The institution would have upwards of fifty participants in events such as running, high jumps, standing broad jumps, and the like. A band would play, food and beverages were supplied, huge tents and game booths were set up for health services, shade, and enjoyment. All of the "athletes" would receive awards for being a party to the event, and there were trophies for those who placed in the top three of their respective groups. It was a great two days. The yard resembled a county fair, and the event garnered local media attention. Becoming personally involved with these athletes as a "god-brother," or chaperone, I came to recognize that there were others in life who had been imprisoned in their own minds through no fault of their own, and they would never be free. It certainly gave me, and other prisoners, a new perspective on our own situation. Things could be worse. A lot worse.

My last Olympiad before effecting a transfer to minimum, I was put in charge of preparing the yard for the competitors. I had a crew of prisoners paint everything so it looked brand new. They cleaned the entire yard. They did a great job. It still looked shabby in the grassy areas, though, where there were huge spaces of brown earth. I asked for sod, but was told none could be supplied from outside the institution. So, I took it upon myself to take a wheelbarrow and a flat shovel around the prison grounds until I found a really nice piece of lawn. I cut away the top few inches of sod, rolling the pieces up and placing them on the wheelbarrow. I then rolled them out into the yard and replaced the worn surface. After several trips, I was satisfied the yard looked great.

A couple of days later, I was summoned to the warden's office. He asked me how the yard was looking. I told him I thought it was good. He told me that when he had problems he liked to stare out the back window of his office and contemplate. He said, "Come here and have a look." I was puzzled, but went to the window and looked out. To placate the man, I said, "Yes, it looks pretty serene, doesn't it?" He then told me to look down. It was then that I realized the grass I had appropriated for the yard had been sitting right outside his second-floor office. "Oh," I said. "Yes, oh," he answered. "If your intentions weren't so good, I would have shipped you out by now. I still can't believe you moved that much ground yourself with just a wheelbarrow. Now, don't do that again. Anything like this, you ask someone first, okay?"

"Right," I said, as I beat a hasty retreat.

‖‖‖‖

I was sitting in the dining hall one day, eating, when a Native man approached me. "Can I talk to you?" he asked. "Of course, what's up?" I asked. "I don't want to fight you," he said nervously. "That's good, why would you?" I asked. "Well, I bought some hash, and now I can't pay for it, because I forgot I ordered some hobby craft, and they took my money," he stated. "Okay … and this concerns me, how?" I asked, confused. "Well, I got it off your friend, and he said it's yours." I was stunned. "Are you fucking serious?" He nodded. I thought for a second and then told him, "Here's what's going to happen. You pay nothing. If my friend asks, you tell him you paid me direct, okay?"

"I can pay next canteen," he offered. "No. No, you won't. Trust me, you owe nothing. You are even. I will talk to my friend." He thanked me and walked away. I was furious.

It was a good thing a few minutes passed before my friend entered the dining room. I needed to cool down. As he entered, I immediately called him over. "Sit down," I told him. "Are you out of your fucking mind, telling people your hash is mine? And don't even try denying it, or I'll punch you out right here." He tried to explain: "The last time I sold hash, guys didn't pay. This time they did, because I said it was yours. I didn't think you'd mind. Sorry." I looked at him hard. "What do you think the security officer is going to do if he gets wind of this bullshit? My ass will be back in the Haven in a heartbeat. You know I'm his number-one target. Fuck!"

I couldn't believe my own friends were causing me problems. Oh well, there was nothing I could do. Worrying about it wouldn't help. I could only hope it never went anywhere.

Not the next day, but the following morning, around six a.m., as I slept soundly in my cell, I was disturbed by the muttering of voices. I heard the lock on my cell door being opened. I continued to try to sleep, thinking it was just the routine opening of cells for the day. Then I heard the sounds of chains unravelling. That reverberated through my entire body. "You fucking goofs," I said out loud. The head guard, now standing in my cell, said, "That's right. Get up. You're being transferred to Millhaven for drug involvement."

Ten days later, my friend would follow me back to Millhaven. On arrival, he came right to see me. "I am so sorry …" he started. I cut him off. "Sorry doesn't matter. It won't change anything. No one here knows why I was transferred back, and if I were you, I wouldn't tell anybody. If my friends here find out you're the reason I'm back, not even I will be able to stop them from killing you. You know that, right?" He nodded, said thanks. I continued, "Me and you, we are no longer friends. You do not ever speak to me again. Ever." And with that I walked away.

It would take me another year to get back to Collins Bay, and in that time, Cher and I were married. Right in Millhaven. That was about the only good thing to happen for me while I was there.

From the first day back, trouble and turmoil seemed to come with the dawn of each new day. I was in the gym, reacquainting myself with my friends the first day, when I heard a commotion emanating out of one the small cages — rooms that had been erected along the far gym wall. I looked over and saw a head of bright blond hair. I knew it had to be Rooster, and so I crossed the floor and sat on a weight bench just outside the cage. The conversation within became more heated, although Rooster was saying nothing. Then the door burst open. A fair-sized man stormed out, looking enraged. He yelled, "I'll show you right now how much you and your friends mean to me!" As he bent down to pick up a metal bar off the skid next to me, his eyes met mine. "Go ahead," I told him. "Pick it up and see what happens." He knew I had his head lined up with my foot. He stood back up, not touching the bar. "So, you must be a friend of his, are you?" I nodded. "Okay, after supper, you come down here with your friends. I'll be down here with mine. Then you'll be sorry," he threatened.

I was unmoved. I told him, "You just made a big mistake, pal. I didn't just come in here, I just came *back*." With that, I asked the guys working out on the next skid, "Will you guys be here after supper?" The Badger smiled. "We wouldn't miss it."

"How about you guys?" I asked the men on the next skid. "Oh, you know we'll be here, brother," they answered.

As I went around the entire gym, asking from where I stood with my adversary, the picture became clear to him. He went out to the yard. Rooster came out of the room. He was really not a violent man, as violence goes, and was a bit shaken. Saul had been in the gym, as well, at this time, and we laughed it off. In our minds, though, we knew a deadly situation was brewing. After supper, our unit, J Unit, was first to be let out for yard, and so we were in the gym when the man arrived with his friends. I could have predicted who they'd be. It was all my enemies from over the years — Jughead, the psycho, all their friends and associates.

The psycho approached me as Jughead approached Saul. "Where do you guys want to take this?" I asked the psycho. "Nowhere. Our friend is just messed up on the pills and we don't want to see him get hurt."

"Well, if he just wants to fight hand to hand, I'll accommodate him," I said.

The psycho told me it was just a mistake on his friend's part, and he asked that I leave it alone. "Fine by me," I answered. I was assessing things, just as the psycho was. I saw Rooster and his enemy shaking hands, Jughead patting Saul on the shoulder. Things were fine, for now. The psycho walked away, but I knew he would hold yet another grudge over my interventions. I let him go. I was eyeing the new threat.

A couple of weeks later, it was the Beluga's turn to be threatened by the new man. The Beluga had arrived with a new twenty-year sentence. He was traumatized. He couldn't understand how he could receive so much time for soft drugs. He sat in the food servery with me and a couple other lifers, bemoaning his situation. We all listened, offering him support and a hot cup of tea. Then I went out to yard with the Beluga, and after a while left him out there on his own. He was higher than a kite on LSD, and not by choice. He eventually found his way back to his cell and remained there for the rest of the day. The next morning, he stuck his head around the corner of the food servery, and with a big smile said, "It was the tea, wasn't it? You bastards." We all laughed and he joined us. I explained, with our sentences, his "twenty years" looked real good, so he was crying to the wrong group if he wanted sympathy. He never mentioned his sentence to us again.

Now, I had come down to the gym, and one of my associates had informed me that the new man was threatening to ball-bat the Beluga as soon as he saw him. I was told the new man was out pacing the yard with another lifer I knew somewhat. Out to the yard I went, and sure enough, on the walking path, there he was. I approached him, asking if what I heard was true. "Why? You want a problem? You want a piece of me?" he challenged.

I smiled and told him, "Here's what I'm going to do. You want to ball-bat someone. I'll go get you one. Then I am going to take it off you and shove it up your ass. How's that? Sound good to you?"

He put up his fists and started to dance around, with his friend appearing to hold him back. "Let him go," I told the other lifer, "and see what happens."

"He's my friend. Please don't," the other lifer pleaded.

I told the new man that if the Beluga got so much as even his feelings hurt, all the friends in Millhaven would not be able to help him. Then I went back into the gym. That evening as men left the gym and waited in the door cage to be released back to the units, the new man was stabbed multiple times by multiple people. Apparently, in the afternoon, high on his pills, he had ranted at some men that they were goofs and pieces of crap. He survived, but that was his last day at Millhaven.

One other day, rumours swirled of an impending murder that was to occur that night. Saul was involved in an ice hockey game that night in the yard. Since we could get no particulars on who the target was going to be, my associates and I went to the gym. I had Forehead and three others go outside to watch the game, to watch Saul, while I remained inside with a few others. Jughead and his crew were in the gym, as were many others. I sat in front of a locker in the far cage, where I could see everything without being noticed. Jughead came in with two of his associates and sat at the table. He had many more associates outside and around the area. He told me something was going down, and that my friends and I should return to our unit. I told him we were going nowhere. He pulled a large knife out from under his sweater and slapped it hard on the wooden table. "I think you should," he insisted. My toe flipped open the thin locker door and an aluminum baseball bat slid out and down along my leg. I grasped its handle at my knee, then slapped it hard on the table and reiterated that we were going nowhere. I told Jughead that if any of my friends were the target, there was going to be big trouble. He picked up his shank, his friends, and they left. That night, as the teams left the ice to return to the gym, a man was murdered. I liked the man, but he was not an associate or friend. I believed the murder to be totally senseless, but I kept my silence. It was not my business. Not every murder that occurred there was.

Saul came to visit me at my cell one day as I lay reading. He told me Cord had gotten into a fight over in A Unit. I didn't care. Cord was a friend of Saul's, but certainly no friend of mine. Cord hung around a lot with Jughead's crew, and it was one of those guys he had the fight with. Apparently, when it was broken up, Cord felt he had been held onto while his adversary was able to get in an extra punch. At least that was the story Saul was relaying. I told him I couldn't care less. I'd be happy if both men killed each other. Saul informed me he was going out to the yard after lunch with others to confront Jughead's crew. "Good luck," I told him. "You're not going to come and watch my back?" he asked. "No. No, I'm not." I went back to reading. After lunch was over and yard time was called, I watched Saul walk past my cell. I could see he was upset with me. He was one of my closest friends in Millhaven. *Aw shit,* I thought to myself as I got up and put my shoes on. I had to watch his back. I had to make sure he didn't get hurt.

Out to the yard I went. All the interested parties had congregated face to face. I approached two of Jughead's boys and placed my arms across their shoulders. I had one on each side of me. I exclaimed, almost bored, "You guys know that when this fight breaks out, you two are mine. Just a heads-up." They both started to move away, but I just tightened my hands on each shoulder. "Don't even think about running," I said. I watched as Saul and Jughead argued. I had seen the guard come out of his tower with his assault rifle. Then a strange thing happened. Two men I thought were associated with us intervened between Saul and Jughead. One of them started screaming at Saul, and then he took a stance. "You want a piece of me?" he asked. "Come on, make a move, you want a piece?"

Saul was shocked. He just stood there gaping. Everyone in the yard was looking on. I let go of the two guys I had with me and walked over, placing myself between Saul and his new adversary. "Do you want something?" I asked him. "I will take more than a piece of you. You want to fight me?" I was irate.

He was backing off. The other associate that had approached with him tried talking to me. "We're just trying to break this up," he said.

"Sounds like it to me," I answered, not taking my eyes off his friend. I was still glaring at him and coaxing him to make a move toward me. I wanted to hurt him.

Saul spoke up. "Let's just forget this." Jughead agreed. Cord and his opponent were shaking hands. I couldn't believe my eyes. I walked away, calling Saul off to the side. "Don't you ever let me see you have someone dress you down in front of the whole joint like that again," I told him. "And don't ever come to get me to back your goof friend Cord again either. What the hell was that, shaking hands? I'll see you later," and with that said, I went into the gym, angry and disgusted.

卌

I was glad a few months later when I left Millhaven — more so than previous times. I was tired of all the drama, deceit, treachery, and lies that idle minds in devious men concoct. I needed a rest.

I went to Collins Bay for the fourth time in as many years. Shortly after I was situated there, I was told I had to attend a brand new program. It had been in society for some time, but now it was to be a "pilot project" inside a federal institution. It was called the Brentwood Recovery Program. I'd never heard of it, but it was either do the program or return to Millhaven. My institutional PO was one of the facilitators, along with a Catholic priest and an ex-convict. My PO and I did not like or understand each other. Still, given the alternative, I went into the program.

The Brentwood Program turned out to be the second-best thing that happened in prison (my marriage to Cher being first). It was first, though, when it came to opening my eyes to the rest of the world. To reality.

I had always truly and firmly believed that 85 percent of the world's population, at the very least, were substance abusers and more were criminally minded. I was shocked to discover how wrong I was, with the abuser ratio being less than 5 percent. In my world, the one I grew up in, it seemed everyone had an addiction problem of some kind. I also came to understand that just because I perceived a person one way, it did not make it necessarily so. And it didn't give me the right to cause harm to them. What affected me most was realizing that everyone was a human being, with people of their own who loved and cared for them. When I hurt them, their people hurt, as well. I hated to think I created innocent victims. In all my altercations, I had not once given any thought to the hurt I was causing the guy's mother, wife, children, family, or friends. If there were ever a program I would recommend, Brentwood Recovery was it for me, hands down. No other program or course I ever took compared to its insights and knowledge. My PO came to know me as a person during this time, realizing I was not the monster or demon that over-told and overstretched tales had made me out to be.

$$\cancel{||||}$$

Tony Danza, the actor known for his roles in the series *Taxi* and *Who's the Boss?*, came to Collins Bay to use the prison as a set for a new movie about a prisoner-turned-lawyer in the United States. Because they needed the prison yard area, and I was the prisoner who led the yard crew, I was summoned to a board meeting with the warden, his administration, the prisoners' committee, and Mr. Danza and his film crew. Showing up for the meeting last, I took the only chair left available, and that was to the left of Mr. Danza. At the conclusion, all the prisoners asked for his autograph. Afterward, he turned and asked me if I wanted his autograph, as well. I looked at him, confused, and then asked him if he wanted mine. He looked at the warden, and everyone that knew me started laughing. My response was a surprise only to the outside guests.

The prisoners' committee then got the photographer to take pictures of each of them standing with their arm around the star. When it was my turn, I told him I knew his history and therefore wanted pictures of him with me in "boxer" poses with our fists up, facing each other, squaring off. Mr. Danza really found my uniqueness to be quite refreshing. We went out to the yard with the crew and all his extras, and I offered my "experience" to the director as to what exactly this prison yard looked like with ongoing activities so that he could instruct his actors and extras during his shoots. Mr. Danza asked the director to include me, but was informed that would be in breach of their contract with the prison. I assured Mr. Danza I did not wish to be in the movie anyways. I'd already been given all the coverage I ever wanted on the newspapers and TV. He laughed. He impressed me as a very down-to-earth guy, and we got along great during his work there. The prison received a full-size billiard table and accessories for their assistance in the making of this movie, which was greatly appreciated and well-used by the prison population.

9

Headed Home

AFTER BEING BACK at Collins Bay for over a year, and close to nine years into my sentence, I was afforded a transfer to Warkworth Institution near Campbellford, Ontario. While I was waiting for the paperwork to be completed, I found myself involved in a major calamity. Irish, one of my friends from Millhaven, was now the chairman of the prisoners' committee at Collins Bay. He was a medium-sized man with an IRA attitude. He came to my cell to tell me one of his friends had just been assaulted with an iron bar out in the yard and taken to the outside hospital. The prognosis was not good. Irish told me he was going to confront the man's attacker. I knew Irish could not physically handle the adversary he named. The man was a biker associate who weight trained and boxed on a daily basis. He also outweighed Irish by a good fifty pounds.

I told Irish I'd go with him, and if it resulted in violence, I would substitute for Irish, but he could not intervene. He agreed. We met at the committee office, where Irish started in right away screaming at the man. The man asked Irish if that was why he was summoned, and then told Irish to go screw himself. He told Irish he was going to punch his head in. That's when I told Irish to go take a seat and stepped in, punching the man in the head and knocking him off the wall and onto the floor. As he lay there, he told me he hadn't been the one who assaulted the man in the yard. He hadn't been outside all day. I looked at Irish, and told him to go check out the man's story. Irish left. I helped the man off the floor and sat him on a chair at the back of the office. Then I made us both a coffee. I asked why he hadn't just said that right off the bat, and he answered that he didn't like Irish or the tone he was being yelled at in. As we sat there, awaiting Irish's return, eight bikers came walking into the office. They were all the man's friends. They looked at the swelling around his left eye and asked what happened. He told them he'd been hit for "piping a guy out in the yard," and he told them it wasn't him that did it. The leader, Roger, was a big man, and he asked who'd hit him. I said that I had. Roger said that maybe someone should hit me, and I didn't disagree. That's when he punched me in the left temple. He hit me hard, very hard, but I could take a punch. I told him right away that one punch for one punch was fine, but if he threw another one, we were going to fight. I then told him to pick up his friend and leave the office. He did, along with all his other "brothers."

One of the Millhaven guys happened to witness this event, and within ten minutes most of my Millhaven monsters and demons were crowding into the committee office. They wanted to retaliate on my behalf. I told them it was my mistake. Mine and Irish's actually. Irish had the wrong information on who the culprit was that "piped" his friend. I told everyone to leave it alone. I didn't have a mark on me and the biker's friend was sporting an avocado on his left eye.

The next day, I was told Irish needed to see me down at his office. When I walked in, he was standing there with a prison guard, a keeper. In their hands, they had the file of the man I'd hit. Irish showed me where there was a sexual assault on it. The keeper told me he would be happy to place a "toe tag" on the man. I told him he'd also be happy to arrest me for any offence. Then I turned to Irish and berated him for continuing this conflict and listening to a "copper." I told them both to fuck off and left.

That night, the bikers asked me to come see them on their range. When I entered, Roger was there, all tearful and apologetic for having hit me over a sexual offender. I told him he'd done the right thing. No one knew the man's history then, and he'd retaliated on emotion, defending a friend. As far as I was concerned, it was over. However, Forehead and others would not let it go. Irish kept stirring the pot. Forehead felt the bikers had overstepped in their assault on a friend of his. Me — a Millhaven guy.

Two days later, Forehead and his sidekick would be charged for murdering the sex offender in his cell. During the ensuing investigation, my cell was constantly being torn apart. I'd watch from outside, listening to threats from the prison staff that I'd be getting charged, as well. It would never happen. If I had thought for one second Forehead was going to murder the man, I would have intervened by punching the man out and sending him out of the institution alive. Forehead was later convicted.

Soon after, my paperwork finally arrived; I was off to Warkworth Institution, which was considered "high minimum" security at that time. I was happy. To get away from my nemesis in the security officer at Collins Bay, and to show my new wife some progress, some light at the end of a long, dark tunnel.

Warkworth, at the time I arrived, housed quite a number of first-time offenders and very few men who had cascaded through the penal system like I had. Warkworth was also the next step down for some prisoners from Kingston Pen, the "protective custody" institution in the Ontario region. Men imprisoned there were not acceptable to normal institution populations.

The morning I arrived, I was placed in a reception unit. At lunchtime, I went with everyone else down the outside corridor, or "breezeway" as they called it, to the dining hall. On the way back, I was confronted by the president of an outlaw motorcycle gang. He was standing there with two other men. One was a stranger to me, but the other guy I'd met in Millhaven and had known for years. "Are you calling me a rat?" the president asked.

I told him I'd called him a rat for ten years, and would do so for the next ten. He was a rat, a police informant.

"I straightened everything out with your friend Rod," he said.

"That's nice. Did you straighten everything out with Cleveland?"

The man turned ashen. He had not expected I would know someone he took the stand against in open court.

"Look, I'm not here to bother you. I'm here to go home. So, just get out of my way, stay out of my face, and we'll get along fine," I told him.

The man I knew from Millhaven confronted me at suppertime. I told him I know what I know. He didn't believe me. Two weeks later, though, after the outlaw president was taken out of the institution and the Toronto papers came in with a two-page spread confirming what I said to be true, he believed me. I could not have cared less.

I didn't realize how many protective custody inmates were at Warkworth until I was in the gym one day watching a ball-hockey game. There were a lot of spectators on the sidelines. On one team was a very large but agile man — the star player. When he had the ball, and made end-to-end rushes, bowling over everyone in his path to score a goal, the fans would be electric, cheering, clapping, and whistling. I asked an associate from Toronto who the man was. "Oh, he's the Mississauga Rapist. You know, the guy who raped and killed all those women years ago. He's okay now, though. He wants to be castrated and released." "Really?" I said, realizing my associate had not even blinked an eye. He was okay with cheering this type of person on. I watched the rest of the game. And the following game, I watched as he smashed young men, first-timers, into the stands, onto the hard floor. And the crowd cheered.

I joined the opposing team for his next game.

The first game I played in at Warkworth, the first shift, the man picked up the ball behind his own net and began racing up the floor. He deked around one of my little forwards easily and swung out to the right wing. A third of the way, he darted to the middle of the floor, then angled his body to push up straight through the centre of the court. He made it to centre ice. I hit him on the dead run, in the centre of his chest, lifting his bulk off the floor. As his breath left him, he flew, landing on his back and sliding along the floor back the way he had come. There was no sound from the fans, only the sound of his helmet rolling toward his own goal. I picked up the ball on my stick and passed it to my little forward. He had no problem scoring a goal, with the goalie transfixed on his star player, now lying prone on the floor.

The recreation officer had been watching from his second-floor office, as he did most games. Now he was beside me, ordering me to follow him to his office. "You can't do that here," he yelled. "This isn't Collins Bay 'war hockey' here." He looked at me for a response, so I gave him one. "I watched the last two games, just like you did, and I didn't see you come running down when he was crushing these one-hundred-pound kids into the floor. Besides, I was just going after the ball."

"The hell you were," he spat out. "I don't want to see that again."

"Well, tell him not to hit either," I answered.

"Listen, you," he said, "we can send you back to Collins Bay or Joyceville, but him we're stuck with. I can't suspend you from play, because it actually was a fair hit, but I'll be watching you every time you're on the floor, and one assault and you're gone out of this institution. Do you understand me?"

"Sure," I said, and I went back to the game. When I was on the floor, the "star player" wasn't. And he stopped steamrolling people.

I hated every day I spent at Warkworth. Two weeks after I got there, I was summoned to their Keeper's Hall at the request of the unit managers. There were four of them — one from each living unit. "We're thinking of sending you back to Collins Bay," one said. "Do you realize we have men here who haven't eaten since your arrival? They're too afraid to walk down to the dining hall." I told them I was just there to do whatever time I had to do before being transferred to a work camp, my next step toward home. I told them I had not threatened anyone, and it was not my fault if some men were afraid because of their pasts. "I haven't said a bad word to anyone here," I told them.

"If you do, you're gone," another keeper told me. I was allowed to return to my cell.

Strangely enough, although there were a few men whom I knew from previous institutions, my closest association was with my shop boss, though we never discussed anything other than sports, politics, and sports again. He was ex-army, an ex-boxer, and although he was a Boston Bruins fan, I didn't hold that against him. He was a stout fellow with a punched-in nose and scarred eye. He was a blue-collar kind of man. Any serious or hard jobs that he had to supervise, he would put me on them. He supported my bid for "camp," and would back me up whenever other staff members would question my sincerity about staying out of trouble.

||||

Ron showed up at some point in my term at Warkworth. My old friend from Millhaven promptly informed me that he had found God. That he was a true Christian. He certainly did put on a command performance for everyone around him. I would never believe Ron, regardless of my hope for him. I would meet many "pretenders" in my time. I could always differentiate the real and the fake Christians. The real ones had an aura, a calm assurance of peace and contentment. I always believed in God, but I would never pontificate, nor press my beliefs on others. To me, that was my own personal decision. Those who didn't know me were amazed at my knowledge of "the Word." My particular scripture is Ecclesiastes 7:20.*

One day, Ron came to me after a visit with his wife and child. He'd had words with another inmate who'd been carrying on inappropriately with his wife in front of other visitors, including children. The inmate had told Ron to meet him in the yard later that day. Ron did not want any violent encounters that would set his progress back. His "Christian" walk would be a red flag for the man and his crew. I knew they'd definitely be awaiting Ron. I thought about it for a few minutes, then I went out to the yard. Just as the man was meeting up with his friends, I interrupted their conversation with one of my own. I knew I was not perceived by them as a Christian, but as a Millhaven monster. I told them I was very unhappy with my new environment, but what made me dislike the place even more was looking at their shaved heads and hearing their white-Supremacist bullshit. I implored them to attack my friend. It would give me an excuse to exact my violence upon them. Then I left. Ron would come to me hours later. He'd met up with the "gang." It turned out they were really nice fellows, and the one from the visiting room assured Ron there would be no further acts of indiscretion. "Praise be to God," Ron said. "He must have touched their hearts."

"Sure," I answered.

Sarge would show up after Ron. He transferred in from Quebec, where he'd been arrested in a drug lab with my oldest brother and received a substantial term of incarceration. Right away, he had issues with an older biker and his entourage of "young guns." They seemed to harass him at every opportunity. Sarge was a tough man, and had defended me when I

---

* "Indeed, there is no one on earth who is righteous, no one who does what is right and never sins."

was a young man outmatched by my opponents. The biker knew I was a threat and backed off, encouraging his charges to do the same. But one of them came to visit me in my cell; he did not feel I looked tough. He asked what my position would be if he and Sarge had an altercation. My opinion was that it would be none of my business in a one-on-one fight. Frankly, I thought the kid would not have a chance against Sarge.

Then I injured myself one day at work and had to be taken to the outside hospital in Campbellford. I'd split my left index finger in half, and it looked like a snake's forked tongue. The hospital stitched it up, put a splint on my finger, and wrapped it heavily in gauze.

When I returned to Warkworth hours later, the young gun showed up to tell me Sarge and he had a fight, and Sarge was in another outside hospital. I was quite surprised, but all I could say was "Okay." Ten minutes later, another associate showed up to ask if I'd heard about Sarge. I said I had. Then he gave me the particulars: the young gun had lured Sarge into a side room in the gym to fight; then three of his associates had attacked Sarge from behind with goalie sticks. One swing had fractured Sarge's skull.

I took the gauze and splint off my hand and went to the young gun's cell. I told him to pick up his friends and meet me outside so we could go somewhere away from everyone to talk. He knew I now knew what really happened to Sarge. I went outside to the cloistered area, sat on a bench, and waited. Ten minutes later, the young gun came out. He had two guards with him. They were escorting him to the hole. His three friends came out shortly behind him, much in the same manner.

Sarge would return to the institution a couple of weeks later, and remain until his release, but he was never the same man. His experience caused him to cease any future criminal activity, and he became a driving force in educating young men on the perils of a criminal lifestyle. He even became a member of the Legislative Assembly of Manitoba for a while, and authored a book, before his death from cancer.

$$\cancel{||||}$$

My case management team was preparing my case for transfer to "camp" — minimum security. As was mandatory for lifers, I required a recent psychological report, so an appointment was made with the institution's new psychologist. When I arrived, the first question out of his mouth was "I understand you beat people over the heads with iron bars to have them bring drugs into this institution for you, is that right?"

"Pardon me," I said, shocked.

"Are you denying this?" he asked.

I was confused. "I wouldn't be in Warkworth if I did things like that, now, would I?"

"So, you deny this?" he continued.

"Of course I do. I never did that in any institution."

"I further understand you are a member of a Jewish mafia?"

I was sure this "professional" must be high on drugs, or have the wrong interviewee. "I have never heard of such an organization," I told him truthfully.

"So, you are denying this, as well?"

"Look," I said, "I'm of German descent. How many blacks do you know in the KKK? Of course I'm denying that."

"Well," he said, "If all you're going to do is sit here and deny everything ... you may as well leave."

So I got up and left.

Two weeks later, I received his report. Not only did it eliminate any chance I had for a transfer to minimum, but it raised red flags as to my suitability for anywhere less secure than a special handling unit. I was incensed. I phoned my family. I talked with my case management team, as well as my shop boss, about the report. The warden received a call a couple of days later from a lawyer my family hired. He informed them he'd be coming to Warkworth with a battery of psychiatrists and psychologists to conduct their own testing.

After the warden talked to everyone involved, he called me to his office. "We have a problem," he said. "Do you know a guy named Brainiac?"

I hadn't heard his name in years, and I knew he'd been deceased for quite some time. "He was the chemist on a conspiracy charge with me in 1975," I told him truthfully.

"His father is best friends with our lead psychologist," the warden informed me.

"So?"

"You do know he's dead, right?"

"Yes, I heard he died out in Quebec years ago. What does that have to do with me?"

"His father blames you," he said bluntly.

"I was in Millhaven when he passed," I said. "I hadn't seen him in years. Besides, the guy died of hypothermia out on some property he was running a lab on in Quebec. What could that possibly have to do with me?"

The warden told me the new psychologist, not knowing his way around, had followed the direction of the head "shrink," Brainiac's father's best friend. And that was what my report was based upon.

I told the warden my lawyer was going to have a field day, and I wasn't backing off.

"I want you to give me two months," he said. "You'll see my new psychologist again, and your report will support your camp application."

"So, you want me to have to pay for their mistake?"

"Please," he said.

That was all I wanted to hear.

Two months later, when I walked into interview number two, I told the man exactly what I thought of his conduct in my case, and I made sure his boss heard me through the closed door, as I had some choice words for him, as well. Two weeks later I received a proper report. I was fit for camp.

I was supposed to get escorted passes out of the prison, but due to the tall tales about my history, the guards in my unit were wary of taking me out. After watching them take out other prisoners over and over, while I remained stagnant, I confronted them: "Do you really think any one of you are worth my jeopardizing my freedom after being inside this long? Get your wagon, and get me out of this institution."

The next day, a guard from another unit appeared and introduced himself. "I look after lifers," he said, "and I'm going to start taking you out in society this week. Is that okay?"

I smiled and told him that would be perfect.

I completed all my passes without incident, and shortly thereafter left for Beaver Creek Institution.

It was fantastic there. The institution held just ninety men, most of them elderly. The food was great, and there was lots of it. Wild game in the form of raccoons, skunks, deer, moose, and even wolves would find their way on the property at times. The institution had a water reservoir in case of fire, but it served as a huge swimming pool in the summer months. I would weight train for a couple of hours each day, jog three to five miles, and then go swimming. Life was good.

Of course, like every other institution since Millhaven, the stories and my reputation preceded me, and again would cause me problems.

‖‖‖

A large blond man from Hamilton was pointed out to me shortly after I arrived. I was informed he was a lifer, as well, convicted of murdering two women. While I was in Warkworth, he'd been at Collins Bay with many of my past associates, including Big Red and the Beluga. The blond had worked with the institution's security officer to have them arrested on drug possession charges and even testified against them at trial. Both were acquitted, but, as a reward, the blond was transferred to this work camp.

He knew my history even before I'd seen him, and he ran to security, swearing I was there solely to kill him. The staff recognized his paranoia for what it was. As much as I did not appreciate what he had tried to do to my associates, I had no other design than getting out and going home to Cher. That said, we did have one confrontation.

I'd cut through the back door of the rec building, heading back to my living unit. The first room I passed through was a small area with pool tables. I overheard a young man saying, "I'm not calling you a rat. I just said everyone else is." The young man was cringing in a corner, with the big blond facing him. "I'm going to beat your face in," the big man threatened. As soon as he took one step toward the young man, I said, "I don't think so." As I said it, I took off my parka and threw it on the pool table. His parka lay on the other end of the table. He picked his up and exited the building.

One thing I got to do while I was at camp was speak at a local high school, to a class interested in penology. I attended with the institution's liaison officer and another prisoner, a big bearded ex-biker. While I spoke to the class, the ex-biker personified his image with crossed arms and a stern look. An inevitable question eventually arose. "What about homosexuality in prison?" a student asked. I said I had no experiences to share, but that that was why the liaison officer had brought the other man. They all turned and looked to the big bad ex-biker. He was caught off guard and began to stammer. When he finally spoke, he said he knew nothing about homosexuality either. I turned and winked at the class and said, "Sure, he doesn't." They all laughed. The more he protested, the more they laughed. He finally gave up. We went back to the camp, having fulfilled our obligation to the school.

My assigned classification officer was a problem from the day I arrived. He was very nervous of my prison reputation and put a lot of stock in the rumours and horror stories about me being a serious threat. He was visibly shaken whenever I attended his office, which was very disconcerting. I tried hard to ease his concerns, but he continued to shake. The man was an avid birdwatcher in his spare time and would go on early morning treks around the camp's treed property with some of the other inmates to look for birds. He'd whistle their calls as he spied each type. I went on a number of these treks, just trying to establish some communication with him, but to no avail.

Eventually I was granted unescorted temporary absences, three days in duration each month, to either my home or a halfway house. On my first pass home, after ten years of incarceration, I spent the day with my wife, Cher, but Rooster had convinced her to let me go out with him for a couple of hours to see some of the guys. We went to a bar on the Lakeshore strip. While I was in the bar having a Coke, Saul called. He spoke to Rooster, and then I got on the phone. He was upset. None of the guys had been looking after him, and he was sick, he said. I explained I was only on a three-day pass. It wasn't like I was released. He asked me to do my best to help him, and I promised I would. After hanging up, I asked the guys about his situation; they seemed nonchalant about it.

The following morning, I got up and got dressed. I told Cher I had to stop by and see Saul. (I did not tell her he was in a reformatory.)

When Saul walked in to the visiting room, he was surprised to see me sitting beside his sister. He was handed a couple of ounces of hashish, which he secreted away. Then he was shown rolls of Valium. He protested being able to handle them himself, but directed them to a friend at a nearby table. Once that was done, I got up to leave. "Where are you going?"

he asked. I had only been there five minutes. I smiled. "I told you, I'm on a pass. Do you think I want to waste what little time I have in this place, when I could be getting lucky. I'm out of here." His sister and I left. In the car, she giggled. "You are a wild man."

On one of my three-day passes, my classification officer changed the destination to a halfway house instead of my family home. I was incensed. He actually seemed very pleased that he'd upset me. The day after I returned, I watched as my "worker" took lunch in the dining hall with the warden and his senior administration. I was in the middle of the line of fifty prisoners awaiting our lunch and I called over to him.

"Can't you see I'm eating," he growled.

"I only have one question," I begged of him.

"What is it?" he relented.

"Do you know anything at all about birds?" I asked.

He put down his fork and stood up. He puffed his chest out, proud as a peacock. "I know everything about birds," he said, so that everyone could hear. "What do you want to know?"

I grabbed my crotch area, pushed it forward, and asked very loudly, "Would you take this for a swallow?"

The deputy warden spit green peas out of his mouth and onto the warden's new suit. Everyone in the dining hall was laughing, except my worker and me. He sat back down and I continued on through the food line, eventually sitting on the prisoner side of the dining room, at which point the head of security approached me. Everyone knew I had problems with this case worker, and the head was no exception, but he told me that if I pulled another stunt like that, he would have no alternative but to ship me to a higher security institution. As he left the table, though, he looked back and smiled. "That was a good one, though."

But I still had to deal with my worker. At my first parole hearing in Beaver Creek, I entered knowing I had the support of my family, the Toronto community, and the halfway house where I would be residing. I also was told, and shown on paper, that I had had the support of my worker, and thus the institution, for my day parole releases. During the hearing, the worker petitioned for me to serve further incarceration. The board members ruled in his favour. I was irate.

Over the next few days, security had their hands full after an influx of illegal Valium arrived at camp. After the interrogation of other prisoners, I was transferred back to Warkworth after it was alleged that I had been found in possession of a number of the pills. On court day, two officers from Beaver Creek appeared. I'd learned a bit watching the Lion defend me in Toronto, and I asked that the second officer not be permitted to hear the first's testimony. The court judge acquiesced.

The first guard said he found the pills in my bathroom. On cross-examination, he admitted that the bathroom was one provided for the entire range, and, in fact, everyone in the institution had access to the area. I asked why I was the one charged. He told the court I was high, that I was under the influence when they came to extricate me. I didn't argue. I then told the court that the second guard was a true Christian, and that if he said I was high, I would accept the maximum penalty. However, I told the court, if he said I was not high, I expected the judge to do what was right.

The second guard took the stand. Under my cross-examination, he turned to the disciplinary court judge and told him, "If he's trying to tell you he was under the influence, that he was high, he is a liar. I was assigned to escort him from his unit, and I stayed with him for eight hours after. He was as straight as an arrow." The judge informed him I was not the one saying I was high.

I was found not guilty of all charges.

I petitioned regional to send me to another camp, but they ordered me back to Beaver Creek. Upon my return, the inmates who had told security I was responsible approached me. They knew I knew what they'd done. They told me they were sorry, that they didn't want to be transferred themselves. Their wives and children would never forgive them. They knew I was a bigger fish for security to fry, and so they had thrown me under the bus. I just told them to get away from me.

The deputy warden was also awaiting my arrival, and motioned me over. "My classification officer screwed you at your hearing, so you screwed us. I'm willing to call it even. I'll make you a deal. No more flooding this place with pills, or anything else, and I promise we will get you home where you belong, with your family, at your next hearing."

Then, life was great.

One hot, sunny day, months later, as I lay by the pool sunbathing, the warden approached with a unit manager and my PO. I lifted up my flip-top sunglasses. "Yes?"

"Will you be putting in for day parole out of here anytime soon?" the warden queried.

I looked around the property. "Why would I do that?" I asked, seriously.

The three men chuckled. The warden said, "That's what we thought. You have it too good here. I'm directing your parole officer here to put you in for a hearing." Then they walked away.

So, finally, after eleven and a half years, I was released from federal custody on day parole in Toronto.

卄卌

The Rooster picked me up the morning of my release. After we'd been travelling for about forty minutes, he turned to me: "Is everything all right? You haven't said a word."

I told him I was just thinking about the past eleven-odd years, wondering if I had been fair with everyone. He reminded me I had made 95 percent friends and 5 percent enemies, and no one could ask for more than that. I'd made a couple of errors, fighting with men who hadn't committed the acts of wrongdoing I'd thought they had.

Then I thought back to my youth, to when I'd lost my way. Everyone had been so busy with their own lives, they didn't notice mine was heading in the wrong direction. No one had intervened. I was young and naive, and I had only criminals assisting me in my life choices. But, no matter what, I was responsible for me.

And just like I had when I left the Guelph reformatory twelve years earlier, I was determined to begin a straight life this time, to stay upon a proper path. But just like all those many years ago, it was not to be. The past decade plus would turn out to have just been a warm-up for more time I would waste in prison. Time wasted out of my life.

PART TWO

It's easy to smile at the end of each mile
When life goes along like a song.
But the man who's worthwhile
Is the man who can smile
When everything's going dead wrong.

— Ella Wheeler Wilcox

10

Debts and Threats

THE BLACKTOP ROLLED ALONG in front of Rooster's BMW as we sped toward Toronto. The sun was shining and the fresh air poured through the open window and across my face. I was looking forward to a new start in life. I felt (overly) confident that only good things were in my future. I knew I had a great deal of community support awaiting me, all the help I would need to succeed.

My friend the Dreamer was the superintendent of a building and had arranged a ground-floor apartment for my wife and me. One of my brothers-in-law had secured legitimate employment for me with his company as a machine operator. I had my wife, her family, my family, and many others to fill my days and nights. My old friends were either in touch with me, or easily found. The boys were ecstatic I'd been released, even if it was only to a halfway house in the northwest end of Toronto — the boys being my oldest brother and a plethora of the men I had become associated with in the criminal subcultures of Toronto and the penitentiaries of Ontario. I also had a few friends who had straightened their lives out, away from drugs, crime, or both. And they held hope my criminal lifestyle was over.

After thinking briefly of my past prison life and the people I now left behind, my mind focused on my nephew Froggy. I was very concerned since I'd learned he had been diagnosed with leukemia, and was now in a

Toronto hospital recovering from chemotherapy. Froggy had weighed heavily upon my mind. He was only fifteen years old. He had been a good kid his entire life. He worked after school store-clerking, and he never got into trouble hanging out with the wrong crowd as I had done in my youth. I could not believe such a bad thing had happened to him.

Rooster found the halfway house easily. I went inside and presented myself to the director of the house and her staff. I was given a room key and left what little property I had brought with me in the room. I was told I could leave for the day until my seven p.m. curfew. I went back out to the car, and Rooster sped me through the city, down into the familiar East End, where I met up with Cher at her parents' home. Rooster gave me some money and left.

After greeting the in-laws, Cher and I grabbed a taxi to go visit Froggy. He was overjoyed to see us. I could see right away the extent of his illness: bald head and greyish-green pallor, sunken eyes and thin frame. I smiled at him and we talked until the nurse told us visiting hours were over. Cher and I then went to our new apartment in East York. She'd seen it a few times already, but I hadn't. It certainly wasn't extravagant, but it was a two-bedroom and would satisfy our needs. Cher had semi-furnished the place with the help of the Dreamer and my oldest brother. We went out for supper after spending an hour or so of alone time together. I dropped her back at her parents and then took the long cab ride back to the halfway house. I had no car, and I didn't have a driver's licence anyways — something I never felt necessary to obtain in my criminal past, but was now regretting not having.

My room on the second floor was large enough for me, and since I would be at the house for only the required seven hours, during which I would be sleeping or showering, it was sufficient.

I met with the director of the house again in the morning. She was surprisingly young for her position, and she was more than good looking in my view. Everyone else that resided there agreed. We chatted about what each of us expected of the other, and I gave her an idea of my itinerary for the next two weeks. I didn't have to commence work right away, so I spent my mornings and early afternoons at Froggy's familial home. He had been released to spend his last fortnight of life at home as there was nothing more that could be done to treat his leukemia. His parents had exhausted every avenue, but they still continued to hope for a cure. I'd stay with Froggy each day until his parents came home from work. Cher was working days, as well, and I'd head to our apartment to await her arrival each day.

I was quite surprised that I was not experiencing the culture shock so many of the men I had served time with over the years had told me they'd experienced. I didn't feel out of place in the stores, on the streets, or anywhere else in the community. I attributed the lack of anxiety to the fact that I had never really lost sight of "the street" while I was incarcerated. I'd never gotten used to being in jail.

It didn't take long to notice that our entire apartment building always smelled of curry. The Dreamer hadn't told us that most of the building's tenants were of East Indian descent, and that the building would always smell of curry. I didn't like the smell; neither did Cher. What bothered her more, though, were the cockroaches. I had the Dreamer get industrial-strength gas bombs to eradicate the pests, but within two days of his efforts the roaches would return. Cher didn't like coming to the apartment at any time, but she'd come there briefly just so that we could have private time together.

Rooster would pick me up some days and we would go driving around to meet some of his friends and clients. He loved the fact that people would pay him their debts once they saw him with me. I never knew what he told them, but I'm sure it wasn't that I was a nice man. And I was sure that they were not really friends of his so much as they were drug dealers. I didn't care. I had a great time in his company. He'd been the best man at my Millhaven wedding and had been a great friend when we were "doing time" together.

Froggy passed away. To honour his request, I hadn't gone to see him during his last two days of life; he'd asked his mom (my sister) to tell me that he did not want me to see him looking so terrible. The skin on his head and face had split open in several areas and had turned a sickly green. He was in a lot of pain despite the amount of morphine being channelled into his small, frail body. It wouldn't have mattered to me how he looked. I loved my little nephew, and I knew he idolized me. Still, I'd been helpless to combat this terrible disease that was taking his life.

After his funeral, I returned to his parents' home along with the rest of my family, feeling his loss, feeling defeated. I was grieving, and seeing my other family members in their grief only heightened my emotions. I was mad at the world. I couldn't understand, knowing all the bad people in my life, how a fifteen-year-old kid could have come to such a tragic end.

I didn't handle the situation well at all. I broke away from the family and went over to an area of Danforth Avenue where there were many bars. I went into a number of them and immediately picked fights with the doormen, the bouncers, or both. I wasn't drinking; I just wanted to hit someone. I'd begin the argument as soon as I was asked to check my coat at the door. I was fortunate not to be arrested that day. As I said, I went into a number of bars, so I picked a number of fights.

Unbeknownst to me, at the same time my oldest brother was not so fortunate. After the funeral, he'd received a phone call from his girlfriend in Quebec. The police had arrived on her doorstep looking for him. He was on a lengthy parole release, too. The police were looking to charge him in connection with the theft of an eighteen-wheeler and its content of stereos, TVs, and other electronics. They'd left a phone number for him to call, should he decide to turn himself in or make a deal with authorities. Otherwise, they'd catch up with him on their own terms.

The following day, he met me at my apartment. He told me he'd called the police and arranged to postpone his arrest until after he attended a fundraising "stag" for the Crab's family. The Crab, one of my brother's closest friends, had passed away recently, too, quite unexpectedly, and left behind a young son with his young mother. My brother had agreed to turn himself in to the police after the event.

The next night, the Dreamer picked me up to take me to this stag party. There, I saw a host of men I'd known in the many different criminal subcultures over the years. There were rounders, bikers, and organized crime family members — not just the average guys, but the cream of the crop. The Crab had been well-known, well-respected, and well-liked. Many of the guys there came up to me to chat, shake my hand. Some were introductory meetings, but most were men who I had served time with or committed one crime or another with. After a while, I was approached by one gang member I knew from my past. He said hi and offered me his hand. I told him I couldn't shake it. We'd been friendly once, but that was before I was told he was involved in the homicide of a close friend. My oldest brother witnessed the exchange of words and became concerned I would assault the man. He had the Dreamer drive me back to the halfway house.

The following day, I saw my brother again. He was surrendering to the police, but wasn't confident his confederates were going to honour their part of the deal in returning the stolen merchandise. He asked me to involve myself in ensuring his freedom. I couldn't say no. We went to see his associates and he introduced us. Later that day, he turned himself in to investigators.

The next night, I received a call from Bernie, a friend who lived nearby in the East End. He told me there was a large contingent of police and trucks in the parking lot behind his house. They appeared to be busy picking up a large amount of merchandise that had been left there under several drop cloths. Bernie was confused how anyone would know that vacant parking lot was there, it being hidden from normal traffic view; let alone, he wondered aloud, who would be using it as a drop site. I told him not to worry, it didn't concern him.

At his hearing, my brother was reinstated on his parole and freed.

I went to work at the factory job my brother-in-law had arranged for me. The job was fairly easy, and my co-workers were nice. I had a Nicaraguan foreman, though, who seemed not too pleased with my arrival. He thought of himself as somewhat of a ladies' man, and took offence to the attention I garnered from the female workers. I didn't want their attention, nor did I encourage it, but still the foreman would scrutinize my every move, hoping to find fault in my work. After a few weeks, one of the bosses asked if I could work a twelve-hour shift as another employee needed a half day off to attend a family crisis. I told him I would, but that I would have to talk with the halfway house director first. After I spoke to her, she called the boss, then told me I could leave the house a couple of hours early on the morning in question for work purposes.

The morning after I worked that shift, I was told I was grounded to the house for the long weekend. I couldn't go out for the next four days, not even for one minute. I was upset and confused. The director told me she had agreed to allow me to leave early, but that I should have come back a few hours earlier the night before so as to complete my required seven hours' nightly residency. I hadn't even thought that to be an issue and no one had mentioned it. I was ticked off.

The director also took the time to further tell me she was disappointed I did not spend any time in the halfway house other than that which was required of me. I told her I had to work, that I was also working on fixing up my apartment, and had a life to build with my wife and family. I had been away a long time. I pointed out that she had a large number of "residents" who did nothing but hang around the house and stare at her — most of them parolees convicted of sexual offences that I found highly offensive. I told her I was surprised she even noticed my absence. She told me she had checked the costs of my taxi fares from home to the halfway house, and on a daily basis they pretty well equalled my factory earnings (she was right). She wanted to know how I could afford my travel costs. I told her Cher worked, as well, and I received a lot of family assistance from both our families. She still wasn't happy that I was uninvolved in her halfway house, or with her. But I continued to meet the conditions of my parole, at least as it pertained to the halfway house.

One morning, I awoke with a pinched nerve in my neck. It hurt like heck to even try turning my head, so I called the factory to get the day off. They put me through to the Nicaraguan foreman. When I told him my situation, he said he didn't care if I was injured. He wanted me at the factory within the hour. I was never good with ultimatums, so promptly told him to put his job where the sun don't shine. I hung up, then made another quick phone call. Within five minutes, I had an interview scheduled for the following day with a roofing company.

I had never shingled a roof before, but the next morning I showed up on the job site and talked to the boss. He was a man around my age, and we seemed to get along. He hired me on the spot, albeit at a minimum wage. I notified my worker of the employment change.

After five days on the new job, the boss pulled me aside and told me he couldn't pay me the minimum wage. I told him right away I would take a pay cut, because I needed to maintain employment for my parole. He laughed, then told me he was giving me a four dollar an hour raise.

I enjoyed the outdoors work, ripping off old shingles and replacing them with new ones. I would then drive the garbage off to the nearest dump site. About a month later, the boss was riding "shotgun" with me as I drove his truck. He noticed there was an open beer in the cab, and told me I should be leery of that because of my parole situation. I laughed and told him I could not see law enforcement pulling over his old truck full of garbage, and besides, I was more concerned that I didn't have a driver's licence. He couldn't believe I'd driven his truck for a month without being licenced. He took the wheel.

After that, he gave me another substantial raise. I was very good at the work, but I was also good with the customers. He'd get into the odd argument with a paying customer, and I'd intervene and mediate to everyone's satisfaction. He'd laugh when, every once in a while, a lady would come out of the house with lemonade for the other workers but then tell me mine was inside the house. I'd never take any of them up on the offer, of course, but he found it funny.

‖∦

Cher and I gave up the East End apartment after a few months. Me, I liked the solitude of the apartment, the hours of privacy, but it was no good to me if my wife would not live there with me. That was too much solitude. The Dreamer was upset, but he understood about the cockroaches, and the curry smell.

Cher's brother and his wife and daughter had been living in the second-floor duplex of their parents' home, but they had recently decided to move north to Richmond Hill for work. Cher asked her parents if we could take over the residence. They couldn't cover their mortgage without renting out the second-floor unit, at least not without straining their budget. They agreed. The apartment had a separate entrance, and Cher assured me her parents would not interfere in our relationship. I liked them anyway, so I agreed to the move.

One day Saul phoned me from his sister Carrie's house. I was surprised to hear from him, and that Carrie only lived two blocks from Cher's parents. I went over and we talked about old times. He was trafficking hashish. Me, at this time, I felt hash was a soft drug that would be, or should be, legalized along with marijuana, and in my opinion was far less volatile than alcohol. Even the courts and law enforcement had softened their perception of simple possession of the drug.

A great many of my criminal associates trafficked in hash. During this time, my oldest brother asked me to connect his older friends with one of mine for the purpose of obtaining some hash to traffic. I did, but never followed up on any of their business dealings. That is, until my brother's friends failed to pay their bill.

I told my brother to let his older friends know I'd hurt them if they didn't pay my friend. He was upset with me, but I told him it was his fault for involving me in the first place. Now I had to get involved. I was also upset that no one had given any gratuity to me, which was common courtesy when one arranges a deal between two parties. My brother gave his friends the message, and they quickly paid their bill.

I often found myself being an intermediary between supplier and trafficker. I seemed to know most of the criminals, and held the respect of both sides. The suppliers were confident they would remain anonymous, safe from arrest while receiving their money; the traffickers were happy they could be supplied in advance with no funding.

Gerry, an old rounder from the East End, sought me out one day to make an offer. Apparently, he had a large amount of hash he couldn't sell. Gerry's forte had always been break and enters or fencing stolen merchandise. He asked me to put him together with a dealer. I told him I needed to know his price and how much quantity he expected to move per week. He asked me to meet him at a local bar the following afternoon.

The next day, I had Carrie pick me up in her Camaro and drive me to the bar. Gerry hadn't arrived yet, but we were fifteen minutes early. There were about a dozen men in the bar, but nobody I really knew. I did recognize a group of four men seated at a table. I'd met them at a house where my friend Bernie had been moving in with his new old lady. I'd helped him bring over what few belongings he owned. That relationship lasted only as long as Bernie's paycheque, and then he was beaten up by these men and thrown out the door.

A guy at the pool table asked if I wanted to play a game of billiards. As I was playing, Carrie kept coming over, telling me she wanted to leave.

I kept telling her to hang on until Gerry showed up. Once the game was over, and the appointment time had passed, I finally relented and left the bar. Once we were in the car, I angrily asked her what her problem was. She knew I was going there to meet Gerry and that I might have to wait, so why had she kept bothering me to leave? She told me that while I was playing billiards the big, bearded man at the next table kept telling her that she was leaving with him, and that if I said anything, he'd kill me. She was scared.

At that point, we were just pulling out of the parking lot, and I told her to stop the car and stay there. I went back in to the bar and directly toward the big man. "You going to kill me?" I asked. He went to answer, but I wasn't listening. I punched him square in the face, knocking him off his chair. He jumped up and I hit him again, knocking him unconscious. I then dragged him by his coat collar across the floor and into the men's washroom, where I laid him half-sitting against the wall. As he came to, I kicked him in the face. He rolled over onto the floor, asleep. When I turned to leave, the man's friend approached with the bouncer. "I don't think I liked that," he said to me angrily. While he was talking, I was in motion. I hit him full force with my right elbow on his temple. He hit the floor, unmoving. "Did you like that?" I quipped. I looked at the bouncer. He put his hands up and stepped back. I turned to leave, but I was full of adrenalin and anger. On the way out, I stopped at the table where the four men who had been involved in the assault on Bernie sat. They admitted they knew Bernie, but didn't remember meeting me. As they moved to get up from the table, I started knocking them out. After I walked away, two other men came in my direction from the billiard table. Carrie had come back into the bar, and she hit one from behind with a pool cue, breaking it. The other one looked at the carnage on the floor behind me. "Do you really want to do this?" I asked. He stepped aside, and we left. The owner was yelling at Carrie that she was barred from drinking in his establishment for at least a month; as for me, I was barred for life. I couldn't have cared less. I never went there anyways. I was just glad (and surprised) that the fights had gone so well for me. Gerry never did show up, but, in retrospect, it turned out to be a pretty exciting day just the same.

The next day, my oldest brother called and asked me to meet him at a local restaurant. When I entered, I saw him sitting with an old acquaintance of ours, a local biker who'd been arrested with us on the drug lab bust back in 1975 and been acquitted. The biker told me he wanted me to go to his clubhouse with him to meet his "brothers." A great many of them drank at the local bar I had just fought in the day before, and they wanted to make sure I knew who they were in case I should venture into that bar again. I laughed and told the biker that I would not be going back to that bar. The place was a dive, and I had only gone there as a rendezvous point. His brothers had nothing to worry about. The biker asked if I could find him some hash for personal use, so I gave him my number and told him to call me. Later, I met up with him at a nearby laundromat. A friend could not provide me much quantity to give the biker, but enough that he was more than happy.

The same biker had an enterprise going with my oldest brother and another biker from a different club. I knew the third man, Bo, from Collins Bay, but I never knew about their business until one night when my brother's biker friend made a big mistake. He called Cher on the phone and told her he needed our address. She informed him she was not allowed to give it out unless I told her to. He started screaming and threatening her. She called Rooster on his pager. He tracked me down at a friend's apartment. I was with Saul and another ex-convict named Slugger. I called Cher, then I called the biker's clubhouse. The biker got on the phone and told me I was in serious trouble, and that "the enterprise" was no longer in his control. My fate was "out of his hands," he said. I had no idea what he was talking about, and I cared less at that point. He'd threatened my wife, and that was my focus. I told him to meet me where he'd seen me last, then made a few calls to men I'd known at Millhaven. Saul made a couple of other calls, as did Slugger. I was not "hitting the mattresses," I was taking the war to them right away. I'd learned long ago waiting to see what happens in a dispute is often a fatal mistake.

I entered my house with three of my associates. Two carried long arms in the form of a shotgun and machine gun, as well as some other less noticeable firearms. I'd also brought a female family friend with me who Cher knew. I told Cher she was going with the lady to stay at a hotel room for a few days. Cher was extremely frightened. She was also extremely pregnant. She had no idea what was going on, and had never seen so many well-armed men in her life.

After she was safely away, I walked out on the street. My friend Bernie was walking hurriedly toward me. Slugger, not knowing him, almost ran him over, coming right up on the sidewalk with his car and cutting Bernie off just in front of me. Bernie yelled that he had seen armed men between the houses on both sides of my street. I told him I knew and to get out of the area. Then I hopped in one of the cars. We picked up our men as we rolled slowly down my street, then drove off to the laundromat in a four-car tandem. When we turned the corner near our destination, all we saw were police cruisers all around the place. I lived close by, and this was the only time I had seen this much law-enforcement activity on this corner. That caused me consternation, but did not deter my anger. I was not leaving this confrontation unfinished. I drove down to the clubhouse, where we announced our arrival with a few gunshots. No one would stick their head out of the clubhouse door that night, at least not during the few minutes we were there.

The following afternoon, my oldest brother called and told me he had to see me. That it was really important. He said he was at a local restaurant with Rooster, so I walked over. As I got close, I noticed it was not Rooster with my brother, but his partner, the biker. I circled the area a few times looking for others before I entered. My brother had one of my sisters with him and the female friend I had left with Cher the night before. My brother asked if I had been high the night before and misinterpreted the situation with his friend. I didn't take my eyes off the biker. The female friend assured him I was not. She'd been with me at Slugger's. The biker told me they heard gunshots outside their clubhouse the previous night, and asked if that had been me. I told him emphatically that it was. I also told my brother to shut his mouth and not say another word. I was furious. He'd gotten me to this meeting under false pretenses, and not only had he brought a "civilian" with him, but that particular "square john," my sister, was a family member. I knew this was to ensure that I didn't seriously hurt his friend. My brother very much appeared to be taking sides against me, although he didn't know the whole circumstances of the dispute. I was not happy at all with him. I told his associate that he had known me when I was an eighteen-year-old kid, long before I had gone to the penitentiary. I told him I may have been perceived by him as a weak link then, but times had changed. I was a far more powerful threat than my brother, Bo, him, or his bike club if I chose to involve my criminal associates. The biker tried to explain to me that Bo had ripped off the product, and his club was not sure my oldest brother was not involved, and that was why they were interested in "just" talking with me. I reminded him his enterprise had nothing to do with me. I then told him if he or his brothers ever spoke to my wife, even breathed on her, he would find me waiting for him in his living room with his family, and that he would not like it at all. He said he'd made a mistake (I agreed), and asked if there was anything he could do to ease the tension between us. I told him I had spent a great deal of money, actually thousands of dollars, the previous night on procuring weapons, and I asked if he would be interested in paying me for them. He was stunned. I told him my friends were all Millhaven monsters, a myth many believed, and anytime he wanted a problem with me, he would be accommodated. It would be in his best interest if he just kept his little criminal enterprises away from me. I had no time in my life for his minor-league dramas anymore. I took my "straight" sister with me when I left.

The following day, at Bernie's house, Bo showed up. He told me he'd just arrived back in town and learned of the disagreement. He couldn't believe they thought he'd ripped them off, or that my brother had went against me. I told him it was over as far as I was concerned. I didn't care to discuss the matter. He'd started the commotion when he took the product out of town without telling his two partners. He did have a reputation for ripping drug dealers off, but this time he'd arrived back with the money, so they were all happy. I could not have cared less. It did not concern me. They'd upset my wife, and that was something I told each of them they would never ever want to do again.

After Bo left, I asked Bernie how they knew each other. I'd known Bernie since he was a young lad, and I always considered him a friend. Bernie said the Dreamer had introduced them. I told Bernie to be careful. Bo was a "heavy" from the London area, an enforcer for his outlaw motorcycle gang. Bernie was just a little guy and not too knowledgeable in the criminal underworld. Bernie assured me he was all right.

Not two weeks later, Bernie called me over to his flat. Bo was there again. He'd given Bernie a few pounds of weed to sell for him. Bernie had fronted the product out to guys he thought were his friends, but now his customers were refusing to pay. Bo didn't seem to care; he had other plans in mind for Bernie to work off the debt. I wasn't surprised. Bo probably gave Bernie the weed hoping for just such an outcome. I knew that Bo's plan would entail Bernie doing crimes that Bo didn't want to do himself. Bernie would likely be arrested and sent to prison for a long time. I told Bo that wasn't going to happen. Instead, we all hopped in a car and went to visit the people who owed Bernie money. After we collected it all, Bo turned to me and, smiling, said it was the first time he'd gone out collecting where he had played the "good guy." I was not so amused. When we were alone, I gave Bernie heck. I told him it was the last time I'd pull his butt out of the fire. Of course, we both knew that wasn't true.

Bo hung around town at the Dreamer's apartment. When a friend of my oldest brother's showed up there from Quebec, I got a call. The man was looking to purchase a large quantity of weed and gave me his buying price. I talked to a friend, but the two of them couldn't agree on a price, so I told the man he may as well return to La Belle Province. Bo spoke up and told the man to go get his money, said he'd get him his product. I looked at Bo long and hard. He had as much chance of getting that product as I did of getting a pardon from the Canadian government. Again, Bo was a known rip-off artist.

I told Bo to go get his product and I'd take the Frenchman to get his money. When I left the Dreamer's place with the man, I put him directly on a bus back to Quebec.

A couple of days later, the Dreamer called and told me to tell my brother not to go to his apartment. Bo was there, and he was mad. He was looking for my brother and me. Said I'd better stay away, as well. Bo had said we were avoiding him.

Ten minutes later, when the Dreamer answered his door, I strolled in. He was stunned. Bo was sitting on the couch having a drink. He asked me what I was doing there, and I told him I was avoiding him. He told me he was mad that I'd let the Frenchman get away. I told him he was out of his mind, first of all, if he thought for a second I would let him rip off one of my brother's friends, and second, if he thought he could handle me in a fight, let alone both my brother and I. He calmed down very fast, and we agreed to forget the whole incident.

Bo came to me later that week asking for my help. He was in trouble with his club, and they wanted to see him. He didn't want to go alone. He wanted me to pick up a few handguns and go with him to the clubhouse. I knew it was an in-house disagreement, and that they would kiss and make up, but if I was with him I'd become their enemy for no reason. I told him if he got hurt, I'd respond, but no, I wouldn't go with him. His meeting turned out as I thought, and they were all brothers once again. However, months down the road, after another disagreement, one of his brothers ended Bo's life by putting a fire axe through his skull as he lay sleeping in a chair.

‖‖‖

Cher got pregnant not long after my release from the work camp, and in due course gave birth to our first child, a girl she named Kelly. We had a deal as to who would provide the name based on the sex of the newborn. Although I lost the deal, I won. I'd wanted a daughter I could dote on, and now I had the finest one in the world. Kelly would make me proud every day of her life.

I was in the delivery room when Kelly was born. I had never had such a wonderful experience. I spent each day at the hospital until I could take them both home. At work, I couldn't wait to get home just to hold the baby.

I loved Cher just as much as I could love anyone. She would always be my life partner. But I was lacking in character in many areas. I had never had a stable relationship longer than a few months, and during those times I had been expected to do nothing but provide. I didn't recognize the work that was required to maintain a relationship, a household, let alone raise children together. I would never raise a hand against my wife or children, but there were times when I put the problems of my associates ahead of my new family. There were also times I placed my own self-gratification ahead of my responsibilities. Basically, I was an asshole when it came to relationships.

11

Back in Blue

CHER AND I BECAME EMBROILED in an argument one afternoon and I stormed out. I walked over to Saul's sister Carrie's place. There were four men in her living room, each with the hope of "dating" her that day. She was quite the promiscuous lady, and each of her suitors knew that. They also knew each of them was there with the same hope. I found it hilarious.

When I noticed Carrie had a bit of a black eye and some swelling on one temple, I asked what happened. She told me she'd given a guy she met at a hotel some of Saul's product, but instead of paying her when he was supposed to, he beat her up.

I was incensed. Losing product is an occupational hazard. No dealer likes to lose profit, but it happens, whether through police pursuits or rip-offs. Beating up, especially a female, was just not tolerated in my criminal circle. She assured me Saul would take care of it.

Carrie and I went out later, after getting rid of her four suitors. They were not happy, but they weren't prepared to defend her against the man who ripped her off and assaulted her, let alone confront me. We went for a drive through Toronto's East End. On the way back to her house, we picked up a number of police cruisers, which chased her car into her backyard. As I got out, the cops clamoured behind the roofs and hoods of their squad cars, guns drawn. "Don't move," they yelled. They were all screaming and swearing and making threats. I was smiling back at them. I grabbed my crotch and told them a few uncouth things about their mothers. Carrie was screaming for me not to resist as the police made a slow and careful approach. They had me put my hands on the roof of Carrie's Camaro while they searched me, her, and the car. One cop walked up beside me and showed me a twenty-five-gram piece of black hash. "What's this?" he asked seriously. "It's yours," I answered. "I'd put it away before your friends here ask you for some." He grabbed the hair on the back of my head and slammed my face into the roof of the car.

"Hurt yourself?" I asked. I was handcuffed while being read my rights. We were taken to the nearest police precinct. I was charged with four counts of break and enter with mischief and for the piece of hash. Four houses in the East End had had their front doors kicked in earlier that day. Apparently, the police contended, I'd been looking for the man who'd assaulted Carrie. Three of the four homes contained the man's friends, while the fourth was just a wrong house occupied by two very gay men. I was also charged for providing a false name to the police. While Carrie was released on her own recognizance, my fingerprints came back and I was held on a breach of federal parole. I had to appear in Old City Hall the following morning.

卌

The old bullpen hadn't changed a fraction since I'd last spent time there. I watched as a pretty good fight ensued between a middle-aged Portuguese man and a young black who had put his hand in the older man's pocket in an attempt to relieve him of his wallet. When the black man's friends decided they were going to involve themselves, I intervened, along with a couple of other men, and told them to stay out of the fight. It ended with the wallet still in possession of its rightful owner.

I was ordered detained on all charges, save the possession of the hashish, for which I was granted personal bail. That didn't matter. I was going nowhere other than the Don Jail.

When the justice of the peace called me out of the Old City Hall bullpen to sign the paperwork for the bail on the possession of narcotics charge, the guard on the door to the hallway opened it up and asked if I was ready to leave. I told him I most certainly was. Six other guards came flying at me from their office, screaming at the cop to relock the outside door. "Where do you think you're going?" one cop asked. "Back in there," I said, pointing toward the nearby bullpen. "That's right," they said, knowing I would have left had they been two steps slower or less observant.

When I arrived at the admitting desk of the Don Jail, I saw a number of the guards that I'd come to know over the previous years. When I stripped down to exchange my clothes for jail blues, a young guard barked at me to touch my toes. I knew it was standard procedure: *Lift your arms up over your head, open your mouth, tousle your hair, and then bend over to touch your toes.* I was in no mood to be taking orders from a rookie, especially with the attitude he was expressing. I told him to touch his own toes. He threatened to place me in the hole. I told him to go ahead. The old sergeant overheard the argument and came around to ask the new guard what the problem was. When he told the sergeant, he was informed that there wasn't a hole in their jail that I hadn't already been in. He told the rookie to just leave me alone. The older guards escorted me immediately up to 4C south range.

As usual, there were a number of my former associates there. The Don now had outgoing telephones installed on each of its ranges, two phones per corridor, so I called Cher. She was not impressed at all with my arrest, but even less so with *who* I'd been arrested with. Cher knew Carrie's reputation for being very promiscuous with anyone with a criminal record, and mine far exceeded most. As much as I tried to convince her, she would not budge. In her mind, I was definitely having an affair with Carrie.

Saul sent a message in for me to call him. He wanted me to plead to any deal that would have the charges against his sister dismissed. This didn't surprise me as Carrie had said the same thing even before we arrived at the police station. I assured Saul that Carrie would not be going to jail, but if he thought I was about to jump on a sword just so she didn't have to report to the bail offices once a month, he was using far too many drugs. I told him sarcastically that I noticed his lack of concern for me.

One of the men I knew from Collins Bay told me the guards had let them know that morning that I was on my way in. He told me a guy sitting at the middle table was concerned that I'd want to fight him. I found out who he was, and what he'd done to make him think I'd want to assault him. I walked over and sat across from the man. He looked up at me through the two swollen black eyes he was sporting — courtesy of Metro's finest, according to him. Art was his name, and he'd knocked out a friend of mine in a floor-hockey game at Collins Bay earlier that year. That was what he'd been worried about me finding out. I introduced myself, and informed him that if he had knocked me out, my friend would laugh his head off just as I was doing now. Floor hockey in "Disneyland" was a game of war hockey, and everything involved stayed on the floor. I told Art there was absolutely no problem between us. He was happy. We would actually become good friends during our stay. We occupied the same cell, now that "double-bunking" had come into effect in the Toronto-area jails.

A couple of bikers I knew from the Pen, plus a couple I knew from the street, were living on 4C south at that time. My friend Joey's kid brother Devon was also on the range, facing several bank robbery charges. A few days after I arrived, I saw a short, medium-sized man come on the range. He was around thirty. I was at a table reading when I noticed him change the channel of the range television. Within seconds, Tarzan approached him. Tarzan was a huge, muscular biker. He grabbed the little man by the front of his shirt, lifting him off his feet, and slammed him up against the wall. "You fucking asshole," he screamed in his face, "I'll kill you."

"Put him down," I said, stepping between them. "He doesn't know any better."

Tarzan looked at me, then set the man down and walked away. I turned to the little guy and told him, "Don't touch the TV again, just watch what everyone else does, and you won't get hurt, okay?"

He thanked me, shaken by the beating he'd almost received. Not long after, we were all locked in the cells for count. A half hour later when the cell doors were reopened, Devon came into our cell with a big smile on his face. "There's a guy in my cell who turned himself in on traffic tickets just so he could kick the heck out of you," he told me. "Really?" I replied. I went down to Devon's cell to see who this man was. When I entered, I saw the little guy sitting there. I told him I heard he was looking for someone. He nodded and gave me the name. When I told him that would be me, he turned white, his eyes teared up, and he croaked, "I'm going to die, aren't I?" I sat down beside him and asked him to tell me his story.

He was a resident in one of the houses whose door got kicked in. He'd been at work, but his wife and kids were in the house. They'd been untouched, but traumatized from seeing their front door sail down their hallway. He'd gotten very angry. He got my name from the newspaper, but his wife had given him a totally different description of the person now seated beside him. I told him to relax. I was not going to harm him. In fact, I was going to help him. After all, I was well aware of who kicked his front door in. I told him to call his wife and tell her to expect a visitor within the hour. I told him to tell her to accept whatever she was given. He made the call, and then I used the phone. I had him call her back an hour later. A man had delivered enough cash to pay for their door, to pay his fines to get him out of jail, and to pay their rent for a few months. She was very pleased with her little man, and she was on her way to pick him up. He was very grateful. I told him not to worry about it, and I apologized for the ordeal his family had suffered. As he left, I watched with great admiration the little guy who had the backbone to purposely come to jail to confront me, to defend his family — even if it was very stupid of him.

When the preliminary hearing began for Carrie and me at the College Park courthouse in downtown Toronto, the first witness was one of the gay men. He took the stand and said he and his partner had heard the front door crash in. He was overly animated, much to the judge's irritation. He testified that his partner and he were on the second floor. He identified both of us as being the intruders. I called Carrie's lawyer over for a conference. When it was his turn to cross-examine the witness, he asked when exactly it was that the witness had seen Carrie's face. He testified he never did see her face, but that he could positively identify her because the police had told him it was her. The judge questioned the witness and then threw him off the stand. He then dismissed all charges against Carrie. I, however, was committed to trial for the one break and enter with mischief. I was not too concerned. I knew at a trial I would be found not guilty. Carrie was very happy. She asked when she could visit me. I told her not even when I was dead would that be all right. That was the last time I spoke to Carrie.

I returned to the range at the Don. Art had gone back to the Pen, but California had come back on new charges. He told me he'd been caught off guard at a local restaurant by the bikers he had the controversy with. The leader told him he'd have a fair fight with the one biker believed to have started the initial altercation. California obliged, and promptly whipped his opponent. He was told the feud was over. He was so happy to have had my intervention on his behalf when we'd met earlier. California was in very good shape. He was in his prime, and he trained every day, stretching and boxing. Me, I'd read my books and newspapers. I'd train once in a while with the others, but just to keep from getting too lethargic. One never knew when someone would show up and want to fight just to gain a reputation. I'd seen that occur on occasion, but never with me, at least to my knowledge.

One day, mid-morning, the cells were left open. I lay on my bed reading my book. It was far more comfortable than sitting at a table on the range. California came in with his friend Punchy. "Have you heard what's going on down in the 'jungle' range?" I looked up from my book and shook my head. "The black guys are taking the white guys' food off them at every mealtime," he said.

"So?"

"Well, that isn't right. Some of those guys haven't eaten in days," he said.

"I guess the white guys should either fight or move then, eh?"

"There's too many to fight," Punchy chimed in. "There's like thirty-five black guys and only five whites. They'd get killed."

I looked at them and said, "So, I guess you guys came to say goodbye. You moving down there to even things up, are you?"

They looked at each other, disappointed, then left. I went back to my book. I had enough problems without worrying about what went on in other parts of the jail.

An hour or so later, I walked out onto the range to stretch my legs. I noticed a small, thin newcomer sitting at the middle table by himself, but paid him little attention. Lunch was served, and a half hour later the food trays were taken away. About a half hour after that, the landing door opened and the sergeant of the guards walked onto our floor area. Behind him came eight black prisoners surrounded by guards. The sergeant opened the outer grille of the sally port that led onto our range and had the blacks enter. Once they were all inside the metal-barred cage, the sergeant told them to try pulling their bullshit on this range. Then he buzzed the inner sally port door, giving them access to our range. I was sitting at the end table watching this as I read a newspaper. They entered, but all but one stayed near the front three cells.

The largest man, who the other black men referred to as the Terminator, made his way down along to the first table. The little white newcomer stood up and confronted him over taking his food for the past few days. He challenged the much larger man to a fight at the end of the range. They both walked past me and squared off. The little guy danced around for a few seconds, then moved in to land a punch. Instead, he was punched in the face and sent flying. The large man turned to leave, but the little guy picked himself up and told his opponent he wasn't finished. He danced around, moved in, and got punched in the mouth again. The big man turned and smiled at me. When he went to walk away, the little guy called him on again. He had blood running from his nose and mouth. As the larger man got closer to him, I put my paper down, got up, and stepped between them. I put my hand on the little guy's chest and slowly pushed him away, telling him that it was over. Then I turned to the big man and told him it was not over for him. I punched him square in the face, sending him back into the cold metal bars that ran the length of the corridor. I took a fighting stance, expecting him to charge at me. He came off the bars, spun, and ran screaming up to the front of the range, yelling for the guard to let him out. I was stunned. The big man left the sally port and was taken around the corner onto the north range. I sat back down with my newspaper.

The little guy came over to thank me, but I didn't say anything. I thought he'd shown a lot of courage confronting a no-win situation even though he was in the right (which is why I stepped in). He went back to the middle table. California, Punchy, Davey, and a few of my fellow prisoners/associates from the East End came over. "That was great of you to step in," California said. "Was it?" I asked. "You guys came bugging me about this 'jungle' bullshit this morning all upset. Now, those guys are standing right in front of you, and what do you do? Nothing. That's fine by me. If I have to fight each one, I will, but then I'm not going to be too pleased with any of you, I can tell you that." I went back to my paper.

"The boys" went into a huddle, then went to the front of the range. They were each scrappers in their own right, and the black men from the jungle range provided little opposition during the melee that ensued. The guard found he had seven beaten men in front of the sally port screaming for help, so he had no choice but to let them in the cage. He called the sergeant, who entered our range for the second time that afternoon. Only this time he was smiling at the men he'd brought up earlier. "You guys don't like the pen range? What's wrong?" he asked, sarcastically, then added seriously, "Okay, I'm going to take you all back down to your range, but if you pull any more racial shit, you'll be coming right back up here." He signalled the guard to let them out of the sally port, and the seven followed him through the landing door and back toward the jungle.

The following morning, we had a new guard working our range. After breakfast, I approached him at the sally port and told him I was ready. He asked what I was talking about. I told him that our range had been involved in card tournaments with the range on the north side, and after three days we were down to the final game, and I needed access to the north side to finish it. The guard unwittingly buzzed me onto the north side.

The Terminator was seated alone at the middle table. I had not made it past the first four cells before he recognized me, and my intent. He got up, and as I arrived, he tried to deke around the table to get past me to the front of the range. I'd already calculated this move and slid across the metal tabletop, catching him in a full nelson. When I was stable on my feet, I lifted him off his and slammed his head — and more so his face — repeatedly into the metal bars of one of the cell doors. He screamed loudly for help until he was knocked unconscious.

The guard who let me in was now racing along the outside of the range bars, yelling at me to let go of the Terminator. I dropped his bleeding hulk onto the range floor, went back to the south side, and picked up my book. A stretcher was brought up to take my opponent away.

The rest of the day was normal routine. The south side range was pretty upbeat over the latest events. Me, I was just bewildered about men who came to jail thinking they could physically exact their prejudices and biases on others and not be held accountable. I couldn't believe how stupid that train of thought was, but then, upon entering jail, most of these men had no idea that the concrete and steel were the least of their concerns. Not having any experience, they didn't understand how quickly power can shift from one group to another. These eight men had just found out.

The next morning, Mr. B. was assigned to work our range. He was a huge black man. He was always polite, and he was one of the few guards who I'd never seen assault anyone. For that reason alone, he garnered a lot of respect from us prisoners. I was expecting a visit that morning, and so I asked him for the razor. I had to stand in the sally port to shave, as was the protocol. Halfway through, the phone rang. Mr. B. answered, spoke to someone, and then hung up. He looked over and smiled at me. "That call was for you," he said. "Is my visit here already?" I asked. I knew it was far too early for visiting hours. "No, that was the jungle range. The men down there want you to know that the white men are getting their food now." Mr. B. looked pretty pleased about that. I pretended to feign indifference, but inside I was trying hard not to smile. As the boys went out to court and back, they said the others were blaming the Terminator for their actions. They'd been afraid of him, and only followed his lead so that they didn't get beat up. I didn't care; I was just happy not to hear about it anymore.

The next time I went to court, I ran into the Terminator as I arrived back at the Don. I was still handcuffed, which was unsettling, especially since he was not. He was being released out the same door I had entered. He stood there talking with another black man, his eyes and face still somewhat swollen. He told his friend that he was *never ever* coming back to jail. I was happy to overhear that. Maybe the Terminator had learned from his mistake.

I'd talked with the lawyer about getting my bail set so I wouldn't have to sit in the Don any longer than necessary; once bail was set I could be transferred to a penitentiary and brought back for court. "Doing time" was much more comfortable in a federal institution.

The Supreme Court building in downtown Toronto stands at the southern end of stately University Avenue. Its hallowed halls and prestigious courtrooms command the respect and dignity of the common people, as well as its own officers of the court. On this day, I had been scheduled to appear before one of the distinguished judges. There was no way I could miss this appointment. I was transported early in the morning from the Don via police paddy wagon and arrived at the bullpen hours before court opened. My lawyer was seeking to have bail granted for me on the charges of break and enter with mischief times four.

The court proceedings were halted as I walked into an old and familiar courtroom. I was placed in the prisoner's box. The same four hard plastic chairs were still fastened in place, as I remembered them. That day, the first seat was occupied by a very large and very muscular Jamaican man. The last seat was occupied by a thin white youth seeking bail on car theft charges. I took the third seat. Court resumed.

The Crown attorney addressed the judge, referring to her notes. It was the sentencing hearing for the Jamaican. In his case, the court was told, a young girl had visited her terminally ill aunt in a west Toronto hospital. On her deathbed, the aunt had given her niece a gold chain as a memento of the love they shared. On the subway on her way home, the young girl was accosted by the Jamaican man, who tore the chain off her neck and then returned to his seat. (*What a scumbag*, I thought.) The girl pleaded for the chain back. She informed him of the personal value it held for her. He promised that if she got off the subway at his stop and waited until he was in a taxi, he would return it to her. (*Well, at least he was a scumbag with a conscience*, I thought, continuing my silent appraisal of the situation.)

But once they were both outside on the street, the Jamaican grabbed the girl and hit her. He then dragged her behind a nearby church, where he beat her until she was barely conscious. (Sitting there, listening, my heart began pounding. My neck and ears were beginning to burn with anger.) The big man, continued the Crown attorney, then threw the young girl's battered body on the cold, hard asphalt, took her clothing off, and raped her. (I was now on fire.)

The Jamaican turned his head my way but continued turning until he was facing the back of the courtroom. I glanced back and saw that the little girl was in the last row, seated beside her mother. The Jamaican actually smiled at her, a big smile, baring his teeth. He leered at her for a few seconds before he started to turn his head back around to face the judge. As he did so, his eyes met mine. We were only three feet apart. I snapped.

I unleashed a volley of spit from my mouth right into his face. The man reached to wipe the spit off as he rose from his chair. Neither of us being in restraints, I kicked him under his jaw as he rose. Now we were both standing. He put up his fists to fight, but he was too slow. I was already in mid-swing, connecting with his right cheekbone with a left hook, knocking him over the end of the prisoner's box wall. He went sprawling out onto the courtroom floor. I followed over top, landing on his prone body. I hit him in the face and head with another six to eight hard, solid punches before courtroom security tore me off of him.

The Jamaican was no longer smiling. He was in tears and yelling for help. I was placed back in the prisoner's box. He was made to stand over by an empty juror's box.

The court had fallen silent the moment I had spit in his face. The Crown attorney began to speak again. The judge had ignored the interruption, but now he interrupted the Crown. "I've heard enough," he said. He sentenced the rapist to seven years in a federal penitentiary, plus another year consecutive for the theft of the young girl's gold chain. He ordered him deported back to Jamaica, but not until he'd served the full term of his sentence. Then he told courtroom security, "Get that man out of my sight."

A court officer approached me and half-whispered, "You just made my day." I told her to put me in the same bullpen as the man when I was finished court, and I would make her week. "We can't do that. He's asked for protective custody away from you," she said.

My case was called next. The Crown attorney read out the allegations. She opposed bail being granted and began to expound upon my criminal history, then upon my character. The judge shut her down. "There is nothing you can tell me about this man that I don't already know. Sit down," he ordered her. Then he turned his gaze toward me. I knew I had just disrespected his courtroom. I honestly felt sorry about that. "Do you have any sureties available to you if I was to grant bail?" he asked. "Yes, Your Honour," I replied, nodding to the people in the body of the court who were there for just that reason. "Well, you are not going to need them," he said, "I'm granting you personal bail on all of your charges, and I want you to have a really good day.… Next case!" he said, looking to the Crown.

Court security motioned for me to rise and leave the box. As I stepped out, I heard a small commotion at the back of the courtroom. It was the little girl pulling away from her mother. "I don't care. I'm talking to him," she yelled to her mom. Then she made her way through the courtroom, up to where I stood. "Mister," she said, with tears in her eyes, "I want to thank you so, so much." I knew from listening that the girl was only fourteen, but up close, she looked more like twelve. She knew from the court proceedings that I was a convicted murderer, but in her eyes I was her "avenging angel." I told her, "I am so sorry about what happened to you. Sorry no one came by to help. But don't you let him ruin your life. There are a lot of good people in the world. That man, I'll look after him. Don't you worry about that. If I don't get him, I have friends that will." I then offered a soft smile, and said, "You are welcome." Courtroom security then took me back down to the bullpen.

In my past, I had been acquitted of very serious criminal charges, I had been found not guilty by a jury of my peers. I had charges dismissed and charges withdrawn. But I never had a better day in a courtroom in my life than this one. I felt so bad for the little girl. I never cared about bail being granted. I could not actually be released anyway. Not without seeing a federal parole board panel. (I would be exonerated of those break and enter charges, eventually.)

The following day, a major Toronto tabloid reported on the rapist's case and sentence. The reporter also made it a point to inform the public that the rapist had been served "prison justice," as well.

12

A Joyceville Journey

NOW THAT BAIL WAS no longer an issue, I was transferred to the assessment unit in Kingston, and from there sent over to Joyceville Institution to await a court date. I'd never served time in this archaic penitentiary just east of Kingston, but I knew a few of the prison hierarchy there, men who had cascaded down from Millhaven and Collins Bay. A couple were in the prisoners' committee. Right away, they got me a job as the Allied Coordinator in charge of all the institution's social groups. I also got to order and sell magazines from a large room near the gym called the Con Shop. It was a good job for me.

After I'd been there a week, I had to attend an agenda meeting with the committee and the administration. The following morning, the warden and his deputy came to see me in the Con Shop. They wanted to know who I was, because, they said, every time they'd posed a question during the meeting, the committee members all turned their heads to seek my approval or comment. I told them I was just a guy who'd been around the system longer than the others, and my opinion was respected by the committee.

The committee members were very good with me. They would share their hash or grass with me. We'd sit around reminiscing about our times together at Millhaven and listen to good music. There were two main problems within their office at that time. The most talked-about was the new directive being handed down from the national offices in charge of the penitentiaries — a new initiative that involved the integration of "special needs" offenders into normal population institutions. Everyone seemed upset and anxious about it. Basically, it would place prisoners amongst us who were convicted of offences we found repulsive or who had informed on other men. In the past, whenever one of these men found themselves accidently amongst us, they were assaulted quite quickly. We were now being told that they'd be placed beside us on purpose, and whoever assaulted a special needs offender would be transferred to higher security. Everyone in prison wants to be released as soon as possible, but not everyone possesses great anger-management skills. It was definitely a dilemma. The second problem was that there seemed to be a pretty significant leak amongst the group. It was felt that whatever they discussed, security was being made aware of. Being a newcomer, I had no idea what information was involved, and I cared even less. As it happened, though, not long after I was there, it was disclosed by a guard that the vice-chairman of the committee was the leak. The guard and vice-chairman had an argument over a separate issue just prior to the revelation. It was let out that he had a criminal record that contained sexual offences, and that this was the leverage that was being used so he'd inform on his fellow committee members and their associates.

Not long after this information was leaked, the vice-chairman took a pretty good thumping in his office. He went to the hospital that night. The next morning I was summoned to the security office. The guard in charge of security told me he knew I'd assaulted the man and that I'd be transferred as soon as he had one grain of evidence. I denied any involvement, but I was sure I was going to be transferred yet again for something that I hadn't done. That afternoon, the security officer found me at work and apologized. He was wrong, he said. I had no involvement. My associates on the committee were very happy their leak was gone.

Not long after, I was returned to Toronto East Detention Centre to face trial. In court, the Crown called witnesses, but none showed up. I wasn't surprised. The only one I knew he would have was the gay man who'd testified before, but after the preliminary judge had scolded him, I didn't think he'd want a repeat performance. The break and enter charges were dismissed.

Now, I just had to address the lone drug possession charge. I had to go to the Old City Hall bullpen for that. When I was summoned, two officers took me out of the bullpen, handcuffed me behind my back, and walked me through the main floor of Old City Hall to the elevator. When the doors opened, I saw California sitting on a bench outside the courtroom with one of his friends, an exotic dancer, or stripper if you will. She got up right away and approached me. As she went to kiss me, the cop on my right pushed her sideways and I saw a plastic-wrapped piece of hash go flying over my left shoulder, landing on the floor behind me. I couldn't pick it up, being hand-cuffed from behind. As I turned back, she jumped up again and kissed me hard. I turned my attention to California as the police were growling at her. He looked at me, and then looked where I was motioning. He spotted the package on the floor behind me. He got up and grabbed his friend and they both headed for the stairwell. Just then, one of the cops noticed the package and yelled for her to stop. California had her by the arm, and they ran down the steps and out of view. A number of uniformed officers gave chase.

I was stood against the wall outside the courtroom. The detective in charge of my case, after finding out what had happened, threatened to charge me for possession of the hash on the floor, but the escorting officer informed him I never ever really had possession of it. I smiled at him. Then the escort told him I'd received a second kiss, and it was believed I had something in my mouth. The detective ordered me to open my mouth. After swallowing hard, I complied. He was upset. All the cops standing there were upset. They brought me in the courtroom. The court, unaware of the altercation that had just transpired outside, began to hear my case. The Crown wanted another year remand. He informed the court the cop involved in the seizure of the hash over a year prior had just been involved in a high-speed chase, hit an elderly bicyclist, killing the man, and then had crashed his cruiser into a building, injuring himself. The court seemed as though they were about to acquiesce to the request, so I called the lawyer over and told her to make a deal right there. I was not about to serve any further sentence for a measly piece of hash, and I was sure the intellect of the parole board members would understand. I pled guilty for a three-hundred-dollar fine, or, upon failure of payment, fifteen days in jail. The judge ordered this term to be consecutive to any sentence I might be already serving. My lawyer told him he could not do that. "Give me one damn good reason why my sentence shouldn't be consecutive?" he barked. "Because he's already serving a 'life' term, Your Honour," she whined. He turned to me and said, "And that's the only reason. Three hundred, or fifteen days concurrent." I smiled at him and told him not to worry, his fine would be paid that day, and it was.

After being processed at the East Detention, I was taken to a transfer range instead of the pen range, to wait until a staff member was available to take me over. Not long after, a short, elderly Italian man came in, his clothes covered in cement dust. He'd been arrested the night before and had bail set that morning. I knew this because he sat at the same table as I did, and was talking to another prisoner. The other prisoner told him he could use one of the phones on the range to contact his wife, and then he told the man how to have her and his lawyer come over with the deed to their home to bail him out. The Italian thanked him and went to the phone. He hadn't been on one minute when a tall black man walked up beside him and took a full swing with an open hand, hitting him in the right ear. He landed a few feet away on his butt. "I'm the corridor man here," the black man barked at the injured man. "Don't touch my phone." Then with a smile, he grabbed the dangling phone and hung it up.

The Italian was in pain, teary-eyed, and full of apologies to the bigger man. About five minutes later, the black man made a phone call. I waited until he began his conversation, then got up, walked over, and, with a full swing, slapped him hard in the right ear, landing him on his butt a few feet away. I picked up the phone and told the person on the other end that their friend would have to call them back later. I grabbed the corridor man off the floor and marched him over to a corner of the range by his sore ear. I had him sit facing the corner and told him not to move one inch, to think about why he was sitting there. I growled in his ear, asking him who he thought he was not allowing someone to gain their freedom just so he could chit-chat. The older Italian was clearly afraid and didn't want to use the phone. It was easy to see he was not used to jail, or the violence within. He told me he didn't want any trouble. I told him he'd better get on the phone and call his wife, or the corridor man was going to be going to the hospital. The black man told him to please use the phone, and so he did. I told the corridor man to shut his mouth and keep facing the wall.

When the guard showed up to take me upstairs to the pen range an hour or so later, I told the corridor man he could move from the corner, but that I would be back down if I heard of him mistreating anyone. I was pleased with myself over that incident.

I was not on the pen range very long before I was transferred back to Joyceville. The city jails do not like to house lifers, as there is too high a risk that some meathead will make the mistake of bothering a dangerous one, and all lifers are perceived as dangerous. After the classification officer at Joyceville saw the outcome of all my charges — the three-hundred-dollar paid fine — he immediately had me apply to be transferred back to Beaver Creek work camp. I was granted the transfer and reacquainted myself with the camp. I had few problems there this time. I was very happy about that.

When I saw the parole board there, I was re-released on my full parole, and my oldest brother came to pick me up. It was a clear day as we drove back home. He apologized to me for not being able to assist me financially. He told me he thought he would have been able to, but that him and his three cronies were still waiting for a fence to pay them for a score they'd pulled the month previous. It was worth a hundred thousand dollars to them. The fence had been paid, but he kept telling the boys there was heat on him, so he didn't want to touch the money. My brother and his friends were to meet the man that very afternoon. I listened with interest. He also told me about a man he had resided with in a West End apartment who had terrorized his daughter, my niece. I did not like to hear that at all. I asked him if he wanted me to tag along for his meeting. One of his cronies was a friend of mine I wanted to see, and he'd been the brains behind the score.

When I arrived home, I dropped my effects on the living room floor, gave my wife and daughter a kiss, then told them I'd be back shortly. Cher was stunned. I gave her the two hundred dollars I had left the prison with — all the money I had to my name.

My brother and I went to the restaurant in Mississauga to meet up with his boys and the fence. After seeing my old friend, and meeting his new ones, I excused myself and sat at a stool at the bar. I was sure any fence would not welcome a stranger at the table.

As I sat there, an Italian fellow I knew from the Don Jail strolled in and came right up to me. I didn't like the guy. I'd had to collect money off him once for my friend Downtown when he'd tried to welch on his payment. He was very congenial, though, and we talked for a minute. He told me to hang around and we'd talk when he concluded his business with the four men seated at one of the tables. He pointed to my brother. I couldn't believe it; he was the fence. I took him out to the parking lot right then and we had a discussion. He hopped in his vehicle and left.

When I came back in, my brother signalled me over and asked what was going on. I told him I had a prior relationship with the man, and that he'd be returning within forty minutes with all of their money. The gang couldn't believe it. They'd been trying to get their payment off the Italian for weeks. My brother believed it, though.

After the Italian returned with their money, the four were so happy they each gave me twenty-five hundred dollars. Then I was happy. My brother drove me home, where I gave Cher the ten thousand dollars. She was happy, and forgave me for running right out. We spent the night together at home. Though my infant daughter was acting strangely toward me, I knew she'd remember her father in time.

The next morning, a man arrived looking for my brother. My wife had met him previously with my brother while I was incarcerated. He stayed and had a coffee. My buddy from Kingston, Big Hal, came in. He was a three-hundred-pound giant of a man. The stranger told me he used to live with my brother and another fellow out in Mississauga. Right away, I knew he was speaking of the man my brother had told me had terrorized my niece. I asked if he still lived there. He did, and so did the other guy. I told him we were taking a drive. I wanted to meet his roommate. Big Hal came along after I told him why.

When we arrived, my brother's friend gave me his apartment key. He didn't want to go up. He wanted no part in the confrontation. Big Hal and I went up, but no one was there. After looking around, we left. I had Big Hal take me to a nearby bar. As soon as we entered, I saw an old friend at the bar talking with a stranger. I went up, shook his hand, gave him a hug, and began to idly chat. After a couple of minutes, I asked him, since he lived in the area, if he'd heard of the man I was looking for. It turned out to be the stranger beside him. I asked the man to have a seat at a table with me, told him who I was, and about the story I'd heard with regard to him and my niece. Right away, he became very nervous and offered to buy me a drink. I declined, saying I'd buy him one. Then I placed a rough gold nugget weighing approximately fifteen grams on the table in front of him. He froze, his eyes widened, and his mouth dropped open. He knew it was the nugget he had sitting on the end table beside his bed. I told him he was very fortunate not to have been home, or we would not be having this conversation.

Big Hal, who stood behind him, now took the 9mm handgun out of his coat pocket and pressed it against the man's temple. He looked at me and asked, "Can I shoot him now?" The man was in tears, and pleaded with me not to let Big Hal shoot him. He swore he had not terrorized my niece, and asked to speak with my brother. I got him on the phone. Big Hal kept asking to shoot the man, and I just kept telling him to hang on for a minute. After the conversation, the man handed me back the phone. "Let him go," my brother said.

I told the man he was lucky, but only for now. I hadn't talked with my niece yet, but I would be getting back to him.

Big Hal and I left and drove back to my home in the East End. My brother was there when I arrived, and he was irate. He started to yell at Big Hal, but I stepped in and told him Big Hal had only done what I told him to, and if my brother had a problem with that, he could deal with me. He told me he didn't appreciate me sticking my nose in his business. I told him he shouldn't have mentioned the incident to me if he didn't want me to react. He knew how protective I was of my family and friends. He should have known I wouldn't let the slight go unanswered. He told me it was his business, and he was going to handle it by making the man pay money for his indiscretions. That made me upset. I told him I did not care about money, and I really didn't. That was a major difference in our traits. He was so mad he ordered me out of his house. I had to remind him that he was standing in mine, but I also told him if he was truly upset with me, I had a big backyard we could go into to settle it. He left.

His former friend left his apartment and moved out to B.C., I'm told, the same day he met me.

One of my brother's partners was in the business of "short-term" loans involving large amounts of money for high interest rates to high-risk clients. He solicited me on a few occasions to convince people late on their returns to pay their bill. I was paid huge commissions. But I would make sure of two things before each collection: One, that it was a legitimate loan. And two, that the people had the money to pay. I knew from my discussions with other collectors I had met in jail that these were the two basic tenets if one was to be successful. Otherwise, the people being approached would feel they had no option but to involve law enforcement; and that would not end well. Especially if one were on parole. On my last collection, I was given the address for a man named Dino. He owed upwards of eighty thousand dollars. When I arrived, a middle-aged Italian lady told me her husband was out for the day, but he would be available the following afternoon. When I came back the next day and knocked on the door, I got the surprise of my life. When the door opened, I was staring into the chest of a giant of a man. When he confirmed his identity, I did not hesitate. I hit him under the jaw as hard as I could, knocking him back and to the floor. I kicked him in the head, and then leaned over to tell him to pay his bills. I left.

After going for lunch and settling my nerves (I had almost crapped myself when I saw how big he was), I went to see the loan shark. In his office, I told him I was not at all pleased that he hadn't warned me about the potential physical threat his client posed. He laughed, telling me if it had been easy, he wouldn't have needed my services. Then he handed me my commission. He told me when Dino got off the floor, he went to his bank and had his payment placed into the loan shark's account. I quit after that.

13

Movies and Mayhem

AT THIS TIME, I WENT to work for the film industry. Rooster's friend Chuck was a staunch union member in IATSE, the International Alliance of Theatrical Stage Employees, and had worked in that field for years. He had me fill out an application with his name attached, and in no time at all I began getting called to work a couple of days a week. I'd assist people setting up props for the TV series *RoboCop* and *Road to Avonlea*. It was easy work, and the money was more than satisfactory. I'd probably actually work only two hours a day and spend the rest of the time sitting around the sets, but I'd get paid for the full ten or twelve hours. Over the next two months, I worked on other projects, too, including *Canadian Bacon* and *Johnny Mnemonic*. I'd find myself sitting at tables, eating catered food besides the likes of Al Waxman. (He and I hit it off pretty good, but then he had no idea of my criminal history.)

My older brother eventually came back around. One day we drove out to meet a few of his friends in a strip mall near Pearson Airport. When we walked into one of the stores, two men were in the waiting room. My brother took me into an office and introduced me to his friend behind the desk. I went back to the waiting room while they had their talk. When my brother came out, he introduced me to the two men and began conversing with them. I left and went back out to the car. My brother soon came out, told me to come back in the store, that he was going to be a few minutes yet. I told him the French guy seemed okay to me, but the Italian was either an informant, or, even worse, an undercover. He told me I was crazy, and that he had both men checked out. I told him to check again, but in the meantime, I'd stay in the car. He went back in.

On the drive home, I told him never to bring the Italian around me. I told him I could tell that man was well aware of who I was even before I met him, and that only made sense in my mind if he was some type of law enforcement working a case that involved me. My brother told me again that I was crazy. I said fine; just keep him away from me. In the next month, I saw the Italian twice, and each time I walked away as soon as he appeared.

One morning, I received a phone call from my little friend Heath, an older man in his fifties who'd been a long-time heroin user and trafficker. He asked me to stop by his apartment. He had a serious problem. I drove directly over. He was in his apartment with his tow truck–driving son and the son's new old lady, who was a stripper. Heath told me that his stash had been ripped off the night before. He couldn't figure it out, as the only ones who knew where his stash was were him and his son. I thought about it for a few minutes. I was pretty sure I had figured out the security breach. Privately, I told Heath he was going to have his son drive him to the West End so he could pick up more drugs. Heath told me he had no money for that. The rip-off had left him broke. I told him not to worry. I told him to just take his son for an hour drive, but leave the stripper with me. I told Heath to tell her she was being left to keep an eye on me so that I didn't rip him off for anything in the apartment. Heath and his son left.

I sat beside the stripper and began to talk. After five minutes, I called Heath on his cellphone and told them to come back to the apartment. He and I had to go somewhere. When they got back, I told Heath the stripper had been with his son when he went to the stash, and she had told a friend where his stash was and how to rip them off. I told his son to stay with the girl, and not to let her make any calls or leave the apartment. I told him his father was depending on him, and so was I. The girl was frightened but unharmed.

Heath and I went to an apartment building in the East End. When I knocked, there was no answer, so I left Heath at the front door and I went outside the building. A minute later, I unlocked the apartment door from the inside and let Heath in. We made a drink and sat to await the tenant's arrival.

Two hours later, a big long-haired biker came strolling through the front door and down the hallway. He spied Heath right away, and growled, "What the fuck are you doing in my house?" Heath said he was there to get his drugs back. Heath weighed less than a hundred pounds. As the man approached, he noticed me sitting across the room in his La-Z-Boy chair. I held a drink in my left hand and my right arm was draped down over the side of the chair. "Who the fuck are you?" he demanded. I told him I was Heath's friend, and we weren't there for conversation. I told him I had talked to the stripper, so he had just better give Heath his supply back. "I don't have fuck all, and both of you had better get out of my house right now," he screamed. I lifted my right arm and fired a bullet from Heath's .38 revolver across the living room and into the drywall within inches of his left ear. "Are you going to give him his supply back, or do I have to shoot you?" I asked, adding nonchalantly, "I really don't care either way."

The man took Heath down to his bedroom and gave him back the drugs. I told Heath to wait for me in the car. I made the man and myself a drink, and I explained to him who I was. I told him to go to his clubhouse and ask his brothers who I was. I told him not to bother Heath, or the stripper, or anyone else I knew, or I'd be back, and he'd already seen how easy it was for me to find him and get into his house. Heath never had any trouble from the man again.

I took Heath home, then I made my way back to my place. It was late afternoon, and Cher would be wondering where I'd been. She knew I had the day off of work. I pulled up in front of the house and went through the backyard and up the steps to our second-floor apartment. Cher was in the living room watching TV with our four-year-old daughter. Kelly had gotten used to me being back home by this time, and she reached for me as soon as she saw me. I picked her up off her mother's lap and sat on the couch, putting her on my lap. I'd started to joke around with her when I heard the first loud bang downstairs. I knew that sound; the door being kicked in. I set Kelly on the couch and headed back down the hallway. I heard a second bang, and knew it was the other downstairs door being caved in. I crossed the kitchen and knocked the back door open.

Out on the back porch, I looked down and saw a biker standing in the backyard, holding a handgun. I charged toward him down the stairs.

As I turned at the midway landing, the biker pulled out a badge and screamed, "Police!" I stopped dead. The threat to my family was over. He approached me, telling me to back up the stairs slowly. Other undercovers came around the corner of the backyard and others poured out of my in-laws' back door and joined their counterpart in subduing and arresting me. They had me lie on the porch while they searched and handcuffed me. Then they stood me up and marched me back through the kitchen, down the hallway, and into the living room. As I came through the door, I saw a big black cop in a bulletproof vest holding a shotgun on my four-year-old. I told him to take his gun off her or I would put him through the living-room window. The lead detective screamed at the man to take his weapon off the child.

They sat me down on the couch beside Cher and the lead detective said he had a warrant to search the premises. I told him to be my guest. I knew the house was clean. Within two minutes, he came back in with a fellow undercover and a large metal tool box. I looked at the box, then at Cher. She had tears in her eyes.

The lead detective informed me they'd just arrested my older brother a few blocks away for trafficking methamphetamine, and they'd arrest me, my wife, and her brother (who lived downstairs) with the same as soon as they opened the locked box. A cop came in with huge bolt cutters. Inside the box were weigh scales and a large bag of meth. The cop told me my brother had left it there that afternoon, just before he went to make his deal with the men he didn't know were undercovers. I was stunned, angry. I looked at Cher and told her everything would be okay. The cops had waited until I came home to hit the house. Their informant had told them he wouldn't testify against my brother if I were free, and so they'd waited. Other police had raided a rural mansion west of Toronto, where they seized lab equipment and a couple of handguns. They believed my brother had made the meth in a lab somewhere, but were unsure of its actual location.

We were all taken to the nearest police station and placed in cells. The following morning we were transported to Old City Hall to be arraigned. Cher and her brother were granted bail. My brother and I would appear later and be given detention orders denying us bail. With both of us being parolees, it didn't matter. We were transported to the Don Jail, where we were processed, dressed in jailhouse blues, and placed on a court cell range until it was determined which range we'd be housed on.

Since we hadn't landed on the court cell range until late afternoon, we were there for the four o'clock suppertime. I wasn't hungry, so I called Cher, who'd just arrived home. The first thing I needed to know was that our daughter was fine. Upon our arrest, the police had let her be placed with a neighbour until my sister-in-law could make it over.

As I was on the phone, my brother grabbed his yellow food tray and sat at a table nearby. I watched as he unravelled the paper napkin that contained his plastic cutlery. As he was doing this methodically, a young black male walked over, picked up my brother's food tray, and headed down to the back of the range. My brother was stunned. He looked down at the empty space where his tray had once sat and then he looked over at me. I broke out laughing. "Welcome to the new Don Jail," I told him.

He hadn't been in this institution in a long time, and was unaware of the new culture that existed in many of the jail's areas. He got up and went down to where the food thief had just sat down. My brother slapped him in the side of the head, retrieved his food tray, and came back up the range to his seat at the table. I kept talking with Cher, and she asked what was so funny. I told her I'd tell her in a minute. I was watching for what I was sure would follow. The young black male had gone over to a group of his associates, rubbing his ear, and now they were looking at my brother. After a minute, they made their way up the range. As they approached him, I said, "Hey, guys." They looked over at me. "That's my brother. You know, same father, same mother. You might want to think about what you want to do next, eh." They retreated back down the range.

An hour or so later, we were placed on a regular range. There were a large number of black men, but most treated us with respect, and we reciprocated. Only one man really gave me a hard time about using the phone, so after arguing and finding no other solution, I finally relented and beat him up. That was the only way to make him understand he did not own the phone.

A week later, we were taken back to court. As I entered the court, I saw the black cop from the house with his back to me. I shouldered him hard into the wall. When he spun around, his eyes met mine. "Threaten any more kids with your shotgun lately, asshole?" I snarled. He didn't answer.

When I got into the prisoner's box, I called the lead detective over. I asked him how much experience he had on his job. He told me a great many years. I told him he must have dealt with enough criminals to know my wife and her brother were not criminals. He nodded. I told him I didn't care that he had involved me in my brother's case, but if he continued against my wife and her brother, I was going to involve his family as soon as I was released, no matter how long that took. I gave him my word on that. He knew I was deadly serious. He went and talked to the Crown. All charges were dismissed against the two civilians in our case. He told me he just didn't want them to take ownership of the drugs if they weren't charged. I promised him that was not a concern. They didn't even know what meth was.

When we returned to the Don Jail, we were placed on the pen range of 4C south. I wasn't surprised by the decision to relocate us. The previous range that housed us, 4A south, had been an unruly environment when we arrived, and we had our disagreements in the beginning. The situations that arose had been remedied to our satisfaction, such as the noise level and the telephone access, but some of the senior residents of 4A south were not too pleased with the changes we effected. They'd been happier when they were running the range. They still were, only with some trepidation. I suspected they had expressed their feelings to the jail staff they were familiar with. It didn't matter to me. My brother and I were both happier with our new accommodations amongst some of our old associates.

My brother had a new lawyer. I knew he had burned a bridge in some fashion with the Lion, but he'd never talk to me about that. Knowing my brother, he'd probably opted to terminate the relationship because of financial obligations that he'd made but not honoured. I didn't believe I was in any danger of a conviction on these new charges, and since I didn't wish to cause a rift with my older brother, I allowed his lawyer to arrange a lawyer for me. I didn't realize until the preliminary hearings that my new defender was a Bay Street lawyer with zero experience in criminal cases. His forte to this point had been corporate law. It would fall upon me to open his eyes to the criminal court system.

The first cop to take the stand was one of the undercovers who'd executed the search at my house. I told my lawyer the man was lying. He assured me the cop couldn't lie under oath. I chuckled. The lawyer was serious. He was greener than I'd imagined. I told him to ask the cop a certain question I knew would be answered with a yes, then told him to ask another to which I knew his answer would be no. The lawyer told me both could not be true. I told him that was exactly right. The lawyer did as I requested. He asked both questions in a roundabout manner to the witness. I was right. He caught the cop lying. The lawyer looked at me in shocked disbelief. "Now," I said, "I'll show you as each one takes the stand that every one of them will lie to you."

This lawyer was nothing like the Lion, who always expected non-truths. He was a seasoned veteran in the criminal court arena. He caught lies like a frog catching flies. Most of the drug squad police I encountered had a propensity to slant their testimonies to secure a conviction, and thereby pollute their evidence. A few would just outright lie while holding the Bible in one hand and wiping a tear from their eye with the other. The new lawyer had a totally different outlook on the taking of the oath by the time the week was done.

I didn't have him attack the second officer, as he was the one I'd mistaken for a biker in my backyard. He told the judge in all his experience on the force, that day was the only time he had ever seen an unarmed man rush toward him and his loaded revolver. My actions had unnerved him for a few seconds, but then he realized he didn't have his badge showing. He acknowledged that I had a young wife and daughter in the house. The judge gave me a look of appreciation as a human being, and as a man, for trying to keep them out of harm's way.

The next witness was the Italian I'd warned my brother about. He took the stand and immediately identified himself as a paid police informant. It had been his occupation for the past five years. He testified as to the plan and execution of a speed manufacturing operation, and his involvement in setting my brother up to manufacture and to sell the product to the undercovers. My brother looked over at me, but I didn't have the heart to tell him I had told him so. The Crown attorney was more than satisfied with the evidence the informant provided against my brother, but then asked his chief witness to zero in on me. The witness testified he'd seen me twice, and both times I'd left as soon as he appeared. In fact, his testimony would pretty much exonerate me of any involvement or wrongdoing.

Because we attended court daily, we had to stay in the court cells at the Don. It would take the corridor men only a minute to learn we were experienced prisoners. The first night, I lay on the bed as my older brother stood at the cell door watching the hockey game on TV. Halfway through the game, a young black man changed the channel to BET (Black Entertainment Television). Men started to voice their displeasure, including my brother. The younger man told everyone to shut up. He was in his prime, all muscled up and just back from the Guelph reformatory with a huge attitude. He came up and told my brother to be quiet. I got up and exchanged places at the cell door. I told the man to change the channel back to the hockey game. He talked to the corridor man, and then informed me I was not on the pen range now. I informed him the pen range was not a place, but a state of mind, and when the doors opened in the morning, I was going to hospitalize him. I told him to enjoy his music, and then I went back to lying down. Moments later the hockey game came back on.

The following day in court, the next few cops testified that they had followed my brother to my house one day. He'd picked me up to go with him while he reported for his parole downtown. They'd followed us until he dropped me back off at home. My brother had wanted me with him that day to see if he was being followed. I told him I hadn't seen any tails, but now here were the cops testifying as to our route that day, including the side streets and laneways he'd driven. My brother was giving me the business in my ear the more he heard. I kept saying I didn't know how, I never noticed them. Finally, the last cop to testify on the surveillance team disclosed that they had followed the car in a light aircraft. He'd been radioing our location to the ground team, who were taking notes but keeping their cars out of view. There was no way I could have seen that tail, not without a sunroof. My brother relaxed his verbal abuse.

At the end of the preliminary hearing, my brother would take a plea on his charges. Mine were withdrawn. When court was over, the lead detective came to see me down in the bullpen. I was surprised. He asked if him and I were all right. I knew he was concerned about my previous threat, but he'd done the right thing in dismissing my wife and brother-in-law, so I told him of course we were all right. I was so glad it was over.

My brother and I were transferred out quickly to the Millhaven Assessment Unit. He would be classified for Collins Bay. I had a parole hearing in Millhaven, and after the board understood what had happened, they reinstated my full parole. Cher was there to take me home.

When we arrived back at my in-laws' house, we went in to say hello. They were surprised to see me home so soon. My mother-in-law said the police had been there earlier that day looking for me. Not just regular police, but CSIS — Canada's spy agency. I was shocked, and couldn't understand what business they could possibly have with me. Not only that, but I didn't even know I was being released until that morning.

She gave me the card the police had left, and I phoned the detective. She wanted to see me the following morning, and we made arrangements to meet at Old City Hall. After the call, I went upstairs to relax. Cher came up and told me her parents and siblings were traumatized by the police incursion of their home and the subsequent annihilation of the ground floor during their search. Her parents didn't want me to reside at their house any longer. They were nervous the police would strike again with me being home.

I phoned one of my sisters who owned her own home nearby — a two-storey four-bedroom detached house with front and backyard. She lived there with her one daughter, and was more than happy to accommodate Cher, Kelly, and me. When I told the in-laws I understood their anxiety, and thanked them for their past support, they were relieved. They became very upset, though, when they realized Cher and Kelly were moving out with me. I couldn't believe that they'd think otherwise. I wouldn't leave my family behind, no matter how welcome they were at this residence. I told them they were more than welcome to visit us anytime at my sister's. We moved that very day.

The next day I went with Cher to see my parole officer, and afterward we walked over to see my Bay Street lawyer, whose office was nearby. He was happy I'd been freed. He told me a friend of his had just opened up a metal manufacturing plant, and that I could secure work there. I told him of my Old City Hall rendezvous (with CSIS), so he attended with Cher and I. The detective showed me pictures of men they had labelled terrorists. Actually, they had arrested them all. She asked if I knew any of them. I told her I knew them all. They had put them on 4C south while I was housed there. How could I not have met them? My lawyer assured them I was many things, but not a subversive, or any type of threat to my own country. I was amazed at how ludicrous this sounded. CSIS was satisfied, and they apologized for inconveniencing me and my mother-in-law.

The following morning, I went to the metal factory, talked with the owner, and began work as a labourer for a measly eight dollars an hour. It was hard work, but it was honest, and it kept me too busy to be involved with any of my old criminal associates. I was determined not to involve myself with anyone in any criminal activity. I wouldn't ask anyone for financial assistance. I just wanted to make it in life legitimately.

I worked five and a half days a week and it would take me an hour and a half on public transit to get to and from work. The factory had just been gutted from the previous owners, so there was a twenty-foot-high, twenty-foot-diameter pile of garbage. My first job was to separate the metal, wood, and paper garbage into three large metal bins. I filled each of these more than twice before the pile started to disappear. After the pile was gone, I was placed on bending metal pieces manually in jigs, and then on pressing machines. The owners would not pay me on a "piecework" salary, as they said I would have cost their company too much money. After I'd been through every other machine, I was put to work on the high-speed grinders. That was a difficult job, and one that took a lot of care and attention. After six months, I was told I would be promoted to the foreman's position in the fabrication side of the plant. When the position became available, though, the owners brought in an experienced worker from another metal company who they had a prior relationship with. I was not happy about that. In lieu of their decision, they gave me a raise and promoted me to foreman in the shipping and receiving department. They told me when the one owner returned to his native France, I'd be placed in charge of the entire factory as plant manager. That sounded good to me. (Cher was happy. She was pregnant again.)

I would unload all the trucks that came in with the raw metal and load the trucks with finished product. When the French owner left, his one partner brought in another man from another company to act in the position of plant manager. I was deeply disappointed and angry again. The owner took me aside and told me the new man was a "genius," and that he could not forego the opportunity to employ him. I asked some workers who had worked at other companies if they knew the new man. They did. Both previous companies that he had been employed at went bankrupt. They also told me the new man was the cousin of the boss's wife.

I continued in my capacity as foreman in shipping, but I also would see the new guy standing around each day doing nothing to help the company or its workers. I slowly hoarded away the nickels and dimes until I could buy a cheap old used car. (That took me several months.) In the meantime, Cher and I moved out of my sister's with our daughter and rented the ground-floor of a duplex with a small backyard and garage. For the first time in the longest time, life for me was normal.

I'd still have the odd incident occur, though. One day, after we got the car, I was driving down Donlands Avenue, taking our normal route to visit Cher's parents, when I noticed a car that had been coming up the avenue on the other side veer up onto the sidewalk just in front of a young boy about ten years old. The car almost hit the kid. Once he saw who the driver was, the boy turned and started running as fast as he could down the street toward the school on the east side. The driver, a grey-haired, middle-aged man, exited the vehicle and gave chase. I stopped my car in traffic, putting on the emergency flashers, jumped out, and gave chase. The boy made it up the wide steps to the school, but as he reached the doors, the man reached the boy. He spun the child around and raised his arm to slap him. I grabbed the man's wrist. He turned to see me standing there. "Let him go," I ordered. "He hit my grandson," the man said. I told him I didn't care and to unhand the child right away. He looked me in the eyes, then let go of the boy. He turned and went back down the steps toward his vehicle. I told the boy to go inside and have the principal call his parents to pick him up. I told him to make sure he told someone in authority inside the school what had just happened to him. He said he would. I went back to my car. Cher was crying. I thought she was upset I'd gotten involved, but she said she was just so proud that I had.

One late morning at work, two transports pulled in to our loading bays. The boss came to tell me he needed them filled by the three o'clock buzzer. It was a Friday, and three p.m. was quitting time. I asked him how I was supposed to do that. He told me to look after the one, the plant manager and city driver would look after the other. So I set to work. By one p.m. I had half my trailer filled. I noticed the other two men had only loaded ten feet of theirs. I went over and expressed my concern. The plant manager told me to just concern myself with my own transport. By two thirty, I'd finished loading my transport. The other two men were headed into the company bathroom to wash up, but they'd only completed a third of their transport.

The two owners then came down into the shipping area. The one owner, cousin by marriage to the plant manager, demanded to know why both transports were not complete. The drivers would be arriving for their loads within the half hour. I told the boss to ask his cousin. He'd put him in charge of the one transport.

All the workers were in the area now, getting ready to punch their time cards. The owner started to scream at the top of his lungs at me, that he had put me in charge of shipping, and if his wife's cousin did not do his job, it was my job to do it for him. I told him he'd hired the "genius," and if things were messed up, it was his own fault.

The other owner pulled me aside. I really liked the older Italian boss. He told me he'd work with me filling the unfinished transport and would pay me a couple of hundred dollars cash out of his own pocket if I would stay to help him. The transports were new customers and he didn't want to lose their business. So, I stayed as a favour to him. I was still very upset with the other boss, though. I'd never had a grown man scream at me in front of a crowd without having a physical altercation, ever. When I arrived home, I discussed the situation with Cher and other family members. I was not used to the treatment I was receiving from the one boss. They all thought I should quit and find employment elsewhere. I agreed. I did not go in to work that Saturday, as I normally did. I spent the day contemplating what I should do about this company, and with my future.

Monday morning, I arrived at work wearing a suit. I picked up my workboots, tools, and gloves. I said goodbye to most of the employees. They were upset at my leaving. Most of them were new Canadians from South America, and I had helped each of them out at one time or another, when they had fallen behind in their quota or had not been feeling well on a certain day. I'd gained their respect. I went into the boss's office and told him I could no longer work for him. I told him he knew my parole situation, and that was the only reason I had not beaten the crap out of him when he had raised his voice to me in front of a crowd. I told him I wanted him to lay me off so that I could collect my unemployment insurance while I looked for another job. He wouldn't do that. He wanted me to take a few days off, and continue to work for him. I told him he had twice promised me positions and then given them to less-capable men because of his prior relationships. I felt I had earned those positions and been disrespected. So I quit.

I was happy to hear a couple of years later that the company had floundered, then sunk. I did feel sorry for the Italian partner, though. The business could have been a success.

|||||

In September of 1993, Cher gave birth to our son, Adam. I'd decided to go back to the film industry to try to get employment, so I sat around the house for a couple of weeks, going out once in a while to talk with potential employers. None were too pleased with my criminal record or my parole status. Cher was getting frustrated. Her family, her father in particular, started commenting on my inability to provide for my own family. They became very vocal on this matter, and I was getting very frustrated with life. Finally, I got a call for a day's work on the set of the *Road to Avonlea* series. Ten days later, I got another day's work. This was taking too long for me. I had no other options, though. I had stayed away from my past criminal associates since my release, but now I was starting to think I may have no choice other than to make money with them. Cher was more frustrated than ever, and she would not stop bitching at me. Finally, I'd had enough. I felt as though I were a total failure as a "normal civilian" working a straight life. I snapped. Cher and I had a long and loud argument that was very unsettling for the children, and I left.

I went downtown and hung out with Bernie. He was estranged from his wife, as well. At this time I knew I had really screwed up. I was now back in the criminal subculture. The King of Hearts was on a tear down in these parts, as were a couple of my other former associates. They were running various drug distribution centres. I was definitely deep within one of the worst depressions of my life. Although I was not dealing, I was certainly in a foul mood, and not a day went by that some guy did not do something to make me angry and incur my wrath.

The whores, however, were all very nice to me. I was offered "free rides" from different ones every day. They'd buy me food or anything else I wanted just to keep my company. My criminal reputation had preceded me into these neighbourhoods. Many of them would tell me I didn't fit into their lifestyle, and they were right, but I had nowhere else I particularly wanted to be in my depression.

One day, one of the whores asked me to accompany her over to a dealer's apartment. When the dealer answered the door, he grabbed the woman by her jacket, pulled her into the apartment, and slammed her hard into the wall, knocking her to the floor. I stepped into the apartment while punching him in the face and knocking him onto the floor beside her. Three men came up yelling some slurs in an English/Jamaican patois, and pulling out handguns. There was an abundance of firearms in this subculture. I looked at them. "You didn't like that?" They stuck their gun barrels close to my head and threatened me. I helped their friend back up off the floor and then punched him in the face again, sending him back down. Now they were threatening to shoot me. I was smiling at them and telling them to go ahead. Since they seemed to be so hesitant, I picked their friend up once again. Before he could be punched again, he asked me to hang on a minute. His nose was bleeding profusely. He apologized for slamming the whore into the wall. He told his friends to leave. He had just discovered they were of no use to him anyways. They wouldn't shoot.

He told me the whore had gotten some drugs off him, but failed to come back to pay him. She told him she'd been arrested right after she left his place, and this was the first opportunity she had to see him, and also, she had his money. He apologized for assaulting her before asking what had happened. He was most interested in me. Not only had I almost knocked him unconscious, but he had never seen a man with guns stuck to his head laughing at the triggermen. The whore told him I was not the average person. She told him I was the man the King of Hearts called when he was in trouble. The Jamaican hired me on the spot to hang around his apartment and make sure he didn't get robbed by other dealers. I had nothing better to do, so I stayed for a few weeks with this Jamaican and his entourage of hookers. He finally got himself arrested downtown. I really could care less. I would just go over to another associate's apartment. It was no big deal to me. I was being cared for at whichever place I stayed.

During a stay at a friend's apartment, a very striking woman came in. Ann had just been released from a provincial reformatory for women. She was in terrific shape. I had seen her once before, but only for a second. Now, she was standing in front of me and asking if anyone knew how to drive a car. A couple of the guys volunteered, but she turned to me and asked if I'd drive her out to the West End to her friend's apartment. I told her I could, but I had no licence. She didn't care, so off we went.

When we arrived at the apartment, there was no one there. After we'd spent some time together there, getting to know each other, her friend still hadn't showed up. We returned to where we had been previously. Ann would not leave my side for the next month unless she was out "hustling." She did not share that part of her life with me, and I didn't want to know. She'd confide everything else to me, though.

One day she came into A1's place. A1 was one of the finest pickpockets I ever met. She would get into a car with a "john," and two blocks later get out, telling him he wasn't her type. And she would have the man's bankroll in her hip pocket. I'd watch in amazement. The entire episode would last less than a minute. Anyways, Ann wanted to know if I had any money. I told her I only had fifty on me. I had a friend who owned a restaurant/bar in the west Lakeshore area, and I was meeting him late morning to get some money. She told me she was off to see a "sugar daddy" and would meet me at the Lakeshore bar.

A1 came with me in a taxi to the bar, which was operated by my friend's kid brother. He was upset. Their father had just suffered a heart attack and his brother had to leave to go to the hospital. I asked the kid if the brother had left me any money, and he told me that he hadn't. I asked him to call his brother on his cellphone. However, the cellphone was on the shelf below and it started to ring. My friend had forgotten his phone at the bar in his haste. The younger brother would not part with any money without his brother's prior approval. I understood that. I called another man I knew who lived nearby, and he told me his in-laws were visiting; they were just beginning to eat a barbeque lunch, but that he would come over in a couple of hours. That was not very good for me. After the taxi fare and the drinks A1 and I had ordered, our finances were less than twenty dollars.

Ann soon showed up in a taxi. Her sugar daddy had not been home, and she needed twenty dollars to pay the cab driver. A1 immediately took the lead and said we were returning to her place in St. James Town. I reminded her we had no money to pay the fare and she just smiled, saying, "Let's go, I'll worry about that." Ann and I climbed into the back seat while A1 sat beside the driver. When A1 went to cozy up to the driver, he brushed off her advance, telling her to stay on her side of the car. A1 looked back at me; she was quite concerned. I whispered in Ann's ear and she giggled. Then she started to rub the crotch on my jeans and put her head down in my lap. This caught the driver's attention in the rear-view mirror, but only for a second. I sat her up, and whispered in her ear. She said loud enough for the driver to hear that she didn't care, and that she was very horny. She slipped the straps of her dress off over her shoulders and let her dress fall below her breasts. The driver was fixated now on his rear-view mirror, admiring her breasts. Next Ann lifted one leg at a time, slowly taking off her panties, and then she straddled me in the back seat. I remained fully clothed. A1 was closer to the driver now, and he was not brushing back her advances. I lifted the back of Ann's dress so that Ann's bare butt faced toward the front seat, and the driver could barely keep his eyes on the road ahead. Ann started to lift up, and down. The driver's forehead began to perspire, and A1 was rubbing his crotch through his pants. A Travelways tour bus passed by the taxi on my left and I laughed as I watched the passengers peering down through their windows at us. Their faces were scrunched right up hard against the glass as they watched Ann's bare breasts bouncing up and down in the back seat.

Within seconds, the moment came that I was expecting. A1's left hand came around the front seat nearest the passenger door, and in it was the driver's bankroll. It was a thick wad containing mostly five- and ten-dollar bills. I tucked it in my front pants pocket. We were now coming off the Lakeshore and heading north to St. James Town. I had Ann get off my lap and put her panties back on. I told the driver I had to stop for cigarettes, so he stopped outside a corner store. I went in and, along with my purchase, had the clerk exchange all the small bills for larger denominations — fifties and twenties. I got back into the taxi, and we drove to our destination. I gave the driver a good tip with his own money. He told me our fare was the best one he had in his career. I smiled at him, knowing that as soon as he went to put his fare away, he would realize his bankroll was missing. He would search around for a couple of minutes, and then try to remember when the last time was that he had actually seen it. Most probably, he would come to a rightful conclusion that we had scammed him, and he might actually come looking for us.

We went into the building we'd told the driver we were going to, walked through the ground floor, and exited out the back door to the neighbouring building that housed A1's place. We had in excess of five hundred dollars, thanks to the driver, and, of course, A1's adeptness at her trade. My friend at the bar would drive into the city the following morning to give me the money he had promised.

These two women would provide me with a lot of excitement while I was down in "crack alley." A1 was "hooked up" with my little friend Bernie. One afternoon, I was walking up the street as they were coming down. A1 was in tears. I asked what was going on, but she told Bernie not to tell me. I was concerned, though, and wouldn't let them pass until someone told me. A1 made me promise I wouldn't say anything to the two men who were standing just thirty yards north of us. I gave her my word. She told me the one man had grabbed her arm and told her she was going to perform a sex act on him. He threatened to beat her up, and had hurt her arm before she was able to break free. I listened to her, then walked up to the two men.

As soon as I reached them, I knocked out her assailant with a punch to the jaw. He lay unconscious on the roadway. The second man jumped back and started to move like he wanted to fight. I was more than ready to oblige him. A1 quickly told the man, who she apparently knew from before, that I was not only a friend of the King of Hearts, but that I had beaten up the King not once, but twice. That made the man put his fists down and he went to go look after his unconscious friend.

As A1 and I walked away, she began to cry. "What's wrong now?" I asked. She told me I'd broken my word to her. I told her I hadn't. I gave her my word I wouldn't say a word to the assailant, and I hadn't. Bernie laughed and told her that I was right. I had kept my word.

Ann and I were sitting in an apartment one afternoon when A1 came in with Bernie. She told us we were going down to one of the hotels to rent a room for a two-day party, compliments of her. We couldn't refuse. Ann had borrowed a friend's Camaro, and so we all piled in. A1 sat beside me in the front, while Ann and Bernie took the back seat. We hadn't driven five city blocks when a police cruiser passed us, heading in the opposite direction. I noticed the driver stare intently at A1. I also noticed when the cruiser made a U-turn behind us and started to follow the Camaro. I asked if anyone had any court issues outstanding, and everyone said no. I was wanted on a Canada-wide warrant, but I also had phony I.D. and was sure I could pass any questioning as long as it didn't entail fingerprints. I kept driving, but as I turned south toward our destination, the cruiser came up on us and honked its horn. I pulled over with the cruiser behind me.

The driver came up on my side and asked for my licence and ownership. As I fumbled through the car's glovebox, the other cop was asking A1 her name. She told him to ask his partner, that he knew her name. The cop on my side told her she was right, and that they wanted her out of the car as they had a warrant for her arrest. I just looked at her sadly and shook my head. If she had told me, I'd never have stopped.

The cop on my side told me to exit the vehicle and place my paperwork on the trunk of the Camaro. As I did this, A1 was taken out of the car and placed in the rear of the cruiser. Bernie hopped out of the back seat. The cop on the passenger side told him to get back in the car, but he told the cop to fuck off and he ran down the street and around a corner. The cop pursued. The driver told me not to move as he took off after his partner and Bernie.

I grabbed the paperwork off the trunk and jumped back in the car, started it up, and made a U-turn so that my driver's door was adjacent to the cruiser's driver door. I told Ann to get out and let A1 out of the cruiser. She jumped into the cruiser and flipped the release for the rear doors. Then she sprang back into the Camaro. A1 followed close behind. A couple of bystanders, seeing this transpire before their eyes, came over and grabbed A1 before she could get into the car. I put my arm around her waist and stepped on the gas, ripping her out of their grasp. I threw her into the seat behind me and slammed my door. I barked at the bystanders for getting involved, then reversed the car toward them. They moved out of the way, but the parked police cruiser could not. I smashed right into the side. I headed north just as another cruiser came around the corner. It veered to avoid hitting us and went straight into the damaged police cruiser. We continued north.

A taxi had now taken up the chase, and I watched him in my rear-view mirror, speaking into his radio. A couple of seconds later, I bounced his vehicle into a tall concrete street light. He was no longer in pursuit of anything.

The two women in the back seat were having a great time with this chase. However, I was not. Another taxi answering his co-worker's call turned his vehicle at the same intersection as I did, and followed me into the Moss Park apartment complex. I stopped to let the two women out and told them to go into the building to the King of Heart's sister's place. As they entered the lobby, the taxi stopped and the driver started to pursue them. I honked my horn, and when the driver turned to look, I backed the Camaro right into the side of his vehicle. I pulled away a few feet, then backed into it again, caving in the side panel. The driver forgot about the women and came running to rescue his car. When he got close, I drove away. A civilian watching this episode jumped into his car and attempted to block my exit. He was just a second too late, though, and I crashed into the front of his car, sending it spinning out of my way. As I made it to the main thoroughfare, I realized I had three blown tires, and both the front and back ends of the Camaro resembled an accordion. The radiator was starting to smoke, too. I had to leave the car behind. It was finished.

I got out and began to walk toward the building I'd left the women at. As I started up a grassy hill, I could see the tops of police caps beginning to appear on the hill's horizon. I turned and ran. The police gave chase. I hurdled a three-and-a-half-foot iron fence, which seemed to pose them difficulty. I made my escape through some buildings, over a couple more fences, and then entered the basement area of a large church. As I walked hurriedly through the hallway, I pulled off the hooded sweat top and track pants I had been wearing. Underneath I wore a dress shirt and blue jeans. As I was stripping off the excess clothing, I became aware that I was passing by a large number of men sitting drinking coffee, conducting an Alcoholics Anonymous meeting. They were all staring at me with their mouths wide open. They didn't move from their seats, though. I walked out through the front doors of the church, crossed the street in plain view of the police pursuing the hooded, track pants–wearing culprit. As soon as I hit the side street, I began running north again, and didn't stop until I was safely in a house in South Regent Park having coffee with a friend. Within minutes, I was watching as uniformed officers scoured through the parking lots outside looking for me. After they left, I made my way up through North Regent and into St. James Town. I arrived at A1's building just as Ann did. A1 was already in her place with Bernie. Everyone had gotten away. The Camaro was done, though.

I stopped by George Street one afternoon to visit the King of Hearts. I entered through the rear of his building. Two hookers answered his door and told me he wouldn't be back for at least a half hour. They said they would entertain me until he got back, but I declined their generous offer. I was looking out his second-storey front window, though, and wondered what five members of a Jamaican posse were doing sitting across the street, looking toward the apartment. The girls told me they were looking for the King, as well. They appeared none too happy. I was sure there was a problem brewing.

I walked out the front of the building, past the men, and briefly listened to them as they cussed and swore. When I got to a main street, I flagged down a taxi and took it to a friend's house nearby. I borrowed a couple of his handguns and a sawed-off shotgun, and had the taxi return me to the King's.

As I walked back up to the building, the King stood out front surrounded by the five angry men. A few had their hands inside their waistbands, and I could tell they were carrying handguns. Since they were all blocking the entranceway to the building, I excused myself as I passed through the congregation. I did not even meet eyes with the King, but just sauntered through. Once I got into the stairwell, I took the shotgun out from beneath my three-quarter-length leather coat and loaded it. I went up to the King's apartment and, after gaining access and throwing the two whores out, went and opened the front window. I set the handguns on the sill, then positioned my sights on the men below. The King looked cowed as the posse raised their voices. But when he glanced up to his window, his posture suddenly changed and he began to dictate his terms to the posse. When they began to get angry, he asked them to take a look at his window. They noticed me with a shotgun trained right on them. I waved and called for them to pull their weapons. I assured them I would shoot them all where they stood. They talked with the King for a minute longer, then left. The King arrived in his apartment, telling me I had freaked him out when I passed by earlier without a glance, but that he was never so happy to see anyone in his life as he was seeing me sitting on his windowsill. The posse had wanted to take over the drug subculture for the entire area. They agreed, after having seen me, that there was enough room for everyone to continue with their own enterprises. They would not bother the King again.

Ann showed up one afternoon as I sat at Cassie's place in St. James Town. She was carrying a brand new leather jacket and a forty-ounce bottle of Bacardi rum. She also had a pocketful of money. She said she wanted to party with me. I asked what the occasion was, and she told me there was no special reason. She gave me the jacket she had purchased for me and I asked where she'd gotten all the money. She told me matter-of-factly that she'd just robbed a bank. I laughed. She told me she was serious. I asked her what kind of disguise she'd worn. She told me she hadn't worn any. I mentioned to her that the banks had cameras, and with a record, she would not be hard to identify. She told me she didn't care. She told me she had more friends in jail than she had on the streets. Sadly, I could identify with that. I knew she was in her own depression just as I was in mine.

A few hours later, she left to go rob a second bank. She had no weapon, only a piece of paper and a pen. She returned shortly after successfully robbing the second bank.

That night we went to visit one of her friends who lived in a flat nearby. He wasn't home, but she had a key. As we went down the hallway, a woman came out of a different flat. Ann looked at her and murmured, "Oh no." I asked her what the problem was. She said she'd taken a cab to her second robbery, and the woman had been with her. She held the taxi while Ann went into the bank. After they left, and Ann left the cab, Ann found out the other woman had been arrested. Yet there she stood in the hallway.

I told Ann the woman had to have made a deal with the police to find Ann; otherwise she'd still be in custody. Bank robberies were not shoplifting-calibre charges. One did not get charged and simply walk free on personal bail. I told Ann we had to leave immediately, but Ann refused to run. She asked me to spend the night with her. I told her I was sure the cops would come. I had a Canada-wide warrant outstanding against me still, but, like Ann, I wasn't running either. I agreed to stay with her until the cops showed up and arrested us. Oddly enough, they didn't show up that night.

The following morning Ann woke me up and asked what I would like for breakfast. She'd already showered and dressed. She went out to the restaurant to get us some food. After an hour, she still hadn't come back, so I went out to look for her. I couldn't find her. I went to Cassie's and made myself a coffee. A1 showed up a few minutes later and told me she'd been looking for me everywhere. Apparently, the police were waiting outside the flat and had arrested Ann when she came out.

Ann would get three years for her fine penmanship and nerve. I'd miss my friend. There were plenty of women who would have wanted to take her place hanging out with me, but none ever could or would. She was a great friend, considering the circumstances in each of our lives at that time.

$$\cancel{||||}$$

The King of Hearts phoned me one afternoon to tell me one of the Row Boat's brothers was in Regent Park asking where he could find me. He wasn't sure if the man was armed, but thought that I might have a problem. He told me where the man was.

Five minutes later, I saw the man standing in the alcove of a corner store. I stood beside him for a moment. He looked just like the Row Boat. I told him I heard he was looking for someone. He told me he was and asked if I knew his quarry. I told him I was the person he was looking for. He turned white. He said he just wanted to know who had killed his brother. I told him I did. I also told him what I had told his other brother. I had no beef with him, or his many brothers, so they had an open shot at me if one wanted to take it, but if one missed, they would all have to answer for the attempt. I was not prepared to give them all one shot at me. I told him that his deceased brother had been given an opportunity to walk away, but that he had to be an asshole and didn't take it. I told this man not to be running around the area acting tough, asking for me. I assured him I'd always show up, just as I had then, and the next time we would definitely have a problem. He nodded and left.

I'd gone back to reside at my sister's home in the East End of Toronto. Bernie and A1 kept too much company for my liking. I preferred some hours alone each day, if only to reflect on life. Cher and I would try to work things out, but every time we'd met, she'd start bitching about the mistakes I'd made in my past, and I'd leave again. It broke my heart to be away from my children, but they were always with her, and she was always arguing with me in front of them. I felt it was better for them not to have to deal with our situation.

14

Hearts and Cowards

A FEW WEEKS LATER, the King of Hearts got himself arrested. His common-law wife and sister showed up on my doorstep, very upset. They couldn't get any answers from the men who were with the King when the police took him. They'd phoned but were hung up on. They went to the door of the apartment, only to have it slammed in their faces. They told me the King of Hearts had sold the tenants of the apartment some electronic appliances he had stolen, and he had gone that afternoon to collect his payment. They knew he'd been in the apartment for a couple of hours before the arrest. Since I had nothing but time on my hands, I told them I'd go to the apartment that night to see what I could find out.

Just before I entered the building, I ran into a black man I'd met in the Don Jail. He was trying to find the King's sister. I didn't know the address, but I knew where it was. I told him I just had to run into an apartment for a couple of minutes, then I'd take him there. We both went up to the apartment. I knocked and they let us in.

The three men were in the living room drinking whisky. I knew the man whose apartment it was. I'd met one of the others before — he lived on the ground floor. The third man was a complete stranger. I asked the man who rented the apartment to come to the kitchen. I asked what happened to the King. He told me the police showed up and arrested him. I told the man I knew the King had been in the apartment for two hours, at least, and if the cops had seen him enter, they would've taken him within ten minutes. I told him I thought the King was pressuring them for his money for his merchandise and one of them had gone out and called the police. I told the man to convince me that I was wrong.

He took a swing at my head with his right fist. I ducked and came up in time to look him in the eye and knock him sprawling into his living room. The stranger was obviously a close friend, because he flew off the couch and ran at me. He should've stayed where he was, 'cause he flew back out of the kitchen faster than he entered, now with a split forehead. After picking himself up, he left. The third man, the downstairs guy, came at me also, but he was more wary. After a few swings, he went down, as well. I noticed the first man had revived and was reaching for something on his table. I grabbed the canister just as he reached it and looked at the label: pepper spray. After asking what he intended to do with it, I sprayed a small stream across his eyes. He hit the floor screaming. The other man was up off the floor and charging at me now, so I sprayed him, too. He hit the floor.

I was very angry at this point. I told the man who'd entered the apartment with me to grab the stereo, television, and games system. I was not leaving the tenant something he hadn't paid for. Plus, he'd put my friend in jail. My associate began to move the articles out to the elevator.

I had the downstairs man sitting up now. He was recovering from being knocked unconscious, his eyes still burning a little from the pepper spray. I told him he was going to store the stolen merchandise at his place until the King of Hearts was free and he could retrieve his property. I told him under no circumstances was the man who lived in this apartment to have the articles, especially after he'd just tried to assault me. He agreed to look after the goods.

I walked out into the hallway carrying the television and saw police coming from both stairwells. Being five floors up, I had nowhere to go. I was immediately arrested. So was the man who had come with me to the apartment.

At the police station in Regent Park, the cops asked for my name and other particulars. I gave them a litany of lies. They took my fingerprints to confirm my I.D. and I was placed in an interrogation room.

After a half hour, the door opened and two uniformed officers entered. They were huge, and had necks on them as thick as my waist. They just glared at me and went to the side of the room on my right. Then two more cops entered and went to my left. They were even larger than the first pair, and they appeared to be none too pleased with my presence, either. I knew what was coming. The detective who'd taken my fingerprints came in. He informed me that I had lied to him about my name, about everything, and that he now knew who I was. In his opinion, I was a convicted murdering piece of crap. I asked him what his problem was, and if my victim had been a friend of his. He stepped toward me, throwing a punch straight at my face. I took a half step back. I was still handcuffed behind my back. His punch connected but not with any effect. As his arm went back, I took a step forward and head-butted him, knocking him back toward the door. After that, all I recall is being punched in the head and hitting the floor, then a bevy of steel-toed boots kicking my ribs, my face, and my head before I lost consciousness.

When I regained consciousness, I couldn't breathe without unbearable pain. After an hour, I was taken to the nearest hospital. The nurse believed the police, who told her I'd attacked them (five huge men) while I was handcuffed from behind and they had merely restrained me. (I seem to recall watching as she got one of their phone numbers.)

The nurse said that the bumps and bruising on my head and the rest of my body would heal within a couple of weeks. But my ribs were cracked, and it would take months before I could breathe again without pain.

I was taken back to the police station, then transferred to the Don Jail. I was charged for assault on the men in the apartment, stealing their (stolen, unpaid-for) merchandise, and spraying them with the pepper spray. I was also charged for giving the police a false name.

It turned out the King of Hearts had only been charged for being in an area forbidden by his bail stipulations and was released the following morning on his own recognizance. I would not be released for the next seven years.

卌

While I was at the Don, the King of Hearts returned. Shortly after, his stepson Paul arrived. Another man came on the range who had been a prosecution witness in one of Paul's previous charges. Paul told his stepfather and me about this. A couple of hours later, the King of Hearts attacked, knocking the man to the floor. The King then got up on the table and jumped in the air. He was coming down on the prone and bloodied man's head when I grabbed him in mid-flight and stumbled back toward the cells. He was screaming at me for interfering. I asked him if he was willing to trust his life that no one on this crowded range would testify against him if he killed the guy. He knew the answer. He calmed down and I told him to go to the front of the range. The guard had heard the commotion and had hit the panic button. The man was transported off the range on a stretcher under the supervision of the jail's nurses. The sergeant of the guards came down the range and checked my hands for bruising. For some reason, they thought I was the one that had attacked the man. They were wrong. But the following day, I was transferred to the London city jail.

This institution was built the same as the Toronto East Detention in that there were two individual living unit pods on each floor, connected by a middle recreational room. It was a relatively new jail, and therefore looked very clean. When I arrived on range, there was a man, Derek, who I knew from Millhaven. He'd gone to court the day after I arrived, and when he came back, he was in possession of a fair quantity of Valium. He gave me a few. The following morning, when we were let out for breakfast, I noticed Derek had stayed in bed. He was okay, but complained he wasn't feeling well. I was still pretty hungover myself from the pills. I was feeling no pain. After breakfast, the guard came around to lock the doors of the vacated cells. He began to argue with Derek to get up and get out of his cell. I asked the guard why he just didn't leave him locked in the cell if he wasn't feeling well. He locked Derek in. Then he continued through the rest of the range. A half hour after he left, I noticed the recreation room just outside our range was filling up with guards. A lot of jail guards. One of the guards opened the door leading onto my range and asked me to step into the room. The sergeant wished to speak with me.

The guards formed a gauntlet for me, leading toward the sergeant sitting on a desk at the far end of the room. I walked through them and asked the sergeant what he wanted. He asked if I was trying to tell his staff how to do their jobs. I assured him that I was not. A six-foot-eight, 250-pound guard grabbed my right bicep in his large left hand. The sergeant told me his range officer was of the opinion that I was trying to tell him his job, and the sergeant informed me that they did not like tough guys from Toronto telling them what to do. I asked the sergeant to hold on for a second, knowing what was about to happen. I turned and told the man to let go of me before I broke his jaw. The guard was stunned and asked me to repeat what I had just said, and so I did. I was immediately bum-rushed from behind by several guards. They knocked me to the floor face first, and fast. One knelt on my back as the others kicked and punched me. After a few seconds, the one got off so that they could attempt to handcuff me behind my back. They managed to get one cuff on, but I was not letting them get both arms too close together. They continued their assault. Finally, I gave up any hope of getting off the floor and fighting them, so I just let them handcuff me. They picked me up and rushed me out and down the hallway to the stairs that led to the hole. I was very angry, and continued to talk at them all the way to the cell. It was not a very polite conversation. They locked me in and left.

After a while, I calmed down and went to sleep.

The following morning, I noticed a shadow cross in front of the bottom crack of the solid cell door. I knocked on the door, so the guard would hear me. He came back and lifted the cover of the observation window. I told him I'd like a cigarette. He told me he was the guard that had locked me in the cell the day before, and that I had said a number of unkind things about him and his mother. I smiled, and told him I guessed that I would not be getting my cigarette. He shut the cover and left. I laughed. I was battered and bruised, but I knew I would heal.

I was held in the hole for the next four weeks until it was time to be transferred back to Toronto for court. They brought me out of the hole, and put me in a cell in the admitting area to wait for the bailiffs. Four guards sat playing cards in a control room nearby. Their door was open, and one yelled to me that he assumed I did not enjoy my stay at their fine establishment, and imagined I would not be coming back. They laughed. I told them that, on the contrary, I would be coming back to London as soon as I was released, and that I would like to buy them all a drink. I asked them which bar they frequented, or where I could find them. They fell silent. You could hear a pin drop. "What's wrong? Nothing else smart to say? You guys are pretty tough out here when it's twenty on one, and you attack from behind, eh? We'll see how you do one on one when I catch you alone."

The two bailiffs showed up a half hour later. One was a heavy-set Chinese man and the other a big Swede. They were frequently assigned these transports between cities. The Swede did not want to escort me back to Toronto until I promised that I would not assault him. The big Swede and I had had words one morning months previous at the Don Jail. He'd been pushing around a young offender and I had offered for him to try his bullying tactics with me. Now, I just wanted out of the London area and back to where I could see my family in Toronto. I gave the bailiffs my word, and we left.

When I arrived at the Don, I was once again placed on the pen range. I'd only be there a few days until court, and then I was shipped out again to await my next court date, this time to the city jail on Barton Street in Hamilton. I was told London did not want me back — a good thing, in my opinion.

After being processed in Hamilton, I was taken to a floor that housed the two overflow ranges used for holding Toronto prisoners. A black guard was my escort. He appeared polite and professional. He brought me through the hallways, up the stairs, and into the guards' control tower on the landing, centred outside two ranges. I could see into the one range, and the prisoners could see me. A few of the men were acquaintances of mine, and they were yelling and motioning for me to get put on their range. I asked the sergeant if I could be placed on their range, and he deferred to the escort. The black guard then asked me if I was prejudiced. I was a little perplexed by the assertion. I told him I was not. He asked me why I wanted to go on the one range instead of the other, and I told him he could see as well as me that guys were calling me to go there. He told me that he thought I was prejudiced and told the sergeant to place me on the other range. I could not even see into that range from where I stood, but that difficulty was remedied when the guard took me in.

Every prisoner in the range was black. They had the television on as loud as it could go, listening to BET. Five or six of the men were standing around a table playing dominoes, yelling and screaming while they slapped the bones onto the table with as much force and noise as they could muster. The guard opened a cell and told me to put my stuff inside. He locked the door, then left the range. He returned about a half hour later and noticed me sitting at a table by myself watching the Country Music Channel on the TV. I'm sure he was told that I had changed the channel on the men who were listening to BET.

He went over to the men playing dominoes and asked if everything was okay on the range. They looked at me, and I at them. They told the guard everything was fine. He told them there would be no guards coming through in the next hour, so if someone was to get hurt, no one would be around to help. He was motioning toward me as he informed them of the opportunity to assault me. I watched out of my peripheral vision, but said nothing. The black guard left the range again. He returned in a half hour, doing his routine walk. After he punched the clock on the wall, he passed the men seated at the table. One of them asked him for a set of dominoes. He said he had just given them a new set that morning. The prisoner acknowledged that, but informed him that someone had flushed a few of the bones down the toilet, so they could not continue their noisy game. The prisoner really didn't have to motion toward me as being the culprit, but he did. The rest of the men at the table were already doing that. What this guard did not know was that I had seen many of these men in the Don, and they all knew they'd be going back there for court. None of them wanted any conflict with me. They knew we'd meet again. The guard went over to the cell he had assigned me, unlocked it, and told me to grab my property.

He took me off the overflow range and marched me upstairs to their pen range. He was visibly upset. He had hoped to see me get beaten up. I don't know why he'd adopted this attitude with me. I'd never seen the guard before in my life.

I didn't know any of the men on the pen range. They all looked at me, but none initiated conversation. I could see, and sense, their wariness.

The following morning, I went out to the yard with the rest of the men from my range. I passed the other pen range, and through the glass saw a half dozen men I'd known from either Millhaven or Collins Bay. They were shocked to see me in their city. Everyone knew I never left Toronto unless

I was in shackles and handcuffs. That had seemed to be a running joke amongst my associates in the federal penal system for many years.

My former prison associates quickly sent word over to the men I was housed with, and they now treated me as one of their own. As it turned out, a couple of the guys were brothers of associates of mine and had heard of me for years. I had a really good time at the Barton Street jail until I was returned to the Don.

I was not at the Don long before they decided to transfer me once again to the Toronto East Detention Centre. I was taken down to the court cell range along with one of my other associates who was also being transferred to the East the following morning. Rome was a mid-sized man and an experienced criminal. After supper, we crouched down on the floor in front of the cell that had been assigned us near the front of the range. Not long into our conversation, we were confronted by a group of men. The crowd formed a half moon around us while our backs were against the wall. Both Rome and I stood up. I looked at Rome and asked if there was a problem. He told me that, during mealtime, he'd reached for a couple of slices of bread, but one black man had grabbed the entire loaf away from him, saying it was his. Rome had taken the loaf back, took his two slices, and set the loaf back onto the middle of the table. The leader of the crowd, the corridor man in charge of the range, told us to go to the back of the range. That was where most violence occurred, and I knew that. He then informed me with much confidence that was where his crowd lived. I smiled at him, and told him that was quite a coincidence. He asked me why, and I told him, "You guys live at the back, but I own the back. Now let's go and do this."

Rome followed me down the length of the range while the crowd made their way down the other side. As I got to the end table, the corridor man told me they were content to just leave the fight between Rome and the bread bandit. I asked Rome if he could beat the man and he assured me he could. I agreed to leave it between the two. Rome won the fight.

A couple of hours later, as we again sat outside our cell door, the corridor man took a broom handle and smashed in on top of the middle table's metal surface. It sounded like a gun went off in the confined range. I got up immediately. He yelled to everyone on the range that it was seven o'clock and that everyone had to go in their cells or he would personally put them in. I'd never had a prisoner lock me up, and I was not about to start. I took off my sweater while yelling to the corridor man to start with me. I started to make my way toward him as one of the veteran Don Jail guards ran up the side of the range informing the corridor man who I was, and that I would seriously hurt him. The corridor man immediately told me I could stay out on the range, and with anyone else I wanted to. Taking the guard at his word, he told me he did not wish to fight.

The following morning, Rome and I lay in our double-bunked cell and watched as the corridor man and his friend delivered four plates of breakfast to our cell. We took only one each, our rations. The men were happy to see us depart for the East Detention Centre soon after.

The day before I was to appear in court, I talked with the King of Hearts and another associate who was friends with the men I had been charged for assaulting. They assured me the three men would not be appearing. When I arrived at the College Park courthouse in downtown Toronto, my lawyer asked if I would be willing to plead. I told him I didn't think so. As I entered the courtroom, though, I noticed the three men were present, and in deep consultation with the police and Crown attorney. I was very disappointed. I really wanted to argue the charges, but I knew I couldn't escape all of them. I pled guilty for a one-year sentence, but I was not happy. The men had attacked me. I had taken the tenant's property, but then, he hadn't paid for it, and it was stolen anyways. I'd only intended to move it to another location. I had no interest in it. I had sprayed them with their little pepper spray canister, but not before one had tried to grab it to spray me. I'd never have known it was on the table if he hadn't reached for it. As for lying to the police about my identity, my ride to the hospital that night was ample evidence of why I did that. Still, I took the sentence and left the courtroom. I was returned to the East Detention, and then put on the first transport to the Millhaven Assessment Unit, where I was classified for the medium-security Bath Institution.

15

Bath Time

WHEN I ARRIVED AT BATH, it had been recently upgraded from a minimum institution to a medium-security facility. The federal authorities were in the process of installing a second perimeter fence, much like the one at nearby Millhaven. I was placed on a range dubbed "Bay Route." There were four ranges, but the one I was placed in seemed to house the more unruly prisoners. Many didn't last long in Bath before they were upgraded and transferred to Collins Bay. Hence the nickname.

Instead of rooms or cells, the living spaces here were divided with partitions. Each man basically had a six-by-seven-foot area to call his own, but the noise of the range was unobstructed. There were a few men I knew from before, including Big Red. The lifers were concerned about a circulating rumour that they'd all be transferred to higher security, as Bath was not deemed secure enough to hold them. There were also major conflicts between some white and black prisoners regarding the use of the weight pits and other areas.

Big Red asked me to take the job of inmate committee chairman. I really didn't want any part of that, but he was my friend, so I relented. He made me an appointment with the warden. When we met, the warden asked why he should approve me to run for this position when I was just a newcomer to his institution. I didn't meet the criteria to be nominated. I told him he had problems that I could resolve, and gave him the names of three area wardens he could call to ask of my experience. He called me back a few hours later and told me I could run for the position in an election. I went and sought out the biggest, toughest black man in the institution and convinced him to take the position as my co-chairman. Together, we won the election by a landslide.

The institution seemed to run very smoothly. We set up regular card tournaments and family socials. We settled any of the arguments between prisoners that we were made aware of. Because our committee was not given an office to meet with our "constituents," I set up a locker, desk, and typewriter in the only area every prisoner had access to at any time — the main-floor washroom. When a delegation of ex-wardens came through on a tour and discovered where our office was, they were appalled. One French visitor called it "an abomination," and they berated the standing warden. We were given a proper room shortly after that.

One day, my co-chairman and I were summoned to the gymnasium and told it was being locked down. A prisoner had climbed into the ceiling area of the gym and made his way along and over to the female social development officer's washroom area. There, he had poked two eyeholes in the ceiling tiles, one set above her shower, another over her toilet. I asked security to just leave it, and we'd discover who the culprit was, but they wouldn't do that. They shut down the gym and had the ceiling refitted with a solid covering. But once it reopened, the female officer still had a major problem — a prisoner was stalking her.

One night, about a week later, as she made her rounds, she discovered a prisoner was openly masturbating while staring at her. She could see him through the glass on the other side of a door. She told him to stop, but he didn't, so she left, refusing to finish her lockdown routine until he'd vacated the gym area. I was informed of this the following morning by a prison guard. There was concern the situation was getting out of control.

I went to talk to the prisoner and discovered him back in the gym area, looking through a glass door, watching the female officer again. We had a very short but intense discussion. That afternoon, my committee was summoned to the warden's boardroom for a meeting with the administration. At the meeting, the deputy warden informed us the administration would not tolerate any more of what had happened in the gym that morning. I innocently asked my secretary what had happened. The deputy warden leaned across the table and angrily told me I damn well knew what had happened. The sexual predator had gotten his cheekbone broken, along with other physical damage. They had had to comply with the predator's request to be moved to a different institution.

While the deputy warden did not appear too happy about the incident, the social development officer was extremely glad, and relieved — as was every other female who worked in Bath at the time.

Another problem involved a prisoner going into other men's rooms and stealing their property. This was happening far too frequently, and many within the population were upset. Even the guard staff had called my committee into their office to discuss the problem. Not knowing who was responsible, there was little we could do.

One night, I had a special needs prisoner come to me and tell me he'd been ripped off. And he knew who the culprit was. A man had been seen carrying the prisoner's locker out of his room and off the range. I went and talked to some of the men on that range whom I had known previously. They confirmed the special needs prisoner's story.

I went with him over to the other unit to confront the man. On the way there, we found the locker. It had been pried open, and cigarettes and pocket money were missing. We continued on to the culprit's room. Once inside, the special needs prisoner demanded his property back. The man denied any wrongdoing and challenged the man to a fight in the gym. The special needs prisoner looked to me, but I couldn't intervene on his behalf any more than I already had. After all, he was a special needs prisoner, most likely serving his sentence for a crime that I would abhor. In fact, in the days before this became an integrated institution, I would most likely have beaten the crap out of him myself.

Once the special needs prisoner left the room, I told the cell thief that I was aware of his frequent indiscretions, and now that I knew it was him, I'd be watching. I told him I couldn't act for a special needs, but if he made the mistake of stealing from me, or anyone who wasn't special needs, I'd be back, and there would be no "going to the gym." He just shrugged me off and I left.

The next morning, as I sat having my morning coffee, two prisoners came in to tell me the cell thief had just been seen stealing out of four more rooms in the other unit. One of the rooms housed a man I'd come to know and like. He was an older prisoner serving a sentence for vehicular manslaughter — he had driven drunk one night and caused a terrible accident for which he was truly repentant. I got up just as the rest of the committee members came through the door. They told me they'd handle the situation. They'd ask the man to transfer out of Bath immediately. They didn't want me involved, as they thought I might have an anger issue with the thief. I told them to go ahead and handle it. I'd just stand outside the door and listen. I stopped en route to talk with my older associate. He was in tears, and not from losing his money and cigarettes. Those could be replaced. But the thief had damaged personal photographs of his wife and family. I told the old man to leave the unit and go to his work location. Everything would be handled.

The other committee members entered the thief's room and talked with the man. The thief didn't think their idea of him moving was as good as his own suggestion that they all pack up their own stuff and leave. He considered himself somewhat of a tough guy, a "reputed" fighter amongst his peers. He was also a little high on pills. He told the committee members to leave before he assaulted them. The committee members were dumbstruck. One asked the rest what they should do. They seemed perplexed. At that point, somebody walked into the room and asked the thief to repeat himself. When he opened his mouth to speak, his teeth were punched out of his mouth, spewed randomly across his bedsheet as his body sailed over top, crashing into the wall. Coming off the wall fighting, he was hit again, only this time his eye became dislodged from its orbital socket. The third punch left him unconscious on the floor. The committee member had an answer to his question — that was exactly what they should do in that particular situation if it ever arose again.

An hour later, I sat in the hole at Millhaven. I'd sit in a closed cell on the administrative segregation range of Millhaven twenty-three hours a day for the next five months waiting to see if I would face criminal charges.

The radio didn't work there, my TV was conveniently misplaced until the day I was transferred, and I was given no reading material. The window was also heavily screened, and so filthy on the outside that no air travelled in or out of the cell. I was permitted a one-hour yard period each day, weather permitting. But by the time the guards would handcuff me through the slot in the door, then leg shackle me after I stepped out, I'd have no more than a half hour of fresh air. Again, weather permitting. After five months of this treatment, I was becoming a little "stir-crazy."

Fortunately, I knew the range cleaner's brother, and so the cleaner would bring me hot water whenever I needed any for my coffee, or just stop by my door and chat through the crack for a few minutes every other day. I also knew another prisoner housed at the end of the range who would send me down a bowl of Kraft Dinner and tuna almost nightly. I was lucky to have that, as the meals were atrocious at best. Most times I would send the entire tray back out the way it had been served.

There were also several other prisoners who were brought down to the seg range from Millhaven's prison population for "acting up," and I knew most of them previously. Although each stayed only briefly, they were good company. Finally, I was transferred to Collins Bay.

When I arrived this time, I was happy to be placed directly on Three Block. My oldest brother lived there on the second floor, as did many of my prior acquaintances. I was assigned a cell, and soon found out that double-bunking was mandatory for new arrivals. I didn't mind that much, especially since I'd been isolated for the past five months. Bandit was a good friend to meet and become acquainted with. He was not a "hard-core" prisoner, but he talked like a gangster from the 1940s, even though he probably wasn't born before the seventies. We cohabited for months without any problem. I'd spend most of my time on the second floor visiting or outside in the weight pit or yard. I only slept in the cell.

Something new at Collins Bay this time was the random urine testing. Everyone was aware through the prison grapevine that oil-based THC products such as grass and hash would stay in one's liver for up to thirty days and show positive for drug use on any test. Chalk-based pharmaceuticals such as Valium also presented the same dilemma for the substance abuser. Many drug users had now — in order to avoid being institutionally charged, losing their jobs, and most probably their opportunity for conjugal visits — ceased to use their previous "preferences," switching instead to substances that were water soluble and detectable for up to only three days. This was not a good thing, though; it was actually a terrible thing, especially for the prisoners, as those substances were mainly hard-core heroin and cocaine. These were far more expensive, and far more addictive. I'll always harbour disdain for this testing program for the simple reason that it took occasional partiers and turned them into heavy addicts.

And Collins Bay was not short on supply of those two products when I arrived. Of course, along with the illegal drug activity came violence. There were constantly drug-related altercations. Being that I had history with a great many of the men, I'd find myself thrust into the middle of many a dispute, if not to mediate then to take sides. This began almost immediately when a stranger tried to stab an old associate of mine but failed. Incidents would compile almost biweekly. It didn't disturb me too much as I was in a heavy depression when I arrived anyways, first for being back in the federal system and second for being transferred to higher security — the transfer signalled a far lengthier term of imprisonment than I had anticipated. Parole for lifers rarely occurred from this institution, so I'd have to serve a couple of years there before I could effect a transfer to a camp where a board would seriously entertain an application for parole. I didn't feel my transfer was deserving of the situation at Bath.

To make matters far worse, Cher had informed me that my son, Adam, had just been diagnosed with autism. Being uninformed, she felt his affliction was caused by my history of substance abuse. Also being uninformed, I believed her and felt total guilt. If I'd thought I was depressed before, this revelation hammered home the reality of what depression was all about.

I eventually moved up to the second floor to a single cell, where I was surrounded by many of my associates and my brother. I weight trained over the course of the next eighteen months, but avoided sports save baseball. As the summer rolled through, and the time came near for the institution to host another Olympiad event for the mentally handicapped, or "Exceptional People," as they referred to them, I was approached by the committee chairman. He told me that he had to resign or be stabbed to death as it was discovered that he had been pilfering the prisoners' institutional welfare funds for his friends and himself. That was not good. He told me he was "muscled" into the actions, but I knew he could have just talked to some guys to negate the threat. He was just as much involved as they were. He asked me to take over the committee. I declined. His problem was not mine. He left, but returned with the warden. I couldn't believe it.

The warden asked if I'd heard about a stabbing incident on one of the other blocks. I had. Two blacks had stabbed a white man over a very small cigarette debt, and the other whites were thinking they should retaliate. The warden was concerned about racial violence within the prison, especially since it was so close to the Olympiad event where many outside guests, including children, would be on the grounds. He told me all his advisors referred to me as the man who could keep a lid on things. I told him to let me think about it for a day. At that time, I was already approved for transfer to the minimum-security Pittsburgh Institution just west of Kingston, beside Joyceville Institution.

I went around to all the cellblocks and talked to most of the men I knew in each range. I also talked to the group who were threatening retaliation. They all wanted me to take over the committee position. The next morning, I met with the warden and told him I'd act as prisoner chairman just until my transfer went through, but I had a few conditions. I needed to put in place my own committee. I needed men released from segregation who had been down there far longer than their indiscretions had warranted. And I definitely needed a barbeque social in the yard for the entire population to bring the prisoners together. He complied.

My first act was to go down to the Social Development and have my co-members hired. There were four men working down there, and they had been there for two years. They were all black men, and they had also been the ones identified to me by the previous chairman as being his musclers. The lady in SD told me she could hire no one, as the four men held the positions I wanted filled. They'd worked beside her for two years and she wouldn't fire them. She was very fond of them. I told her "no problem." I called the four into her office and promptly told them to clean out their offices, that they were all fired immediately, by me. She was upset, not knowing the intricacies of the reason for the change in the chairman position, but she had no alternative other than to comply with my demands. The four had other ideas. They cleaned out their desks and returned to their blocks, but that afternoon they met with all their friends out in the yard.

I went out to the yard alone that afternoon and sat on the baseball diamond bleachers watching the meeting. After twenty minutes or so, my name was being called on the public address system, ordering me to go to the back dock, just off the yard fence. After ten minutes of listening to the repeated call, I went. The head of security and four of his keepers were there. They told me they wanted me out of the yard right away as their parabolic microphones were telling them the meeting out there was concerning my being killed. I told them I was well aware of that. The guards were shocked that I knew, and even more so that I was still out in the yard by myself. I asked them why they thought I had none of my friends with me. Four of the toughest blacks in that meeting were all close friends of mine. They were there to tell the four disgruntled men that they had ripped off the other prisoners for two years, and had now been caught with their hands in the cookie jar, so to speak. My friends told them they were lucky I had mediated a deal with the rest of the prisoners to leave the four thieves alone. That was the last I heard of their complaints.

The outside volunteer representative for their group did go to Ottawa to complain later, but when the warden revealed the facts, the matter was over.

||||| |||

The Exceptional People's Olympiad at Collins Bay in 1997 went off without a hitch. The yard was made to resemble a carnival midway with bright colours and streamers all over the place. After the deputy commissioner of penitentiaries gave his speech and received his applause at the commencement of the games, I was called up to the podium. All the people in the bleachers began cheering, whistling, and clapping. At the microphone, the deputy commissioner told me it was not hard to tell that I owned the place, and that I was obviously the people's choice. I told him this penitentiary was theirs, and I was only their representative. He told me I was a true politician. I wasn't sure if he was insulting me or not. Nevertheless, it was a great two days for the athletes and the prisoners.

A few days later, a Native fellow got into a ruckus with one of the black fellows. For some strange reason, it appeared to be turning into a racial war that was to occur in the gym one afternoon. Most of the black men had gathered in the gym, along one side and up on the stage. The Native men, being a much smaller group, had asked for the help of the white men, and they were gathered out in the yard. I went out to see what was going on.

Once I had all the information, it was decided to try to limit the altercation between the two adversaries.

The leader of the Native men and a biker from Hamilton said they would enter the gym first as the "leaders," and that everyone else should follow a half minute behind. As the two began their walk to the gym, I joined them. The Hamilton tough guy asked me if I had a hearing problem, or just couldn't follow his orders. I told him I represented the Toronto men, and in prison, we took a back seat to no one. They needed my friends, and I followed my own orders. I'd enter the gym with them. He never argued the point. There would have been no point.

When we went in, we approached the leaders of the black group. It was settled. The two men would go into the washroom without weapons, have their little fight, and that would be the end of it. That's exactly what happened, and everyone was happy.

A few days later, I had a disagreement with the leader of the blacks from my block. One could say it got physical for a few brief moments. The following morning, as I showered at the front of the range, the rest of my associates all left for breakfast in the dining hall. Once they were gone, the blacks came up from downstairs. I was already halfway to my cell when they appeared. I didn't see them coming. One of my lifer associates who hadn't gone for breakfast did, though, and called my name just as I arrived outside my cell. I could sense the alarm in his voice, and I threw my towel, soap, and shampoo through my open door and onto my bed. Then I turned around to see what the problem was.

The group was halfway down the range by then. There were five men on each side of the corridor, with the leader in front and in the centre. They all appeared to be holding their waistbands with one hand, which was an indication to me that they were armed. I smiled. I could probably have run in my cell and held the door closed with all my might, praying for help to arrive, but that thought never occurred to me. There was a free-standing table just outside my cell. I took off my bathrobe, tossed it on my bed, and then kicked the table to the far side of the corridor, out of my way. Standing there naked, I said, "Beautiful. You guys are here for me. Let's do this."

They froze. The leader approached me slowly, stopping within ten feet. "I just want to talk to you," he said quietly. I told him he didn't need to have all his friends with him to do that. He again repeated that he just wanted to talk and asked if we could step into my cell. I agreed, but told him to enter first. He asked if I could put my robe back on. He came in and apologized for the misunderstanding the night before, and asked why I felt he had disrespected me. I explained it to him. He apologized to me once again. When we came out, the guys on my range had hurried back from the dining hall after being alerted to the ongoing situation. My guys were now surrounding the black men with our own weapons. I told them to let the men go.

That afternoon I was in the dining hall when one of the young men from Regent who resided in One Block told me the blacks in his block were talking about me. I asked what they were saying. He told me that they believed I was a "devil man," and not to mess with me. I laughed. My other associates told me the only reason they didn't attack me that morning was because they felt sorry for me after seeing me naked. We all laughed about that.

It was not long after that I was finally transferred to the Pittsburgh farm camp for the first time.

16

Music and Methadone

PITTSBURGH HAD A TOTALLY DIFFERENT atmosphere from the institution I'd just left. No daily drama, no drug subculture that I was aware of. Everyone wore their own clothing, including the guards. There were no security walls or fencing.

I worked in the institution's recreation department until the programs I had to participate in — cognitive skills and substance abuse — commenced. While both were pretty simplistic, I felt that many of the men in my classes benefitted from the knowledge each course imparted. I also volunteered to participate in a parenting course. At the conclusion of my "programming," I was asked by a staff member to participate in a program that allowed prisoners to speak in various communities, at group homes, training schools, high schools, and universities. Although the program was substance abuse–oriented, we could inject criminal lifestyles easily into the discussions. I enjoyed these excursions.

I also got to speak at a Prison Fellowship fundraiser in downtown Toronto. I was quite surprised to be the one prisoner chosen by the institution's clergy to represent their group. I didn't lurk in their hallways at every opportunity as many of the religious zealots did. Arriving in Toronto, I discovered a large contingent of different religious denominations present, as well as community representatives. It was very humbling to speak in front of them.

After my programming, I had the opportunity to work for the Festival of the Islands in Gananoque, Ontario, doing general labour to prepare for the upcoming music concerts. It was a great job, considering the benefits: accidentally falling into the cool lake waters each lunchtime, and watching the bands play each night of the two-week event. The first night, the boss told me to just go and enjoy myself. I could go anywhere in the crowd. I started in front of the midway, a small row of concession booths that formed an alley from the parking lot right up to the stage. I walked to one end, then slowly back, watching all the people. I became aware I was not alone. Returning to the first booth, I purchased three sodas and offered one each to two young ladies standing nearby. They declined, then they went over to talk with the Gananoque police chief, who was standing by his marked cruiser in all his regalia. He looked over at me and we both started to laugh. I hadn't been out of the game so long that I didn't know when a tail was on me. I'd actually expected it. He must've given his two female undercovers the rest of the night off, because they left after that.

After the festival ended, I went to work as a volunteer at Martha's Table, a soup kitchen that catered mainly to Kingston's homeless and needy people. Four prisoners at a time were allowed to volunteer at this establishment. We would clean the building, do the dishes, prep food, cook, and just keep order amongst the clientele, which was not always easy. I enjoyed this job only because of the opportunity to talk with the "street people" and offer them encouragement. I also got to meet with the odd person whom I knew from prison, and of course there was a person I knew from Toronto. She'd stop by anytime she knew I was there.

In the spring of 2000, I was finally afforded day parole. I was glad to be going but deeply upset that I'd been incarcerated for the past seven years. I'd lost faith in the justice system as it pertained to me, an emotional scar that I will carry with me always.

I also wasn't happy that I was sent to a halfway house way out in the West End of Toronto. The Keele Centre at that time had (and probably still does) the distinction of having the highest recidivism rate of any halfway house in Canada. In other words, its occupants were returned to prison for one reason or another more than those from any other house. The majority of the residents were men on mandatory supervision. They had very little time left on their sentences, but had been denied early release. To be "residenced" was a further form of punishment for these men, and they had no problem taking off from the house (if they even arrived there from their respective institutions) or failing the urine tests.

I arrived at the Keele Centre with a job waiting for me and a determination to fulfill my day parole opportunity until I was released on full parole to my familial home. The first year, I would devote a lot of my time and effort to my new job as an administration manager with a logistics firm. I'd grasped the concept of the business quickly, and was earning the firm a lot of money from my office chair.

After a year, my mother passed away. She died simply from old age. That was traumatic for me. When I had arrived home the first time, in 1990, I'd been happy that both my mother and younger sister had done well in their lives. At least they had lived normal, comfortable lives after I'd gone to the penitentiary in 1978. When I informed my parole officer at the Keele Centre of her passing the following morning, she asked me if I had proof. *Did I have proof?* I was shocked and angry. I really took that request as one of the worst insults a person could have given me. The PO, seeing my reaction, asked me to leave the centre right away for work. When I got there, the answering machine contained all kinds of apologies from her for her callousness. I was told I didn't have to return to the centre for five days.

A few of the men I knew in prison come through the Keele Centre while I was there. One of them, in particular, was a great friend to me inside. Mario was residenced, and although he was also determined to make it to his warrant, his job was of the illegal sort. Quite frankly, he trafficked in heroin. He would offer to get me high most every night I saw him. He'd want to party with me and talk about old jail times. I'd always decline his offer of drugs, but we'd laugh about events we'd seen or been a part of inside prison. After a time, and right after providing a urine sample to the centre, I relented and got high with him. I didn't see how any real harm could come of that. What I hadn't thought of was the previous test was at the end of one month, and the staff came right back to test me again at the start of the next month. Obviously, I failed. I was arrested and placed in the West Detention.

When I arrived there that night, I was asked by a guy if I had anything to smoke with me. In front of the guard, I told him no. The following morning, the same guy told me he wanted to talk with me in the washroom on the range. I was no rookie, and had watched him send his four friends into the washroom before he approached me. I just smiled at him and nodded. This was going to be a violent altercation, and I was just in the mood for one. I went into the washroom, past his friends to the back wall, where I turned. He told me I'd lied to him. I told him that of course I did. He'd asked me right in front of a guard if I had contraband, and not only that, but since I didn't know the West Detention like I did the Don or the East Detention, I was not so sure he and his friends weren't a bunch of protective custody inmates, pieces of crap in my books.

He was shocked. I was basically picking a fight with them. I was eyeing the four men behind their leader and trying to think of how I was going to be able to stop each one from getting help from the guards once the fight started. I had every intention of beating the crap out of them. The leader must have been reading my mind, because all of a sudden he made a decision for his crew not to bother me any further. I told him that was a good idea. They were punks, pure and simple.

I stayed on the range and watched this crew pull their little assaults on other prisoners when they came in. It bothered me greatly, but since it did not affect me personally, I avoided confrontation. I really didn't want to pick up new criminal charges at this point in my life.

After a couple of weeks, I was transferred to Kingston's temporary detention unit for federal offenders.

When I appeared before the board a month after my arrival there, my day parole status was reinstated and I went back to the Keele Centre and back to work. I'd managed to keep my job at the logistics firm. I'd go home each night after work, around five p.m., but then have to leave for the halfway house around nine. After supper, it didn't give me much time to spend with Kelly and Adam, let alone with Cher, but it was better than being in prison.

After another year at the Keele, I saw the parole board in downtown Kingston for full parole. I was so looking forward to not having to go across town to sleep by myself each night. At the hearing, I ran into a board member who took umbrage with the respect I had received over the years from various prison populations. She seemed even more upset now that my job as an administration manager of a logistics firm paid in excess of one hundred thousand annually, plus bonuses that added up to another twenty-five grand. She informed me, as well as the other board members, that under no circumstances, regardless of any information shared at this hearing, would she grant me full parole. She even got into an argument with my Toronto PO, who was supporting me for full parole release. I was very angry. This board member had no concept of prison life, and certainly no idea of what she was angry about. In my opinion, I hadn't looked for problems inside; I just addressed them as best I could as they arose.

After the hearing, I was sent back to the Keele Centre to remain on day parole. I was so irate, I got high again, then promptly failed the next urinalysis test. I obviously had not used good coping skills.

When the test results came back, the halfway house director and my PO offered to have me placed in a methadone program rather than send me back to prison. Those were the two choices they offered me. They gave me five minutes to decide. Not knowing anything about this program, in five seconds I opted to remain free and be placed on methadone.

That turned out to be a very, very bad decision.

I should have known. Every negative occurrence in the methadone program house was brought to my doorstep, regardless of my ignorance of the events. A man overdosed one morning and I was called back from work to face questioning. I'd never even spoken to the man, and knew nothing about his past or any of his connections. When they had a surprise raid on the house, complete with a strong police presence and sniffer dogs, I was fortunate enough to be gone over a couple of more times than any other resident. The results were negative, but the inference they made was not lost on me or on anyone else, and I resented them for that. Anyhow, now that I was on the methadone program, I began to associate with many of my prior criminal associates. The methadone definitely affected my cognitive thinking in that manner. Most times I could barely stay awake. I did not avoid the boys, as I had been doing for the past two years. Now, we'd hang out together at the coffee shop, the billiard halls, or their homes. Saul used to come in from Prince Edward Island and we'd have a quick meal and chat before he'd be on his way. I knew what he was up to, and how he made his money, but I never would involve myself. Now, on methadone, I began to go with him to meet his suppliers and friends. His business was not mine, so I couldn't get in trouble just for being around. I knew quite a few of them from my past anyhow, and Saul appreciated the company. So did I.

In the late winter of 2003, March 23 to be exact, three years almost to the day from being sent to the Keele Centre, I was arrested out front at six in the morning by the RCMP. The officers laughed when they told me I was being sent to the "island" and I asked what the hell was on Centre Island in Toronto.

I was flown to Prince Edward Island that morning and appeared in court that afternoon. The Ontario RCMP told me that they had been on me for months, and if it was their decision, I would not be charged for anything, but their counterparts "down east" wanted me charged and had gotten their superiors to order my arrest. The Ontario guys implored me not to get their unit mixed up with "those goofs down east." I didn't know who they meant until I met the Islanders.

When I got off the jet handcuffed to an RCMP sergeant, the tarmac was swarming with media. I'd be all over the news for the next few days. The RCMP were certainly trying to justify spending three and a half years and millions of dollars of taxpayer money on an investigation that provided their friends with paid jobs, and them with paid vacations to Ontario. Their results were chiefly ten kilos of low-grade hashish from one of Saul's runners coming across Confederation Bridge.

Saul was in the courtroom along with about twenty co-conspirators. When I entered, he sat alone in a row near the back of the courtroom. He was angry and yelling at everyone. I went and sat beside him. He told me he faced twenty-some-odd criminal charges, including for weapons and opiates. Being experienced, I told him he would most likely have to make a deal at some point. In the meantime, I told him, I knew no one in the entire province. I'd never been there before. Of his co-accused, I had met three, all of whom were from Ontario, and really had known only one. I told Saul I would need his help to retain legal counsel. He told me that I was on my own, he had his own problems.

I was so angry. I told Saul that was fine, and I would remind him of his answer at the conclusion of this debacle. I was arraigned on six counts of conspiracy to traffic in marijuana. I could not believe I was flown this far for what I believed to be such minor charges.

Methadone was not provided in Prince Edward Island, and I was a federal prisoner. Since I was still on the program, I was housed in Springhill Institution in Nova Scotia. Each time I was to appear in court, the sheriff's office of PEI would come and get me at Springhill. We'd drive across the Confederation Bridge at least seventy times before I was finished with their court system.

I was offered twelve months during my first few remands. I was willing to accept that, but Saul and Gino and others I was charged with convinced me to reject the offer and stand by them as they fought the charges. They assured me no one would be convicted and that they would retain my legal counsel before trial. They lied.

I took myself off the methadone program after two years on it, after I'd been reincarcerated for a full year. I was really upset with Saul's friends down east, and I was getting even more upset with Saul by the remand. I needed to have my mind straight and off the influence of methadone or anything else before I chose any actions and continued any farther down this path of personal destruction. I came off the drug cold turkey, losing over twenty pounds of body weight in two weeks and rotting the tops of several teeth from the constant vomiting. I couldn't place a toothbrush in my mouth without vomiting. It was the most physically ill period I endured in my life, but I stayed the course and became drug-free. The methadone doctor, upon finding out that I had not picked up my dose in a month, told me I should have died. I told her I had come close a couple of times. Contrary to the skeptics, I've remained drug-free ever since.

At Springhill, every lawyer I talked to wanted a hundred-thousand-dollar retainer — or more — to defend me. I could understand that from my Toronto lawyers, who would have had to relocate their office, but the east-coast lawyers were way overpriced. They seemed to be of the opinion that this conspiracy involved millions of undiscovered dollars. It couldn't have been farther from the truth. There was no way I could meet that cost, and even if I could, I would have given it to my family before I used it for a marijuana charge. So, I requested, and was granted, Legal Aid. There really was no way they could deny me, or I'm sure they would have.

The only practising Legal Aid lawyer, the only one in their office in the city of Charlottetown, informed me that she was paid to represent me, not to defend me. In fact, she assured me there was no way she was going to challenge the people she broke bread with everyday just for the likes of me. I fired her on the spot and defended myself. I did not have her legal resources, but I was sure I was far brighter than this grade ten, stay at home, divorced country bumpkin, and I had a lot more courtroom experience.

I felt that if the PEI RCMP wanted to prosecute me so badly, I was going to make sure it was as unpleasant for them as it was for me. I received no legal or monetary assistance from any of my co-accused. I spent three years of my life in Springhill fighting these charges and representing myself.

I went through two preliminary hearings and applied for six different motions to be held in the Superior Court. I did all this with no experience and a kook paralegal I'd met in Springhill. During the preliminary hearings, I would cause the judge to hammer on the gavel each day as I hammered away at the Crown's witnesses. I believed I caught many of their lies, and exposed how stupid their investigations were, if not they themselves.

The PEI detachment had ignored heroin and cocaine sales occurring right in front of their very eyes, not to mention just watching a shootout that occurred between two of the conspirators on a crowded street. They let all of these crimes proceed, just in the hope of making a marijuana arrest farther on down the road. It didn't make any sense to me, unless the PEI RCMP just wanted to continue being funded for doing nothing. I was disgusted by this police force that had the gall to call themselves Canadians. I believed them to be no better than the crooks they were supposed to be chasing and in some ways worse. The judge would tell me, when I expressed my abhorrence, that I did not tell their police force how to apply the law in their province. She would also tell me, during one of my cross-examinations, that everyone on this island province knew everyone else, and that they were all friends. When I openly opined that I would have a hard time picking an impartial jury then, she pointed out with a big smile that the problem was mine, not theirs. I just dug in deeper.

I worked through the disclosure evidence with the Finkster — my Springhill prisoner paralegal. He was presumed by many in this prison to belong in a rubber room, wearing a hockey helmet, and at times I would agree, but when it came to researching law, the man was head and shoulders above the rest of us. He was the one who discovered I had been illegally arrested in Toronto and flown out of Ontario without a proper warrant. There was no endorsement warrant from any legal branch of the Ontario justice system. Their warrant was simply signed by a friend of the PEI RCMP, a justice of the peace in Charlottetown. In effect, I had been kidnapped out of my home province. I brought this matter to the Superior Court of PEI under a motion for a ruling on jurisdiction. The Crown attorney cried foul, saying I was producing a red herring. I told him in Ontario we called it a slam dunk, and that he loses. The Superior Court judge in Prince Edward Island, though recognizing the error of the unlawful arrest, would refuse to rule in my favour. In fact, he refused to rule at all and told me to bring the matter up again when he was prepared to hear my motion on abuse of process. I asked how long that would take. He set his sights to prolong my three-year stay in Springhill to four or five years. He was uncertain which time frame. I was miffed. I was returned to Springhill.

Saul had bailed on me after two years of remands, taking a four-month deal on his charges. In doing so, he did the one thing I had asked him not to do, and that was to plead on charges that involved me. He had plenty of other charges to choose from that he could have pled on, but he didn't. Gino and his partner, the other two who had influenced me not to take my initial deal, now, three years later, took their solidarity performance right up to my Supreme Court motions, and then had their lawyers get a severance from me so that they could plead in Ontario to a house-arrest sentence. When the prosecution agreed to their severance, I knew I was on my own. My co-accused had cut and run, leaving me holding their baggage without counsel. They'd made their own deals behind my back.

I was so angered by this, I took the twelve months offered me three years earlier right then, but not before telling the Crown, the cops, Legal Aid, the courts, and anyone else I could see who lived on this island that it made me physically want to vomit just looking at them. There was no way I should have been convicted of anything, but as the Bay Street lawyer had assured me months earlier, I was a convicted murderer, and there was no way the PEI courts would rule in my favour, regardless of the evidence or the rights every Canadian should have. He was right. I had watched the courts toss Canada's Criminal Code book into the garbage, along with the Charter of Rights and Freedoms in my case. By the time I left PEI, I had no respect for its people and prayed only that a tsunami was on their horizon.

17

Et Tu, Brute?

I WAS BROUGHT BACK TO ONTARIO a couple of months later and housed at Bath Institution. After a year inside, I was transferred again to Pittsburgh work camp outside of Joyceville. Some of the older staff from Collins Bay were now working in higher administrative positions in Pittsburgh, and they remembered all too well my attitude toward them back in the day. Of course, back then, in the 1980s, I was a totally different person. I was abusive toward any authority figures. It was not personal, it was just the lifestyle I had grown into, and now had grown out of. Now, I was fifty years old.

There were also a number of "prison rats" scurrying around the complex at this time, acting as though they could be trusted by the "new" inmates. The rats knew I knew their history. In fact, I'd had harsh words with some of them years earlier. This time, though, I avoided them. I went to work in a mattress factory, purposely staying out of everyone's way. After four long years, I just wanted to go home and be left alone. I sent my earnings home to Cher and the kids. After work, I would sit in my designated house until the nights closed in, and I slept. In the morning, I would return to work.

I was not assigned a PO when I arrived at Pittsburgh, which was disturbing, and I had to bother case management to provide me with such so that I could apply to be paroled. I was given a PO after a few months, but after one month, she left the institution. I was reassigned another one who immediately left on training. Finally, after four and a half months, I was able to put in my paperwork for a day parole hearing.

Then I was promptly "involuntarily transferred" to higher security, sent to Joyceville on suspicion of bringing drugs into Pittsburgh. I discovered that every week I'd been at Pittsburgh, someone had sent in a "kite," or written message, to the security officer saying that I was bringing in large amounts of heroin, cocaine, pills, hash, grass, you name it. Not just small quantities either, but by the pounds, at a cost of thousands and thousands of dollars, if one was to believe the prison rats. The security officer, knowing their history with me, believed none of their assertions, but was still duty bound to record their "information." In all the time I was there, not one inmate, to my knowledge, had shown positive for any signs of drugs during urinalysis testing. Not one speck of any type of drug was seized by guards or smelled by their canine units. There was never anything. But one day the security officer went on his annual holidays and someone in administration from my long-ago past gained access to his files and saw the kites as an opportunity to get a shot in at me. They took it.

I was really shaken and upset. I'd never before been shipped out when there were no incidents. It was then that I realized anyone could have me buried with no proof of anything, and all it would take would be some resentment toward me for some past indiscretion I'd forgotten.

I never recovered from this revelation, or from this "involuntary transfer." I would never again trust that my future hinged on my behaviour; it depended more on the behaviour of others around me in the prison. I had told the warden at Pittsburgh that I could swear on my children's lives, something I took very seriously, that I brought nothing into Pittsburgh during the five months I'd been there, but she ratified my rise in security just the same without even a thought. She just wanted me out of her camp, to placate her administrator and his lying rats.

After a week or so in the hole at Joyceville, I was let out into the population. The prison was rife with turmoil. The first range that I was slated for was very loud. My new cellmate was to be a large black man whose friends called him Stinky. I took a look around, picked up the property I had with me, and then walked back out to the landing, telling the guard who had let me onto this range to notify the hole that I was on my way back. He called the committee. The chairman had known me previously, and he knew, as did I, that I would not live on that range long before involving myself in an altercation. He had the guard reassign me to a quieter range.

That worked out okay, but only after I introduced myself to the four young men who thought they ran the range. We came to the understanding that their doors being left open with their stereos blaring down the range was not cool, and their habit of taking other prisoners' food rations was over.

At Joyceville, I was first employed as the health representative for the prisoners' committee. I did very little, but it gave me access to the weight pit area during the daytime when it was not busy. I did that for a few months. When I first arrived, I was also introduced to the lifers at the lifer room near the back gym area. I knew a couple of the men from earlier times, and most had heard of me throughout their incarceration, so I was welcomed. After a while I quit the committee health rep job and went to work at the metal shop for the next eighteen months.

Of course, incidents did arise at Joyceville — the new "Gladiator School" of Ontario pens. At that time, Joyceville's record of violence far exceeded that of Collins Bay. The culture was no longer one of older, more docile men, but younger, more violent prisoners. There were racial issues between the whites, Native guys, blacks, and Asians; cultural barriers between the old and the young, between the Canadians and the new Canadians, the "Scotians" and Jamaicans; and religious barriers between the Muslims and, well, every other religion in the world. To make matters worse, tobacco smoking was now banned throughout the penal system, and most prisoners were not impressed by this change in their lifestyle. The lack of nicotine was affecting daily attitudes toward everyone and everything. It was not unusual to see two or three confrontations a week — beatings, stabbings.

I would eventually be transferred to the minimum-security Beaver Creek Institution in Gravenhurst. But this was no longer the Beaver Creek of 1990, no longer a place for case management teams who worked to assist men in their reintegration, to help them get out on parole, to help them get home. Beaver Creek had now adopted the concept of charging prisoners for anything they could. They'd send men to higher security based only on information from the prison rats, whether the accusations could be substantiated or not. And their rats could do no wrong, even when they were caught red-handed doing things other prisoners would be transferred for. The place was operating under a two-tier system.

I would last two years there and had just begun to apply for my release when I was transferred again to higher security, this time Fenbrook Institution. Although there was a total lack of any physical evidence, a prison rat said I'd brought tobacco into the prison; another rat had vouched for the first one. Because I had a high prison profile, transferring me out was seen by some staff as a big feather in their caps. That was deemed enough reason to take three and a half years out of my life and do irreparable damage to my wife and children. That was all it took.

Fenbrook was a new prison located right beside Beaver Creek. You could throw a rock from one property and have it land on the other. I'd learn immediately that the administrations broke bread together, and therefore I was harassed for the entire first year at Fenbrook. I was not allowed to work as all the other prisoners were; every job I put in for was denied on the basis of my being a "security threat," even if it was just pushing a broom. I was placed on a range that eventually would be made up of a number of ignorant black prisoners, some Muslim, but all with a taste for loud music and, it seemed, for bothering me. They were aware of my lifer status and the fact that I was trying to get back to a minimum, and that any violence perpetrated by me would certainly quash any hope of release. And they knew I knew. Whenever I'd use the kitchen area to cook my food, I could count on them coming in, hanging around the counters, and crowding me in my efforts. If I was not in the kitchen area, they'd be in the living room area blasting video games and acting like twelve-year-olds, screaming and yelling. There were times at two or three in the morning when they'd wake me with their noise. I was not allowed to transfer to a different range. Some staff, I'm sure, were just waiting for me to snap. My anger-management skills were being severely tested. I hated the place, and more so, I really wanted to assault a few of the men on my range.

I had prior associates living on other ranges who, recognizing my angst, offered to deal with my antagonists, but I didn't want any of them getting into trouble over my problem, especially since I felt the idiots weren't worth the punishment my associates would inflict. I'd tell my antagonists, though, that we would not always be in jail, under a microscope; they would not always have the guards to watch over them, and I would look forward to seeing them in society. I knew I never would see them outside prison, but my words gave them something to think about.

After eighteen months, I was finally allowed to transfer back to Beaver Creek. I had to start all over again. I worked at the paint shop, then as a cleaner, and I did the community volunteer program all over again.

After that, I saw the parole board for unescorted passes. During the conclusion of the hearing, I simply told them to do what they wanted. They were going to anyways. I'd already served ten solid years of incarceration for what basically amounted to my passing on a phone message for Saul involving a little bit of marijuana, and for my not being able to afford a proper lawyer. Saul, the main drug trafficker of the conspiracy, served four months more than Gino on our charges. For being the supplier, Gino served nothing but ninety days of house arrest.

At this point in my life, I'd had enough of listening to people trying to justify my further imprisonment. They'd present the old storyline I'd heard for years: I was a "bad man," and that justified any ill treatment toward me. None of these people had walked in my shoes, not even taken two steps. I was aware I'd threatened and scared several people in my past, but in my mind, my actions were justified by the results — people being unharmed as a result of my involvement.

The board members that day were flogging a dead horse, but I encouraged them to have at it, if that was what they felt they needed to do to feel good.

In the end, the parole board members finally granted my passes, but not before extending them to last over another year and a half of incarceration. I definitely wasn't happy. It didn't benefit anyone to continue my incarceration. It only served to hurt my family and me. The term *rehabilitation* had long ago been replaced with *punishment*. And in my mind, *punishment* had progressed to *mental torture*.

||||| ·

After a year and a half, I'm waiting to see another parole board panel. I probably won't be happy with any future decisions; but then, I firmly believe that were I released tomorrow, I would have no one to thank. The time for appreciation is long gone, and I make no secret of that resentment. So, now, I muse that the board will probably want to extract some more time out of my life, just to show me that my disdain for the criminal justice system and Canada's penal system continues to be more than warranted.

There was a time when I was proud of my country. When I believed in justice. That time has long passed. Somewhere along the line, I matured, and I learned that each of us is only as strong as the people who surround us. I'd suggest one choose one's company wisely. In life, I now expect nothing. I have no illusions about anyone possessing a "moral higher ground." I have no aspirations of becoming "successful." I have no ambitions. I have a life to finish living with family, and that's all.

Life is all about taking opportunities when they're presented. Bad people will take advantage of others if there are not people to keep them within the boundaries of humanity. That is fact. Educated adults know people will exalt you to the highest if they can use you, then vilify you to the nth degree if that serves their purpose. One must learn there are different degrees or levels of trust, and one must use them wisely. All a person can do is to try to walk a proper path and avoid the pitfalls and sinkholes that the people in their lives place around them. I recall an old adage that says if a person lives a full life, and at the end dies having five true friends, then they have lived a charmed life indeed. I believe that to be true.

I know I'm a bitter person, but I like to believe I'm also a realist. I've committed many crimes, but I've also paid for them in full, and then some. I believe I'm a person who does not think twice in acting if I encounter a situation that endangers a person's life. I've demonstrated that on many occasions, both inside prison and out in society. I'd probably be made to serve another ten years of incarceration for mischief if I kicked in a door to rescue people from a burning house; but, even knowing that, that door would still come down. I always believed I had to live with my conscience. I've seen enough of life to know that friends come and go, some faster than others. Family will always be family, but they will not always be friendly. True loyalty is a very rare commodity; far more precious than diamonds or gold.

Many of the people in my life who I mentioned in this book have moved on or become estranged from me for one reason or another:

- Moose was murdered in downtown Toronto by a crack dealer.
- Hans would be found dead, his battered body washed up on the shore of Lake Ontario in Toronto. The police investigation, I am told, took all of three minutes. No charges were ever laid. Hans would have appreciated that, but would have been disappointed in others for their lack of retaliation.
- The Row Boat's hooker would commit suicide not long after the initial trial in which she testified falsely.
- Downtown and his wife were killed in a car crash during a police pursuit of the vehicle they were in.
- The Millhaven Badger would be killed in a car crash during a police pursuit.
- The leader of the West End Crew would hang himself in his apartment in 1975.
- Bullethead would commit suicide at home before facing a bank robbery charge in Toronto.
- Slugger would pass away in British Columbia from cancer. He was broke.
- Big Hal would pass away in Kingston from cancer. He was broke.
- Karen would pass away in 2014 from cancer, joining her younger sister and brother.
- Arnold, my childhood buddy, would pass away from pneumonia. He was a grandfather.
- Willy's psycho murderer from Millhaven Max would himself be murdered by his own crew in Quebec.
- Mack would commit suicide while free in society just as the police were closing in on him for a rape/murder. In my view, Moose should have hit him harder in their common room fight.

- The "after-hours alleyway" motorcycle president would die of natural causes.
- John the Hat would be found murdered in the United States.
- Paolo Violi was murdered by his own people in a Montreal club.
- Vic Cotroni would die of natural causes in Quebec.
- My "Family" connection, who wished to aid me in leaving the Lindsay jail, was found murdered on the railroad tracks in Hamilton.
- My older brother's biker friend would be found murdered in the United States.
- My older brother retired broke, but free.
- Lovely Larry would die a free man when the mountain bike he was riding was hit by a vehicle in Brampton, Ontario.
- The King of Hearts and Rod would both die from pneumonia complicated by drug abuse issues. They were both broke.
- Ron would be deported to England, where he gave up religion for a young lady and a "joint of weed."
- Saul would continue to bounce in and out of prison. He remains "serving sentence" on new matters.
- Big Red, the Rocket, Alex, and many others from my Millhaven Max days remain in touch with each other, and continue life as productive members of society.
- Rooster would escape an arrest and conviction with Saul "down east" at great monetary expense to him and his family in the 1990s. He would resume a normal lifestyle after with his wife and two sons.
- Gino's "family" and their families live happily to date.
- California would retire from the criminal lifestyle, broke, and become a productive member of society.
- Jughead would be released at times, but remains in prison "down east," although a leader no longer.
- The Hamilton biker I met in Collins Bay would be murdered in his hometown by gunfire.
- My Millhaven psycho (unbelievably, to the other prisoners who knew him) would achieve parole, and, after a couple of breaches in which he was returned to prison just briefly, remains free in society today.

None of the criminals I met in my "travels" became rich or famous. They're now just simply dead or happily retired. It would appear the criminal lifestyle was not what they had anticipated.

Me either.

To each of us, the days of our lives inside amount to wasted time.

||||||

People of my generation have made and continue to make great efforts toward preserving the planet for the next generations to live on. They labour to improve life in all areas, from the ozone layer, to various ecosystems, on down into the ocean depths. We are mindful of the various species that border on the edge of extinction, and work to increase their survival. We've made great strides in technology and medical research. Even our prison system has made advancements, with the abolishment of corporal and capital punishment. However, the populations within our prisons, reformatories, and local jails continue to swell in numbers. Plans are made to build more institutions for future offenders. Parallel to the increase in criminal offences are the number of victims in society.

Who are we preserving our planet for if we ignore the culture of our youth, these "cool" new-age gangsters? While our societies do acknowledge and promote the positive effects of counselling and interventions with regards to substance abuse, and do provide some programs with direct contact to prisons for the novice criminal behaviour we discover in some of our very young, our efforts are minimal in comparison to the hype that's disseminated to the next generation that a criminal lifestyle will afford them "riches, excitement, power, and fame."

Large parts of my decades of wasted time — literally hundreds of thousands of hours — were spent talking with other people about the mistakes that they made in their lives. I've learned about the different impacts that external influences played in each case. These people all had family and friends, even associates who did not chose the same lifestyle. So, one wonders, what caused these people to act criminally? Was it greed, envy, lust? I believe it's natural that everyone feels these emotions at some point, to some degree, and wishes to better their standing, to earn more, to acquire a better lifestyle. But what is it that causes some people to act in a criminal manner and others not?

Fingers are pointed at many different areas. Books, movies, television shows, and video games that promote violence and influence young minds. Household income and the area where a person grows up, particularly "ghettos" and "projects" like my own Regent Park. Single-parent families, foster care, family histories of drug or alcohol abuse.

Given the shared history, though, most families, like my own, do not exhibit criminal behaviour amongst all members. Why do some kids adopt the criminal lifestyle while their siblings do not?

What I have gathered is that in almost every case of a young person adopting a criminal lifestyle, there are very real associates, whether immediate family or in the larger community, that impress upon and infect the single individual with a negative influence stronger than that of other, more positive influences. I challenge any speaker to ask a group of young offenders how many of them know an older, cool criminal. I believe every one of them would raise a hand. Twenty years later, those same individuals would not raise their hand if they were asked if they thought those same criminals were still cool. That's the message the young need to comprehend. And it's a message best delivered by people who've lived the life and learned the hard lessons the hard way.

The window of opportunity for infection diminishes with maturity and knowledge, and with reinforcement from positive role models who can help build self-esteem and open kids up to future possibilities.

I believe education should focus on those whom the young look to for guidance and direction. I believe society would be better served if group meetings and seminars were conducted by respected, seasoned professionals, and targeted at young adults who are not involved in the criminal lifestyle that our youngsters find so intriguing — young adults who can learn to provide a positive presence in the lives of teenagers and preteens they interact with — whether they be family members, coaches, mentors, or community outreach workers. Their involvement could save a lot of young people from making the wrong choices, and could save them years of wasted time.

EPILOGUE

IN WRITING A MEMOIR, one cannot but put one's life under a microscope, to examine one's faults, one's transgressions, one's failures. This is especially true when one is one of the longest-serving prisoners in Canada's penal system.

I found, as I made my progression through my life story, a humbling, yet therapeutic effect enveloped my soul. As I rewrote each part, each story, my mind provided me with alternatives to problems I had failed to see in that present. I had to forgive myself for who I was then and understand that is not the person I am now. The reality is you cannot change your past; you can only face the future as a better you.

After being released in the late summer of 2014 on day parole to a Toronto federal halfway house, I spent the next two years under constant daily supervision. My resolve not to enter back into the criminal subculture would be tested initially through lack of finances and employment. When one decides to end a criminal lifestyle, one is alone. It is not as simple as saying, "Hey, everyone. Look at me. I'm not going to commit crimes anymore," and the crowd cheers. That is not the reality. Regaining the trust of family, friends, and the community is a long and arduous process.

Accepting responsibility for the past breaches of trust is the only solution to eventually regaining any degree of trust with anyone. A criminal record will follow you everywhere, and you must adapt to the knowledge that it is like a second shadow. It will follow you to your grave. Denied and lost employment opportunities follow an ex-offender. You must work within the limited opportunities afforded you to prove to be a productive member of society. You have to be patient.

I knew I could reach out to family and friends, but pride fed my determination to succeed on my own. After two failed employments, I was hired by an old acquaintance from my teenage years to work for his construction business. A year later, I switched to a far less laborious job, working film support in the movie industry. I continue to do that to date.

I completed a Ryerson University course, Walls to Bridges, which was offered to a select group of students and ex-offenders. In addition, I had speaking engagements at the University of Ontario Institute of Technology in Oshawa, addressing large classes on the guns and gangs issue.

My resolve to refrain from substance abuse is firm. Without question.

And my social life changed dramatically after my release. Unfortunately, Cher and I found we had grown apart on almost every level. We simply did not get along. Although I still maintain contact with her and my children, we are now divorced.

I now live as a bachelor in Forest Hill, Ontario, although I consider myself deeply involved in a relationship with a woman I have known for forty-two years.

I am relaxed knowing that my door will not be smashed in by the police, nor do I worry about violent confrontations with criminals from my past. Neither would further their causes.

I continue to write and am hopeful of a career as an author. I am also amenable to participation in community projects to educate members and youths at risk of the many pitfalls of a criminal lifestyle.

I now have hope for a successful future. Hope I had relinquished forty years ago on a cold fall night.

ACKNOWLEDGEMENTS

I WOULD LIKE TO THANK the Lion for his persistence in the commencement of this work. And also for the friendship and assistance he has provided me throughout the years. I would like to thank my brother Cole for always being my beacon to reality, especially when I was in the depths of my depravity. He will never know how many times his life example affected my positive actions.

I never ever lost focus on the "outside" world, and, in that, found the inner strength to overcome the situations I would find myself in. And for that I will remain forever grateful to each and every one of those who stood by me.

I would like to thank those people in authority who, over the years, attempted to intervene on my behalf when I was being treated unjustly. Whether successful in their attempts, or not ... I noticed.

I would also like to thank the men who helped me to survive over the many years. To those who have passed, and those who remain.